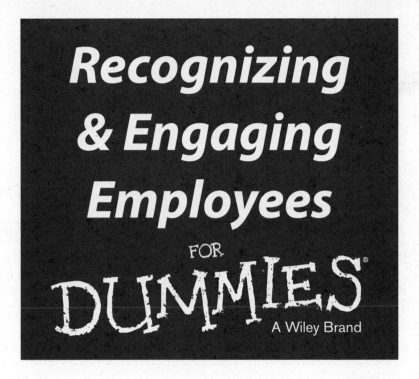

Recognizing & Engaging Employees

FOR DUMMIES®

A Wiley Brand

by Bob Nelson, PhD

FOR DUMMIES®

A Wiley Brand

Recognizing & Engaging Employees For Dummies®

Published by: **John Wiley & Sons, Inc.,** 111 River Street, Hoboken, NJ 07030-5774, www.wiley.com

Copyright © 2015 by John Wiley & Sons, Inc., Hoboken, New Jersey

Published simultaneously in Canada

For general information on our other products and services, please contact our Customer Care Department within the U.S. at 877-762-2974, outside the U.S. at 317-572-3993, or fax 317-572-4002. For technical support, please visit www.wiley.com/techsupport.

Wiley publishes in a variety of print and electronic formats and by print-on-demand. Some material included with standard print versions of this book may not be included in e-books or in print-on-demand. If this book refers to media such as a CD or DVD that is not included in the version you purchased, you may download this material at http://booksupport.wiley.com. For more information about Wiley products, visit www.wiley.com.

Library of Congress Control Number: 2015947243

ISBN 978-1-119-06753-5 (pbk); ISBN 978-1-119-06779-5 (ebk); ISBN 978-1-119-06780-1 (ebk)

Manufactured in the United States of America

10 9 8 7 6 5 4 3 2 1

Contents at a Glance

Table of Contents

Introduction

● ●

You get the best effort from others not by lighting a fire beneath them,
but by building a fire within them.

According to the Harvard Business Review, companies spend over $720 million each year on employee engagement — an amount that is projected to rise to over $1.5 billion per year — yet, employee engagement is at record lows. Just 30 percent of employees are currently considered engaged, according to the Gallup Organization, roughly the same percentage as when Gallup first started measuring the topic over 15 years ago.

What's wrong with this picture? Why is increasing employee engagement so difficult? There's no refuting Gallup's extensive longitudinal research that systematically identified the core variables that distinguish high-performing organizations from their competitive also-rans in the marketplace. But knowing what those organizational pressure points are and positively impacting those variables apparently is more difficult than anyone could have predicted.

Or are these engagement scores the proverbial tail wagging the dog? Are companies spending extraordinary amounts of effort (and money) to chase higher engagement scores while overlooking the fundamentals that are necessary for actually better engaging today's employees?

A painting entitled *The Treachery of Images*, by Rene Magritte, the Belgian surrealist, hangs in the Los Angeles County Museum of Art . . . . The work depicts a man's smoking pipe over the words *Ceci n'est pas une pipe* ("This is not a pipe"). It's basically making the point that the representation of something is not the thing itself. In the same way, engagement scores that represent employee engagement are not engagement itself. Perhaps it's time to focus on the behaviors that truly impact employee engagement, and not just the scores that measure it. This book seeks to do just that.

About This Book

Recognizing and Engaging Employees For Dummies is a reference book that contains a wealth of ideas, suggestions, tools, techniques and best practices of engagement, recognition, and motivation. There are lots of examples and some case studies — many from my own experience in applying these concepts with hundreds of organizations. You can dip into this book anywhere to find advice, examples, and best practices that can instantly provide you help today. Sidebars are skippable, but you won't *want* to skip them, because they provide interesting tangents, tips, and real-life stories that help to bring these topics to life.

I conceived this book to better address the specific actions needed to increase employee recognition and engagement of your employees. I want this book to be helpful to you, whether you are a manager, a team leader, a human resources professional, an executive, or a front-line employee — regardless of your level of experience with employee recognition and engagement.

Although there are many other good books available to supplement this one, including some that I authored — such as *1501 Ways to Reward Employees*, *The 1001 Rewards & Recognition Fieldbook*, *1001 Ways to Energize Employees* (all published by Workman Publishing Company), and *The Management Bible* and *Managing For Dummies,* 3rd Edition, published by John Wiley & Sons — I wanted this book to stand alone as an ongoing resource and an application guide to help you get the best results from your recognition and engagement efforts.

Many of the items I discuss in this book direct you back to your employees for answers as to how they best like to be recognized, ways you can better involve them in decisions, discussions you should have with them about their work preferences, plans and ambitions as well as to just generally get to know them better!

Foolish Assumptions

By purchasing this book I'm assuming that you're a manager, business owner, or human resource professional that is looking for answers and ideas about what you can do to better motivate and engage your employees. You might also be a front-line employee who's looking for ways to get your boss to be a better manager to work for, one who makes time for you, supports and encourages you, and thanks and recognizes you more when you've done good work. Perhaps you're a coach or consultant who works with managers and organizations, trying to help them improve their recognition, engagement, and motivation efforts.

If my assumptions are correct, you'll find that there is something within these pages for you, so long as you are open to considering some new ideas and willing to experiment to learn how best to apply the ideas I include here in your work with others.

Icons Used in This Book

Throughout this book, you'll come across icons that call out different kinds of information. Keep your eyes out for these icons as you're reading:

This icon indicates an especially useful insight or practical nugget of advice. It's usually something quick you can put into action right away.

This icon calls out something that is especially worth retaining. It's usually a key principle or concept that is critical to your success on the topic being discussed.

This icon relays a personal story or company example I've had in my work that relates to the topic being discussed. These are usually fun and interesting asides!

This icon accompanies slightly longer company examples.

When you see this icon, be aware! It describes a mistake or problem you should try to avoid.

Beyond the Book

In addition to the contents of this book, you can access some really great, related material online that you can access anytime at www.dummies.com/extras/recognizingandengagingemployees. These extra web goodies are shorter than the book, and give you quick bit of information and guidance on-demand.

The eCheat Sheet gives you a quick rundown of 14 different engaged workplace behaviors, and the ways in which you should recognize your employees to get them. Sometimes, when a recognition issue arises, you're right in the thick of things at work and may not have time to go back through this book to find the right chapter. The eCheat Sheet articles present info like how to recognize and incentivize employees from different generations in an efficient way so you can solve the problem and keep moving. To access the eCheat Sheet, go to www.dummies.com/cheatsheet/recognizingandengagingemployees.

You can also access some additional helpful bits of information, such as how to get certain business results through recognition, ways to recognize core values, do's and don'ts of workplace recognition, trends that impact managers' roles today, and ten common questions about rewards and recognition.

Where to Go from Here

One of the great things about this book (and most *For Dummies* books) is that it's written in a modular format in which each chapter stands on its own, enabling you to jump around in the book however you prefer. Of course, you can also read it through from beginning to end as well!

Along the way, if you have any questions or comments about what is discussed, please send me an email at bob@drbobnelson.com, and I'll do my best to answer your question. If you're potentially interested in having me present or consult on the topics discussed in this book to your management team, association, or conference, you can contact me directly about that as well. My direct phone number is (858) 673-0690, and I'm based in sunny San Diego, California, USA. Thank you!

Part I

Enhancing Employee Engagement through Recognition

In this part . . .

✔ Discover the current climate of workplace engagement and determine whether your company aligns with current trends

✔ Identify different methods of keeping your employees engaged at work

✔ Get the ins and outs on how to maintain open lines of communication, involve employees in decisions, and provide employees the autonomy they need to do their best work

✔ Understand how recognition drives employee engagement and how you can use this phenomenon to enhance your company's culture

Chapter 1

The Quest for Engagement

In This Chapter

▶ Uncovering what employee engagement is

▶ Recognizing why engagement is important

▶ Exploring ways to best impact engagement

*E*mployee engagement has become an ever elusive holy grail in the management of human resources. It seems that the more companies strive to attain it, the more it slips from their grasp. But the quest continues because the topic is too important to ignore. Without an engaged staff, managers have a tough time accomplishing anything, let alone the best work possible. To reach and surpass business goals, managers and executives must make sure their employees are active, inspired, and feel good about their work.

Despite its importance, few organizations understand what employee engagement is and how it can drive business outcomes. According to the Aberdeen Group (a research firm specializing in employee engagement), engagement levels are dangerously low for many organizations. Now is the time to fix that. In this chapter, I give you a general overview of employee engagement and explore how some of the best organizations are addressing this topic with much success.

Why Engagement Is Important

Some say that employee engagement is simply the use of discretionary effort by employees. Others say it's all about employee connection or productivity or retention. Still others say that it's simply a score on a survey. I feel employee engagement is the alignment of individual and organizational goals and values to better drive business results.

Engagement leads to productivity

As human resources consulting company Towers Watson has noted, "Four out of every five workers are not delivering their full potential to help their organizations succeed." A big reason for that is that workers aren't fully engaged. According to the Gallup Organization, when you compare nonengaged employees to highly engaged ones, you see that the highly engaged employees are

- ✔ 27 percent less prone to absenteeism
- ✔ 62 percent less likely to be involved in job accidents
- ✔ 51 percent less likely to leave their jobs
- ✔ 31 percent less likely to leave in high-turnover organizations

Organizations that make employee engagement a priority see increased organizational productivity, flexibility, and employee retention. Productivity doesn't depend on the number of hours someone spends at work; what really matters is how engaged your employees are during those hours. Employees who are engaged in their work have a greater desire to work harder and are thus more productive.

Engagement creates trust

Most organizations need greater flexibility and agility to handle a changing competitive landscape. Employee engagement creates trust between the organization and its employees so that employees are more apt to be flexible and adapt to changing business circumstances and needs.

Sixty-five percent of hires in a recent year were *contingent employees,* that is, part-time or project-based workers. This trend is projected to represent 30 to 50 percent of the workforce in the future. In addition, 75 percent of all current organizations have employees who work remotely, and 45 percent of companies anticipate increasing that number. This increase in independent workers is forcing organizations to consider how best to manage both full-time and contingent workers within the same organization. Regardless of how their work is structured, organizations will continue to need workers who are engaged and dedicated to do their best to meet or exceed the needs and expectations of their jobs (I talk more about engaging contingent and other nontraditional workers in Chapters 4 and 5).

A few definitions

Here are a few key terms related to employees and the workplace that you'll see throughout this book. If you are uncertain of their definitions, read on:

Engagement: The simplest definition is tapping into employee discretionary efforts, that is, an employee's willingness to go above and beyond in doing his or her job. A definition that's a bit broader is offered by Wikipedia: "Employee engagement is a property of the relationship between an organization and its employees. An 'engaged employee' is one who is fully absorbed by and enthusiastic about their work and so takes positive action to further the organization's reputation and interests.

Recognition: Recognition is a positive consequence provided to a person for a behavior or result. Recognition can take the form of acknowledgment, approval, or the expression of gratitude. It means appreciating someone for something he or she has done for you, your group, or your organization. You can give recognition as someone strives to achieve a certain goal or behavior or upon completion of that goal or behavior. Using recognition, organizations can build engagement and drive success for the company, including all stakeholders. Recognition comes in all shapes and sizes, but the major categories of recognition include the following:

- *Interpersonal recognition:* A personal or written thank you from one's manager or peers.

- *Social recognition:* Acknowledgement, public praise, or thanks provided on social media such as Facebook, LinkedIn, or Twitter.

- *Tangible recognition:* A certificate, plaque, trophy, paperweight, coffee mug, or other memento.

- *Intangible recognition:* The granting of more involvement in decision-making, autonomy, flexibility, or choice of working assignment.

Reward: Something with monetary value (but not necessarily money) that is provided for desired behavior or performance, often with accompanying recognition. A reward can be an item or an experience. Harvard Business School professor Rosabeth Moss Kanter defines a reward as "something special — a special gain for special achievements, a treat for doing something above-and-beyond."

Incentive: Recognition or a reward that is promised in advance for an anticipated achievement that meets certain criteria. Incentives create anticipation and excitement and thus can result in stronger, clearer motivation.

Motivation: The internal human energy available to inspire a person to act.

Motivator: Anything that increases motivational energy.

Demotivator: Anything that reduces motivational energy and/or triggers negative behaviors.

Engagement helps you retain top talent

As the U.S. economy continues to improve, and as current employees seek new job opportunities, holding on to talent will be critical, and doing so can have a major impact on the success of any organization. Engaged employees are more likely to stay longer in their jobs and bring resilience to their organizations. Top employees who are truly engaged remain more committed to staying in their organizations and are less willing to seek other opportunities. Head to Chapter 17 for more on how to better engage and retain high-potential employees.

Looking at Factors Impacting Employee Engagement

There are many factors that impact the design, rollout, and effectiveness of employee engagement efforts. Here, I present an overview of six drivers of employee engagement; in Chapter 2, I discuss specific strategies and actions that companies are taking to most improve in these areas.

Employee fit: Alignment of employee's goals with organizational goals

The number one factor impacting employee performance and engagement is how well an individual employee's performance (and personal) goals align with the overall organizational goals, mission, and core values. This factor is so crucial, in fact, that it might be hard for you to gain support for engagement initiatives unless they are directly tied to performance goals that drive the organization's success and profitability. Therefore, as a manager, you have to act as a liaison to connect the organization's strategic mission with individual values and behaviors of employees.

Having a process in place by which employees and managers agree on performance goals helps drive significant organizational performance. Top-performing companies even support managers with tools and technologies to help initiate performance and goal-setting conversations that better result in this link between individual efforts and organizational goals.

Moving toward a more engaged, accountable workforce doesn't happen overnight. It requires continual and ongoing effort to change ingrained beliefs and behaviors about the role of employees and leaders in an organization so that employees eventually can say — and truly believe — the following:

- "I play a vital role in this organization and am responsible for what happens here."
- "If I see a problem, it is my duty to fix it."
- "My job is justified only if I make a valuable contribution."

Employee communication

Communication is the lubricant of any well-run organization, and it's especially vital for successful employee engagement. In my research, communication ranked highest (95 percent) of all motivational factors that employees most want in their jobs today. Communication needs to be consistent, bidirectional, involve all levels of the organization, and cover all lengths of time (here-and-now, upcoming, and long term).

Of course, managers and executives must be willing to receive and truly listen to honest and open feedback from employees regarding what they, the employees, most need to be engaged. All staff members should be informed about things critical to the company's success and how they each can contribute to that success. Through strong communication, employees feel a sense of responsibility for the success of the organization and can better champion the organization's mission and values, as well as its products and services.

Employee expectations

"What do you expect from me in my job?" is the starting point for all performance and engagement. Therefore, setting clear goals and expectations is vital. These expectations typically come from one's manager. We know from research that the best goals have these characteristics:

- ✔ **They are few in number and specific in purpose:** After all, any of us can only focus on one thing at a time.

- ✔ **They are "stretch" goals:** That is, they are not too easy and are not too difficult. Instead, they have a good chance (some studies suggest about 70 percent) of being achieved with a dedicated focus by the employee.

- ✔ **They are collaborative:** They involve one or more discussions between the employee and his or her manager.

The days of just telling employees what to do and expecting it to be done as expected are pretty much over. To motivate employees to do their best work, you need to explain to them the "why" of their work — its significance and relation to the organizational goals and customers — and engage them by asking them what they expect of themselves (and of you, their manager!). The process of collaboratively setting clear employee expectations creates a strong bond and motivation between managers and employees.

Employees today are inherently motivated to do a good job where they work. I've never yet met an employee who gets up in the morning and says, "I hope I make a mess of things at work today!" They want to help the organization be successful and prosper as best they can, but they can't do this in a vacuum. They need the leadership and support of management to help create the context for their success.

Employee support

Studies have shown that the most important relationship for an employee at work is the relationship between the employee and his or her direct manager. "If you have a good boss, you have a good job" rings true around the world. If employees don't have support from their managers to be fully engaged, they won't fully engage. Therefore, as a manager, your primary responsibility is to support your employees. This could mean modeling engagement and recognition, being there when they want or need to communicate, being available to discuss problems, finding ways for your employees to get extra training and development, and so on.

As a manager, you are also the primary communication link between your employees and the rest of the organization and, as such, can help employees develop so that, over time, they can take on new roles and responsibilities in the organization.

Employee development

Although all development is self-development — that is, employees have to have the ambition, motivation, and skills to want to learn new things in their jobs — your employee engagement strategies should incorporate development opportunities for employees. In most organizations, the role of employee development increasingly falls to one's manager, with the human resources and training and development departments providing guidance as needed.

Employees are more likely to invest in an organization that invests time, energy, training, and so on in them. Career development is the way individuals manage their career paths. It requires the involvement of their managers and others in the organization to help structure opportunities for their learning and growth. Career development is thus a collaborative effort between the organization and the employee that, ultimately, creates greater engagement.

Employee recognition

Employee recognition is fundamental to ongoing support and motivation of any individual employee or group. As I explain in the upcoming chapters, the key to driving an engagement culture is to systematically recognize employees based on their performance. Although money and other forms of compensation are important to employees, what tends to motivate them to perform at their highest levels are the thoughtful, timely, personal kinds of recognition that signify true appreciation for a job well done. Yet managers and organizations struggle to create an organizational culture that systematically recognizes employee performance when it happens. This book will help you to address that challenge.

Employee recognition programs are quickly becoming one of the fastest growing areas of talent management and a key driver of business success.

I discuss employee recognition extensively throughout this book, and I examine the link between recognition and employee engagement much more thoroughly in Chapter 3.

Why Employee Engagement Is So Elusive

As indicated in the introduction of this book, the percentage of engaged employees in the workforce has remained roughly constant at about 30 percent for at least the last 20 years, even though an increasing amount of time, energy, focus, and financial investment has been exerted annually to expand that percentage. Why is this?

Assuming that organizations sincerely do care about their employees and not just about business success and profits, four reasons come to mind: 1) measured engagement variables are too intangible and subjective, 2) the focus of corrective actions are misplaced, 3) one size does not fit all, and 4) the management of change is too complex.

Measured variables are too intangible

Assessing engagement often involves measuring intangible variables, such as employee perceptions, and this may explain why engagement has lagged. Measuring individual perceptions is a slippery slope. The scoring is subjective and can vary due to many circumstances, yet the aggregate scores are treated as objective facts.

How do you systematically impact employees' perceptions of engagement variables like "At work, my opinions seem to count." A company can do 100 things that it hopes will impact employees' perceptions with no guarantees that any of those efforts will work. Quite likely, the company would need to do different things for different people to get a more favorable response. One person may just need to have a comment validated by a manager or executive ("Great insight, Gary!"), while another employee may not believe his opinion counts until a manager acts on the input or idea that was provided.

These observations may explain why organizations are moving away from traditional engagement surveys as the primary means of managing engagement strategies. Although surveys are a valuable way to gauge engagement levels, they do not always yield the kind of information that enables organizations to improve their recognition and engagement efforts. In Chapter 8, I talk more about how to measure recognition and engagement in meaningful and useful ways.

Corrective actions are misplaced

Measuring one set of variables but then focusing elsewhere to try to impact those variables seems like a fool's errand, yet this is exactly how most engagement strategies are structured. Placing the onus of action on the organization and its management rather than the employees themselves with managerial support is a no-win proposition.

Suppose, for example, that you ask employees, "Are you using your full potential at work?" and they report, "No, I am not." How can any manager alone fix that situation? Any potential solutions will at best be a guessing game, and it makes it a little too easy for employees to report, "No, you still haven't got it right — try again" the next time they are surveyed.

Notice how the picture changes if you recast the question to, "Are you taking measures to use your full potential at work?" The focus for change is now on those individuals whose negative perceptions were the driving force behind your decision to take action to begin with.

A better strategy is to focus on the behaviors you want to see more of in employees. You can do that by systematically recognizing and reinforcing behaviors that have the greatest impact on this particular variable.

When writing your engagement survey questions, consider changing the focus of the questions from being *passive* to being *active* so that the questions focus more on your employees' actions. Instead of a statement like, "I'm given adequate information on issues of importance to my job by management," include this statement: "I seek the information I most need to do my job."

This rewording puts employees front and center in driving those variables you are most trying to impact. Unless you place focus on the actions of those who are reporting the need, you'll end up chasing potential solutions indefinitely.

One size does not fit all

Another challenge of engagement programs is the tendency to have a one-size-fits-all approach to engagement and, particularly, to recognition. Companies put in cool programs to drive engagement that are created around the things the person or committee planning the programs finds motivating. Yet, research shows that no motivation strategy or incentive tends to appeal to more than 40 percent of a typical company's employee population. And often, the organization only has the budget to create a recognition program that can appeal to 70 percent of the employee population.

Engagement strategies thus need to be individualized around the personal motivations of each employee, and every manager needs to make the necessary connection with those employees that report to him or her. If you hire a workforce that is universally motivated and engaged by the same approach, that is great, but when does that ever happen in real life? Many companies assume everyone is motivated equally by the same things (such as greater pay), which we know is not the case at all.

Management of change is too complex

As you look at the key factors that impact employee engagement (refer to the earlier section "Looking at Factors Impacting Employee Engagement"), they are each relatively clear and are elements that you can easily focus on for improvement. Often, however, managers and executives make two key mistakes:

- ✔ Over-complicating these issues, sometimes to the point of measuring one thing but focusing on something completely different as a potential solution.
- ✔ Being too ambitious about what they can really change in any given time period.

The result of these errors? The impact of any actions taken become blurred or diminished, and the degree of complexity explodes. The problem is compounded when you overlay the solution on your organization's annual planning and budgeting process, and the speed of change grinds to a halt.

To combat these tendencies, select one thing to focus on and do it right. Clearly focus on a critical area for improvement and then strive to make true inroads in changing that dimension. You'll move much closer to being a culture of engagement if you do a deep dive on just one variable and stick with it over a significant period of time rather than trying to improve a dozen variables across the board. The further your focus drifts from the variables you are specifically measuring, the fuzzier the results you are apt to obtain, and you'll end up about where you started, with no discernable improvement, year after year.

Much has been made over the years of the service-profit chain model where engaged employees lead to engaged customers. However, what is often overlooked is the reverse of this relationship. One research study showed customer satisfaction impacted employee engagement at a much greater rate than the opposite. If an otherwise engaged, motivated employee is constantly dealing with frustrated customers, the employee's engagement level drops quickly. Gallup used to say that if you put a good employee in a bad system, the system wins every time. Employee surveys often ignore these cultural aspects and focus more on the employee's internal satisfaction. For example, are employees empowered to resolve customer concerns on the first contact? Are employees forced to deal with policies that frustrate customers? Do salespeople promise things they can't deliver? These, and other cultural factors, can make or break employee engagement.

Engagement: A Process for Improvement

The best way to think about planning, executing, and improving engagement is a concept I draw from the work of W. Edwards Deming and the total quality management movement. It's called the Shewhart Cycle, and I've adopted it here as the PDRI cycle, which stands for "Plan, Do, Review, and Improve." Read on to find out how it applies to improving your engagement culture and head to Chapter 8 for more details on this approach.

Plan

When you think of planning, you likely envision something elaborate and well-documented, but that is not necessarily what I'm talking about here. A plan can also simply be a desire or intention to take a particular action. You might just ask yourself the question, "If we could do one thing to most improve our department's or organization's effectiveness, what would that be?" or "How can I best make a motivational impact on my employee or work group?" Obviously, the more complex the activity, the more important a formal plan will be, but regardless of the complexity, the greater the commitment to action you have, the more likely the plan will be implemented.

Start with the end in mind. What is the end-state that you want to create in your organization? Focus on desired behaviors and actions needed to move toward that end state. Create measures that will track progress toward your desired end state.

Until a skill or behavior is habitual, some planning is necessary. Although about 80 percent of our behaviors are habitual and require little or no thought, all new behaviors require at least some amount of advance thought, planning, and commitment to instill the behavior in individual practice.

Do

Doing turns intention into action. Many people have good intentions but never follow through on them. If intentions alone were sufficient, everybody would be successful! The best performers understand the difference between intention and performance; they are action-oriented. They know that without focused action everything is just theory. Although their actions at first might be ineffective, they know that it is important to get the learning-by-doing process started. As the famous Nike advertising slogan proclaims, "Just do it!" Systematically recognize and reinforce those behaviors and actions that you've identified could most impact the success of your goals.

Review

After you have engaged in a recognition activity, review it to see what kind of effect it is having. Gaining feedback through a program review is a critical step in the learning process. A review answers such questions as

- How well was the recognition received by the recipient? How did it make him or her feel?
- Was the objective of the recognition met?
- Were there any unintended positive or negative consequences?

With an evaluation incorporating the metrics you established beforehand, access what worked well and what didn't. This review can be elaborate or very simple. Sometimes you'll do this review yourself, based on direct observation, and sometimes it can be a larger evaluation effort that a group takes on with input from employees, management, and any service providers that may be helping you.

After your review, you can do one of three things: Stop giving recognition (fortunately, most people will not choose this option), continue to give it exactly the same way going forward (this option means you felt your efforts were successful), or decide to learn from your experience and improve the way you give recognition to others (the most likely scenario).

Success is an opportunity for positive reinforcement, but we usually learn more from behaviors that fall short of the mark, so failure is an opportunity to learn and improve.

Improve

In this step, you implement the lessons you received during your review, making improvements in your own performance. The more you engage in an activity, review the results of your actions, and improve on them, the better you become at that behavior. Using the PDRI model and the additional recognition knowledge contained in this book, you will get better and better at giving recognition. As you recognize others more often, you'll become more competent and confident in doing so, increasing your skill and effectiveness. The PDRI cycle helps you get better until recognition becomes an ingrained habit. Adjust your plan accordingly and repeat as necessary.

Routines are good, but they do have a downside. They can seem mechanical, insincere, or out-of-touch. Consider these examples:

- The president of a large manufacturing company walks through his plant once a month to say hi to his people. This makes him feel like he's a great manager. If you ask his people, however, they see this behavior as little more than a joke. Says one front-line worker, "Each month, Mr. Johnson asks me how my family is. And each month, I tell him 'I'm still not married, Sir.'"

- In another company, employees report that upper management tends to recognize them more as a show for the benefit of their peers rather than for the employees themselves. In their management team meetings, company managers will talk about the great job one of their employees is doing, but the comments rarely get back to the actual employee being acknowledged.

- In another organization, employee-of-the-month awards are handed out in management meetings, at which the employees being recognized are seldom if ever present. The manager running the meeting traditionally concludes his congratulatory remarks with a comment along the lines of, "If someone runs into Larry, please tell him that he was named employee of the month."

Who best drives employee engagement?

Who should be responsible for employee engagement in the organization? Ideally, senior leaders and the HR department should design and lead the efforts, and then managers should implement them. But who is the "owner" of the effort moving forward? Who should drive the efforts?

According to the Aberdeen Group, for 63 percent of the Best-in-Class organizations the group surveyed, CEOs are the primary champions of successful programs and value motivating employees and supporting engagement initiatives. Yet many CEOs aren't always in the best position to own and execute

the organization's engagement strategy, so it often falls to the managers themselves with the help and guidance of the human resources department. When managers are responsible for employee engagement, they are more likely to link these strategies to performance and results desired by the organization.

Ultimately, organizations have to select drivers that make the most sense for their companies. The key to making sure those driving the initiative are successful is to ensure that they have the necessary resources and authority and embrace the task.

Keeping a Clear Focus as You Improve Your Engagement Efforts

A number of organizations have contacted me for help in improving their focus on just a single variable of employee recognition. They know they need help, based on survey responses to questions such as "I feel valued for the work I do." My first task is to get them to realize it's difficult to change anything based on feedback from just a single variable. It's like trying to guess the shape of a golf ball by looking at a single dimple. You need to expand on that variable to develop a more robust understanding of what is needed. In this case, what does recognition mean to those answering this question? Who is providing (or not providing) recognition? How often is recognition provided? Does recognition vary over time? Does recognition vary with different circumstances? At the very least, you should create an expanded index of variables that all lead to better understanding what employee recognition means for your employees.

I've seen people (somewhat comically) try to interpret what a variable means without this broader understanding of the context ("I think what employees are saying by making this variable low is that . . . "), but why guess on the meaning of the variables you are measuring when you can simply clarify by asking additional questions, conducting some employee focus groups or a pulse survey, or all of the above? The further you drift from the specific variables you are measuring, the more difficult impacting those variables will be.

The thing to remember is that not only are there all kinds of work-based variables to measure and consider, but there are also personal or demographic variables that play into what makes engagement successful. In the chapters that comprise Part V, I go into detail about different issues that impact engagement and recognition.

Chapter 2

Strategies for an Engaged Workforce

*B*y being proactive, positive, focused, and forward-looking, managers can engage and inspire employees — and employees can inspire and engage themselves and their coworkers — in practical ways that yield real results and allow their companies to become stronger, more profitable, and more competitive in even the most difficult marketplace.

Taking control of their circumstances helps employees take control of their jobs — and their lives — and makes positive things happen. Companies that have had increasing engagement scores over the last decade have revealed a short list of key variables attributing to those results, and this chapter focuses on those variables. Here, I show you how to create a framework for managing employees in positive and practical ways to overcome negative times and circumstances. I offer a strategy, a process, and key factors critical to success for you, all supported with examples, techniques, and case studies of how other managers have succeeded in fostering more engaged employees.

Creating a Clear and Compelling Direction

All performance starts with clear goals and expectations. The starting point of any effort to improve or sustain employee engagement is giving employees a clear and compelling vision. If employees don't know (or aren't inspired by) what the organization is doing, they find summoning up the motivation to succeed more difficult. Frances Hesselbein, president of the Leader to Leader Institute, once put it this way: "No matter what business you're in, everyone in the organization needs to know why."

People who perform well feel good about themselves. When employees reach or surpass personal or company goals, their level of engagement is typically at its highest, which then affects other areas of performance. If this spills over to better delivery of customer service or higher-quality products and services, that can then, in turn, have a direct impact on the loyalty of customers.

Assessing employees' understanding of your organization's mission and purpose

Ask employees what the mission and purpose of the organization is. If they don't know, or if you get a different answer from each person you ask, chances are things have drifted or perhaps haven't been clear for some time. Use this opportunity to revisit your purpose.

To gain clarity about the organization's mission, management guru Peter Drucker suggests that you ask these five questions to get at the core of your business:

- ✔ What is our mission?
- ✔ Who is our customer?
- ✔ What does the customer value?
- ✔ What are our results?
- ✔ What is our plan?

Clarifying your vision (and revisiting this process periodically) is useful for deciding what's most important for the organization to focus on to be successful. In addition, the result needs to be compelling enough to inspire everyone. "A vision is not just a picture of what could be; it is an appeal to our better selves, a call to become something more," says Harvard professor Rosabeth Moss Kanter. From that vision, you can shape your *unique competitive advantage,* those aspects that you have to offer your customers that your competition does not. This advantage represents your strengths in the marketplace that you most need to capitalize on to be successful.

Modifying strategies to meet goals

After you clarify your vision for your group and start to revitalize your goals, you should analyze what's currently working and what's not working for the business. For example, established customers may be cutting back on using the services of your firm, but what new clients have recently started to invest with you? What do those new clients have in common, and how can you approach similar clients in the marketplace? Changing times call for changing strategies to meet your company's goals. Engage employees' help by seeking their input and ideas for improving business operations, saving money, or better serving your customers.

A company adapts to changing times

My spouse worked for a computer equipment and software company based in San Diego that saw its future orders drop significantly when customers no longer had the funds to purchase capital equipment. The firm laid off about 10 percent of its employees and froze salaries, but company leaders knew that these decisions offered only a short-term fix for a declining cash flow. Top management got together with the firm's sales representatives and brainstormed what could be done to address the situation, as well as what the competition was doing in response to the situation. Here's what they came up with:

✔ Changing the pricing model to include new options for payment that didn't require the customer to make an expensive upfront purchase of equipment

✔ Offering a new, software-only solution that allowed customers to run needed applications on computers they already owned or on equipment they wanted to purchase from other vendors

✔ Financing the purchase of its customers' equipment so that the customers didn't have to initially tap into resources from their capital budgets

✔ Targeting new markets, such as the federal government (which had more available funds), which the company had never focused on before

All these changes required everyone in the organization to help think through implications for the business and make adjustments accordingly. The result was that the firm was able to get new clients who took them up on their new offerings. Overall, the approach helped the firm generate new sales revenue from new clients in a difficult financial time.

Opening Lines of Communication

People want to know more than just the information necessary to do the work they're assigned; they also want to know what their coworkers are doing and how the organization is doing. To keep your workforce engaged, communicate information to employees about the organization's mission and purpose, its products and services, its strategies for success in the marketplace, and even what's going on with the competition.

In my research, the highest-ranking variable that 95 percent of employees want most from their managers is direct, open, and honest communication. Also, the Families and Work Institute in New York did a study — the National Study of the Changing Workplace — that revealed the importance of non-monetary factors on employees' choice of their current employers. The top-ranked item on the list was "open communication."

Good information, bad information, or no information?

Employees want and need to know what's going on within the organization, even if the information isn't always positive. There's nothing wrong with being honest with employees when the firm is struggling; doing so can lead to increased teamwork and dedication, especially if the bad news is also an opportunity to brainstorm and communicate with employees about ideas and plans for turning things around. Bringing employees into the loop can instill a greater sense of involvement and responsibility, which ultimately leads to increased feelings of value and trust among employees.

I remember working with a defense contractor that was very guarded about sharing information with its employees. Everything was on a need-to-know basis. I asked for the rationale behind this practice and discovered that managers believed that if they told their employees something and it changed or turned out to be wrong, they, the managers, would look bad. I suggested that they give their employees that context and see if they still wanted to hear the latest information, even if it may change. Of course, they (the employees) all did.

Simply telling employees what's going on in the organization and providing them with the information they need to most effectively do their jobs is motivating. In addition, every time you communicate, you have a chance to recognize employees. Exchanging praise and recognition in newsletters, posting an "applause" bulletin board on the company's intranet, and commenting in meetings are just a few possibilities for formalizing communication about employee recognition.

Employing direct, two-way communication

Feedback sessions, departmental meetings, or companywide gatherings should ideally serve two purposes: to provide information and to gather feedback. To maximize employee engagement, keeping employees abreast of and asking their opinions about management's goals and ensuing plans is imperative. Something as simple as a companywide meeting during which you present the state of the organization to all employees can make a world of difference in easing employee tensions and fears.

When discussing major issues like organizational changes, always host a dialogue rather than a lecture, and encourage questions. And if any key updates are going to be shared publicly outside of the organization (for example, in a press release), make sure you tell your internal employees first and invite feedback. Your employees have to feel as though they have the freedom to express their fears and concerns and the chance to receive honest and informative responses.

Exploring communication techniques

Methods for communicating with employees vary depending upon the situation. Group settings require different interaction than one-on-one communication. Following are some suggestions for how to best communicate with individuals and groups.

Individuals

Here are some techniques for effectively communicating with an individual employee:

- ✔ Engage in periodic one-on-one meetings with each employee.
- ✔ Offer personal support and reassurances, especially for your most valued employees.
- ✔ Provide open-door accessibility to management.
- ✔ Invite employees to write anonymous letters to top management about their concerns.

Groups

Here are some communication techniques you can try to keep information flowing in groups:

- ✔ Conduct town hall meetings.
- ✔ Host CEO-led breakfasts and/or brown bag lunches.
- ✔ Maintain a 24-hour "news desk" on the company intranet.
- ✔ Provide periodic state-of-the-union updates on the business.
- ✔ Be open and honest in explaining the situation and challenges going forward.
- ✔ Take questions in advance of a meeting or allow them to be written on index cards, anonymously.
- ✔ Record meetings and distribute the proceedings to those who are unable to attend.
- ✔ Set up a blog site for your CEO, especially if you have satellite offices and/or your employees travel regularly. Doing so enables even distant employees to receive immediate feedback around key issues and updates.

Communicating bad news and dealing with rumors

One of the most common errors many organizations and managers make is not sharing adequate information with employees. In some instances, top management doesn't share information because they're uncertain themselves about something. In other instances, managers feel that sharing information with employees may undermine their own power and job status. So management tries to "protect" employees from fears regarding the potential of job loss or frustration related to the ability of senior management to effectively handle a pending crisis.

Employees aren't looking for a sugar-coated delivery of information. The best way to explain the state of an organization is in a clear, concise, and honest manner. If sales are declining at a rapid or steady pace, every member of the staff has to know. Sharing this information inspires in all employees the collective ownership of the organization's performance. From frontline staff to mid- and upper-level management, everyone shares a portion of the responsibility for an organization's revenue, performance, and future.

By including each employee in an honest, behind-the-scenes look at the fiscal landscape of an organization and the approach or plan to resolve the crisis, you send the underlying message that every single person is a critical part of the whole. That, in turn, creates a greater sense of accountability. Feeling as though they're part of the solution rather than being left in the dark gives employees the confidence they need to buckle down and do their part to pull the organization through a time of crisis.

Open lines of communication across the company can end one of the most detrimental viruses spread throughout an organization: rumors. It's human nature to believe negative statements of supposed fact rather than positive ones. Because most rumors breed negativity, it's crucial to stop them at the source, even openly asking employees about rumors they have heard. Merely talking to employees can ease uncertainty and let them know that you're there to provide information, not keep it from them.

Involving Employees and Encouraging Initiative

When you arm employees with more frequent and relevant information, they're more likely to act on that information in ways that can best help the organization. Honest and open communication shows that you as a manager have both trust and respect for your employees. You can build on that foundation by explicitly requesting and encouraging your employees to get involved in helping the company. This alone can lead to profound results, from improved daily operations to a better bottom line.

According to a survey I conducted of employees in a variety of industries, 92 percent of employees want their managers to ask for their opinions and ideas at work, and more than 89 percent want their managers to involve them in decisions that are made at work. This section explores ways for you to become a more engaged manager with engaged employees who share their ideas and opinions and have some input in decision-making.

Guiding employee focus

Today's managers are discovering that they have to create an environment that encourages employees to *contribute* their best ideas and work, to help seek out new opportunities, such as new sources of revenue, and to overcome obstacles facing the company, such as cutting costs, wherever possible. Workers are discovering that, if they expect to survive the constant waves of change sweeping across the global business marketplace as well as hold onto their current jobs, they have to join with other employees to contribute to their organizations in ways that they've never before been called upon to do.

Managers need to discuss the following topics with their employees:

- ✔ **Employee impact:** Are employees aware of how they impact the company's bottom line, that is, how their jobs financially impact the organization?

- ✔ **Revenue-generating ideas:** How can the company generate additional income? Whether it's new fees, cross-selling, or up-selling, what new ideas could be tried?

- ✔ **Cost-savings suggestions:** How can costs be trimmed, delayed, or eliminated? Which expenses are critical and which are optional and could at least be cut temporarily?

- ✔ **Process improvements:** What steps in the organization's processes can be streamlined, saving time, resources, and money along the way?

- ✔ **Customer needs and requests:** How can employees help others in the company who are focused on customer needs and requests? How can customers' needs be further explored?

- ✔ **New products or services:** What ideas exist for new products or services? How could those ideas be better developed and implemented?

- ✔ **Morale and teambuilding:** Who is interested in helping to improve employee teamwork and morale? How can this be done at little cost?

- ✔ **Virtual employees:** How can virtual employees be better utilized by and integrated into the organization?

Asking employees for their input and ideas

I have yet to see an organization that doesn't have an open door policy, in which employees are encouraged to speak to their managers about any concerns, ideas, or suggestions they have. In practice, however, this policy doesn't always work very well if, at the point of interaction, one's manager is not receptive to the input.

Soliciting ideas needs to be a constant, ongoing strategy. Conducting employee surveys and asking staff questions in a meeting is a start, but to maximize buy-in and motivation, you need to challenge your employees to identify ways to improve on an ongoing basis. Employee engagement should be both a philosophy and a practice. Employees need to understand that you need their efforts now more than ever before, and then you need to create new mechanisms that inspire their ongoing involvement to improve.

Would you like more ideas from your employees? I'm convinced that every employee has at least one $50,000 idea — if you can only find a way to get it out! Yet most companies do little, if anything, to get ideas from their employees. Or if they do decide to take action, it's in the form of a suggestion box that's placed in the lunchroom with (for some reason) a lock on it. The first dozen or so employees who submit suggestions, if they hear back at all, often receive a form letter months later that more or less states, "Here's why we're not using your silly idea . . . ." The result? The suggestion program grinds to a halt. In fact, I recently heard of one company that ended its dead suggestion program because, the company announced, *the company had gotten all the ideas.* How convenient.

They don't feel that's the case at AT&T Universal Card Services in Jacksonville, Florida, where the company gets some 1,200 ideas *per month* from employees. They don't feel that way at Valeo, either. In a recent year, the French automaker received 250,000 ideas for improvement from employees.

Taking initiative at Boardroom, Inc.

Boardroom, Inc., a newsletter and book publisher based in Greenwich, Connecticut, expects every employee — from receptionist to chairman — to submit at least two ideas each week for improvements. Initially established to encourage cost-savings, the Boardroom, Inc., program is called "I Power," and the company credits the suggestion program with a five-fold increase in its revenues as well as untold benefit to the morale, energy, and retention of its employees. Each employee is asked to turn in two suggestions each week; these suggestions are evaluated the same week by an employee volunteer. For many of the suggestions, the evaluator says, "What a great idea!" and returns the idea to the person who suggested it with the implicit permission to proceed to implement the idea.

As Martin Edelston, chairman and CEO of Boardroom says, "Sometimes the best idea can come from the newest, least experienced person on your staff." Like the hourly paid shipping clerk who suggested that the company consider trimming the paper size of one of its books to get under the 4-pound rate and save some postage. The company made the change and did, indeed, save postage: a half a million dollars the first year and several years since. Explains Marty, "I had been working in mail-order for over 20 years and never realized there was a 4-pound shipping rate. But the person who was doing the job knew it, as do most employees know how their jobs can be improved."

The first year of the program, suggestions were limited to one's own job until employees got the idea that the intention was less to complain about things than to try to think how things could be improved. The company now even has group meetings just to brainstorm and share ideas about specific issues or functions in the company.

(continued)

(continued)

And the benefits of the suggestions are not limited to saving money. Says Antoinette Baugh, director of personnel, "People love working here because they know they can be a part of a system where they can make a contribution." Adds Lisa Castonguay, renewals and billing manager, "My first couple of weeks, I was kind of taken aback because everyone was smiling and everyone was open." She recalls her first day of work when she was pulled into a group meeting and, within 30 minutes of walking in the front door, was asked, "What do you think we should do about this problem?"

Lisa almost fell on the floor. Why? Because she had just come from a company where she had

worked for eight years, and no one had ever asked her for her opinion about anything. After she got over the initial shock, she realized that having her opinions and ideas sought after and valued by those she worked with felt pretty good. As a result, she wanted to think of even more ways to help the company.

The impact is both positive and contagious. "People became agents of their own change," says Marty. "There's so much inside all of us, and we don't even know it's there until someone asks about it. And in the process, it just builds and builds." Adds Brian Kurtz, vice president of marketing, "It's a constant flow of communication. People are not sitting in a cubicle, totally insulated from one another."

Involving employees in decision-making

When employees believe they have a hand in decision-making, companywide buy-in and participation is much easier to obtain. If the general consensus among staff is that decisions will be made with or without their input, the likelihood of anyone providing open and honest feedback is quite small. Asking employees for their input shows that you respect and trust them, and it likely increases the quality of the decisions being made.

Ultimately, the responsibility for any decisions that are made remains with the manager, so collecting input from employees doesn't mean you're obligated to use what's shared in every instance.

No one knows how to better do a job than the person who is currently doing that job, so starting there makes sense. For example, if a reporting process is ineffective or costly, talk to the individual responsible for managing the process. Take the example of a receptionist at Champion Solutions Group in Florida, who received expense reports from field sales representatives via overnight delivery. When the company implemented her suggestion that the reports be faxed instead of shipped, it saw a 40 percent reduction in postage costs — and led company leaders to seek the advice of employees for other ways to realize cost savings.

Employees who offer solutions that result in cost savings need to be recognized for their efforts, especially if you want them to repeat that behavior or if you want to inspire others to do likewise. Incentives, such as bonuses, trips, or gift cards, not only reward the employee, but they also inspire others to develop cost-saving ideas of their own. Make the process fun and rewarding. Hold contests, departmental competitions, or other organized events to increase employee involvement and interaction. Ask employees for their buy-in on the type of incentives they value; they may want an extra vacation day or time to volunteer at a favorite charity.

Support for change can't be acquired without involving employees, so you need to ensure that you give employees the opportunity to be involved in the decision-making process. Some simple ways to include employees follow:

- ✔ Asking employees for their opinions on various matters of importance to the department
- ✔ Inviting employees to actively participate in setting objectives and revising goals for the department
- ✔ Establishing task forces made up of employees whose objective is to identify better ways to work

I worked with an organization whose employees are highly engaged in achieving the firm's goals on a daily basis. They do this through "huddles." During the first 10 to 15 minutes of every morning's work group, each employee-owner describes his or her number one priority for that day and any barriers he or she faces in achieving that priority. Everyone in the huddle votes on the top priority and then the group's manager passes the agreed-upon top priority to the next level up which has a second-level huddle that immediately follows the first huddle. At the second-level huddle, the process repeats, along with a review of the previous day's metrics. The manager groups can choose to resolve any or all the barriers that arise and then they, too, vote on the number one priority to be passed on to the executive team for its meeting, which is up next. On Fridays, all groups take a break from their normal "meeting rhythm," as they call it, and ask for "IQs," that is, ideas or questions, that every employee has for achieving that quarter's overarching goals. As a result, the organization was perhaps the best I've ever experienced at systematically achieving its quarterly goals, quarter after quarter!

Increasing Employee Autonomy, Flexibility, and Support

If you're effective at getting employees to take more initiative, you have to provide them greater autonomy, flexibility, and support to help them succeed. All employees need to have a say in how they do their work to make it more meaningful. After you enlist your employees to make suggestions and improvements, you need to encourage them to run with their ideas, take responsibility, and champion those ideas to completion. Allow employees to approach anyone they need for help, give them the authority to make decisions or use resources, and permit them to take the actions that are necessary to get the work done.

In my research on employee preferences at work, "autonomy and authority" and "flexibility of working hours" were two of the top motivators for today's employees. To the extent that you, the manager, or the organization is able to provide those motivators for employees, their morale and performance will be positively — and significantly — impacted, and they'll do their best work possible.

Giving employees autonomy

No one likes to be micromanaged. The vast majority of employees would prefer to determine how they work best. In other words, they'd prefer to be assigned a task and allowed the freedom to develop a work plan that suits them. As a manager then, focus on the end result and allow your employees to put their own imprint on the job — to decide how best to achieve the result. Take it a step further by allowing employees to pick and choose the projects and responsibilities they can work on as a reward for having previously done a great job.

Here is where truly knowing your employees becomes important: Understanding their strengths and weaknesses allows you to properly assign projects and tasks, making suggestions for assignments that you know the employee would likely value and helping that employee develop new skills in the process.

Allowing flexible work schedules

Based on my research, the majority of employees cite increased flexibility in employee work schedules as a top motivator. Furthermore, depending upon the type of work, a flexible schedule can also increase the efficiency of getting the work done.

Technology has opened up new possibilities for how employees work. Gone are the days when communication was limited to fax and phone lines or face-to-face meetings. These days, some businesses operate entirely on a virtual platform with employees scattered throughout the country or world.

Although not every company is able to operate this way, a large percentage of jobs can be done outside the traditional 9 to 5 office schedule. As a result, in recent years, many companies have experimented with flexible schedules or telecommuting options. Consider these statistics:

- ✔ Forty percent of current workers work remotely.

- ✔ Eighty-six percent of employees today report that they wish they had more time to spend with their families.

- ✔ In the last five years, nearly 30 percent of workers have voluntarily made career changes that resulted in a salary reduction in an effort to lead a more balanced life.

- ✔ Almost 50 percent of employees value the option of flexible or work-from-home hours.

- ✔ Fifty-four percent of employees appreciate the option to leave work early to tend to family or child issues.

- ✔ A large percentage of workers would take a reduction in pay if doing so allowed them to have more time for personal interests or to spend more time with family.

Having a sense of balance between the personal and professional parts of their lives is very important to today's employees. Your company can help employees achieve greater flexibility and greater balance by implementing policies that promote life outside of the workplace. Here are some suggestions:

- ✔ Letting employees work alternate hours (arriving early and leaving early or vice versa)

- ✔ Offering four-day work weeks, in which longer hours are worked on fewer days

- ✔ Letting employees telecommute and work from remote locations

- ✔ Offering job-sharing options, where two or more employees split a job

- ✔ Allowing an employee to leave work early or to take time off to compensate for extra hours worked

Many companies have found that offering employees the options of working a flexible schedule or telecommuting increases morale and productivity. For some employees, the attraction is less time spent each week in a car and savings on gas or mileage. Others may enjoy reducing childcare expenses or simply having the opportunity to spend more time with their children. Whatever the motivation, employees appreciate the option of being able to have some control over their own schedules and, as a result, feel as though the company has their best interests in mind.

I once managed a work group that experimented with having employees work from home on certain projects. Those who worked at home logged their hours and were available as needed to discuss work issues. Not counting the commute time that was saved, employees were found to be *twice* as efficient in what work they accomplished. With less socializing and fewer interruptions, the employees were better able to focus on the work at hand. I've heard of similar findings in other studies conducted since then.

Providing managerial accessibility and support

When employees are encouraged to have more autonomy, independence, and flexibility in their jobs, they need your support; however, in one survey conducted by Gallup, 66 percent of respondents said their managers had asked them to get involved in decision-making, but only 14 percent felt they'd been empowered to make those decisions.

In most cases, giving employees the autonomy and authority to act in the best interests of the organization and offering words of encouragement and praise along the way works wonders. Encouraging employees to pursue their ideas and supporting them in that process are also important for yielding positive results in the workplace.

Here are some guidelines for building rapport with and supporting your employees:

- **Take time with employees.** It all comes back to communication: Getting out and talking to employees, spending time with frontline staff, and making an effort to truly listen to employees can open your eyes to seemingly small accomplishments that would otherwise go unnoticed. No matter how small, the roles and responsibilities of every employee are a critical factor in the overall success of an organization.

- **Ask employees what they want and/or need.** Don't assume you or your management team knows automatically. For employees that have been with you several years, don't assume what they wanted five years ago is still the same; encourage open and honest dialogue.

- **Be available for questions from employees.** Managers have to be available and approachable to get employees to talk with them. Whether that means dropping into the break room, holding "office hours," or having a beer with the team after work or to celebrate finishing a project—face time is critical. I know of one manufacturing plant that even invested in an electronic deli type of sign that said, "Now serving number . . . " Employees who wanted face time with a visiting executive got a number and made their way to the main office as that number got close to being called.

✓ **Show understanding and empathy.** It's important for all employees to feel that their managers are on their side, rooting for their success and seeking to help them succeed in any way possible. When employees face life changes, tragedies, or circumstances that demand more of their time than usual, employees need to feel comfortable discussing their situation with their managers or employers. If they're met with understanding and a willingness to help, they won't ever forget it. And the happier and more stable your employees, the better your business fares.

Best, Best and Krieger — a large law firm in Southern California — promotes an open door policy wherein anyone who has questions or concerns regarding personal or professional security is free to discuss those worries with the firm's managing partner. Employees are facing some very real fears, and ignoring these can only make them worse.

✓ **Support employees when they make mistakes.** Employees need their manager's support more than ever when they (the employees) make mistakes. Finding fault and openly criticizing employees is easy — sometimes even in front of their peers. But if you take that approach, your employees will lose a degree of self-esteem and a willingness to act independently — and you may never get those attributes back again.

To help employees sustain necessary levels of motivation, work with them to identify potential barriers to their success. Don't simply assume that there are no obstacles or that all the obstacles are evident. Look to employees for guidance and input, and allow them to point out barriers to accomplishing a task, completing a project, or merely going about their daily duties.

Establishing effective lines of communication that involve and support *all* employees is especially imperative if managerial or other staff changes occur — new managers are put in place, project groups are reassigned, departments are downsized, and so on. No matter how small the changes, employees will feel as though they've lost some sort of control over their situation.

Regardless of the approaches you ultimately decide to take in your efforts to increase employee engagement, remember the following points:

✓ Encouraging initiative starts with taking initiative. Everyone has an idea that can improve his or her job, department, or even the company overall. Find a way to get those ideas out! Do something different, experiment and learn along the way.

✓ Set up a system for eliciting employee ideas and fostering employee engagement that is simple, doable, and fun. If the suggestion program becomes a boring burden, it isn't likely to continue for long.

✓ Stick with it. The best idea may not always be the first one, but the process of valuing your employees' ideas will lead to more and better ideas.

Investing in people at Edward Jones

Edward Jones makes every effort to make its employees feel valued, and the results are evident in the longevity and positive attitude of the company's employees. A survey of Edward Jones employees conducted by *Fortune* magazine revealed that 96 percent of its employees considered the company a friendly place to work, and more than 89 percent felt that managers followed through on what they said or promised. But the most telling statistic is that 83 percent of employees have every intention of working at Edward Jones until they retire.

The vast majority of employees cited their reason for holding the company in such high regard as a sense of truly being cared for. And even though the company has grown rapidly over the years, the culture has remained the same. Employees who have been with the company for decades felt as though principles and values remained intact throughout all of the growing pains.

The personal and professional growth of the company's employees is of utmost importance to managers at Edward Jones. Employees are encouraged to explore new opportunities within the company, which combats the threat of employees becoming bored and looking for new experiences outside the company. Some employees are asked to directly lead or participate in new ventures, ranging from moving within the office in which they're based to traveling overseas to launch new departments, projects, or offices. The philosophy behind this practice is centered on Edward Jones' culture, which strives to develop initiative and drive in all employees. Employees are given the autonomy to forge ahead with new roles or projects they identify, assuming the fit is right. If the employee is lacking in a few key areas, he or she is provided the training necessary to effectively move into the desired role.

Continuing to Focus on Career Growth and Development

Managers need to support their employees in learning new skills and allow them to participate in special assignments, problem-oriented initiatives, and various other activities that expand the employees' knowledge and expertise. They should develop yearly and/or project-specific learning goals with each employee and discuss what was learned, either at the end of the year or in the debriefing of the completed project. Periodically, managers should also hold career development discussions with each employee, perhaps as part of his or her annual performance review, to discuss career options and potential career paths that are available to each employee.

Taking stock in your employees

If you haven't already done so, take time to meet with each employee to discuss his or her job interests and ambitions and create an "inventory of readiness" for your staff. Ask questions such as the following:

✔ Who has skills that aren't currently being utilized in the department?

✔ Who is interested in learning more about other areas of the business, its clients, processes, products, or services?

✔ Who wants to get into a management position some day?

✔ What does everyone want to be doing five years from now?

With this initial baseline of information about your team, you can evaluate who might fit emerging needs, tapping the hidden talents of all employees and expanding traditional roles to help move the organization forward.

Linking needs with employee interests

Although development opportunities are traditional motivators to most employees, during crunch times, such opportunities take on a new sense of urgency. When a needed position is frozen or another position is terminated, how can the work that is left best get completed? When a new project emerges, who in the group is ready to help out? As organizational needs arise, ask, "Who can best benefit from that opportunity?" and approach that individual.

American Express developed a teaching concept called "Label and Link" that the company trains all managers to use. As a development opportunity arises, a manager labels the task as an opportunity and links it to something that's important to the employee being considered for the opportunity. Instead of dumping a work assignment on an already overloaded employee, a manager might say, "Gary, we are forming a new client task force to deal with a new market opportunity, and I immediately thought of you for the team since I know from our past conversations how interested you are in working more directly with our clients. I also know that you've got a lot on your plate right now, so if you feel you are too busy to take this on, I won't hold it against you — there will be other opportunities in the future. But if you are interested, let me know because I'll take whatever time is necessary to help you with the assignment. In fact, it might even take more of my time than if I just joined the task force myself, but I'm willing to make that investment in you because of what I've seen in your potential on our team. Let me know what you decide and thanks."

More often than not, Gary doesn't need to think it over further and immediately accepts the assignment. To some people, this might seem like a trick of some sort, but it's the essence of employee motivation because it aligns the employee's goals and needs with those of the organization. Gary's manager sincerely wants to help Gary learn, grow, and develop.

A manager who is sincere in his or her approach and truly has the best interests of the employee at heart can tap into an energy that employees themselves often don't realize exists.

Another developmental approach is to give employees an opportunity to experience different roles. For example, networking company 3Com believes that allowing those who work behind the scenes — especially engineers — to get out and sell to or visit customers gives them a greater appreciation for the value of the work they do. The employees in technical roles often receive customer feedback second- or third-hand and rarely, if ever, have the opportunity to sit down with a customer directly. How beneficial it is for them to engage in a dialogue that helps them do their job better and avoid feeling as though they are operating in the dark with piecemeal information! When they can hear positive customer feedback first hand, it means much more!

Don't skimp on training

The Container Store has been selected numerous times by *Fortune* magazine as one of the magazine's 100 Best Companies to Work For. The Container Store strongly believes that its employee training programs are one of the major factors in the company's high staff retention rate and overall success. During their first year of employment, new employees can expect to receive 185 hours of training — about 26 percent more than any other retailer in the industry. As a result, for more than two decades, the Container Store has grown almost 20 percent a year.

Though the temptation is great to put it at the top of a cost-saving list, employee training should be one of the *last* things to go if you're making cuts. Employees are the most important assets a company can have; without them, a business simply cannot succeed. Employees can make or break a company, so developing their skills is extremely important. The strengths of your employees can be the determining factor in how or whether your company is able to remain a step ahead of the competition. One of the best ways to keep your workforce strong is through training.

According to a survey I conducted among employees working in industries across the nation, more than 90 percent of the respondents stated that manager support in learning new skills was important to them. Providing such support lets employees know that their development and career advancement is important to their managers and, hence, to the organization as well.

One of the primary concerns management has regarding training is the travel expenses often associated with it. Over the last decade, a large portion of training has been made available online or through other technological venues. Additionally, some companies have embraced the idea of in-house training led by senior management or top executives. All employees can benefit from learning from managers and executives in their own organizations. Programs can be a combination of general topics as well as topics that are company-specific and that use internal managers as trainers. Having internal managers serve as trainers taps into the wisdom of those more experienced both with the topics covered in the training, as well as the organization, its history, culture, and values.

Developing your employees' skills pays off in the long run in employee engagement, employee retention, and competitiveness. Skills refined or learned in training are effective in good times and when times are tough. Southwest Airlines learned this lesson when the company faced economic struggles after the events of September 11. With changes being made throughout the entire industry, the airline decided that all employees had to increase their ability to adapt to internal and external changes. So rather than slash training, as was the norm in the industry at the time, Southwest increased the amount of employee training it conducted.

Expanding employee utilization through cross-training

Cross-training your employees combats their boredom or complacency while simultaneously benefitting the company. If you have a small staff, having employees versed in multiple roles can help in times of layoffs or other reductions.

Make the most of your employees; take time to explore their other interests within the company. For example, a member of the technology department may have had a former career in marketing or sales, or an employee could simply have a strong interest in another part of the company. Work with other managers to provide or discover this information and use it to develop effective cross-training programs. This strategy can be especially beneficial during a downturn or spikes in business to handle peak levels of work activity without adding staff.

Charles Schwab assembled a group of employees from all departments within the organization and dubbed them the Flex Force. When market activity was high, so was Schwab's call volume. This team of employees was on hand to field the additional calls because they had adequate training to do so. Likewise, JW Marriott cross-trains administrative assistants to double as banquet servers when they are short-staffed. In both cases, the companies have seen an increase in productivity and performance, as well as significant cost savings.

Providing development through mentoring

A mentorship program connects senior managers in the organization with lower-level employees who don't report to them directly for an informal development relationship. Providing mentorship programs allows employees who have significant career experience to pass on their lessons to other employees, helping develop them in the process. Employees with a desire to further develop their skills and career path are eager to learn from others in the organization and often welcome mentorship opportunities.

Some companies offer internship programs for employees as well. This is especially popular in a large company, where options for a career path are numerous. Giving employees the chance to experience a behind-the-scenes look at a new role or department can help guide employees in their development. For a predetermined period of time, allow employees who have expressed interest in moving to another role or division the opportunity to work alongside someone currently in the desired position or department. During this period, transferred employees do not relinquish their existing jobs and are assured of being able to return to their original roles when the internship is complete. Even if an opening does not exist or the specific role is currently occupied, when vacancies do occur, the employee who has completed an internship and acquired the necessary skills and knowledge is likely to emerge as a prime internal candidate. This saves the company time and money in conducting an external search to fill open positions.

Shadowing programs are also particularly effective in the development of unlikely relationships among employees. Companies that already have such programs in place have reported a relationship among shadows/shadowers that extends beyond the duration of the program. These connections, especially when spread across departments, do tremendous things for morale, communication, and commitment to the company. Employees no longer feel isolated in their roles or departments and begin to develop a greater sense of belonging.

Young employees in particular are ideal candidates for shadowing or mentoring programs, especially if their current roles do not match their education or desired career paths. Many times, young employees or new graduates pursue an opportunity with a company in the hopes of moving up or on to a job or department that better suits their background and interest. For more information on the unique appeal of job-shadowing programs to younger workers, turn to Chapter 16.

Developing leaders

Some people are simply born to be leaders; others must be developed to fulfill that role. Whether a particular attribute is inherent or acquired, it requires development and reinforcement. Many of the necessary qualities of an effective manager can be learned and even more can be brought to the surface or greatly enhanced during challenging times. The following are some characteristics that demonstrate an employee is ready to become a leader:

- ✔ Focus on learning and development
- ✔ Ability to inspire coworkers
- ✔ Empathy for others and a true understanding of their needs
- ✔ Dedication to employees' personal values and an ability to carry that through in their work
- ✔ Interest in engaging others and instilling teamwork
- ✔ Acceptance of responsibility for their work

You can best develop existing managers (or employees ready to become managers) by combining personal and professional development. All employees should focus on key factors of their personal attributes, as well as their careers — including how they have contributed in previous positions, how they interact with individuals they encounter, what their values and beliefs are, and what skills they need to acquire to get where they would like to be. The motivation to explore and expand on each of these factors has to start with the individual.

Stronger managers can help move a company from middle of the road to great and can be even more beneficial when a sweeping recovery is needed. Investing in programs that provide leadership development is an effective strategy in the long and short term. If cuts to training budgets are necessary, concentrate on eliminating training for skills that can be attained through other means and concentrate specifically on leadership. Chapter 17 discusses additional strategies for developing leaders.

Learning opportunities are personal, too

Training shouldn't end at job-related tasks and knowledge. If employees feel as though they are a part of the process by understanding how their jobs contribute to the overall performance of the company, they are far more likely to work that much harder to contribute.

The best learning cultures promote learning of all types, not just job-specific training. Offering programs that speak to employee emotional and mental well-being is one way of showing you have employees' best interests at heart. For example, if you're revising company financial goals, the new goals will probably impact employees' personal finances. Providing access to resources like webcasts and online seminars regarding financial management or investments is a great way to help employees plan for their futures as well as be more open to changes within the company. Helping employees learn how to better manage their finances can help reduce stress levels at work, as well.

Here are some ways that companies are helping develop employees:

- ✔ **GlaxoSmithKline** offers a seminar focused on personal resilience to teach employees ways to prevent stress and succeed in their jobs. A group of employees is assigned the task of pointing out work-related pressures within their departments and presenting suggestions as to how they might be combatted. Since its inception, GSK's stress management program has reduced work-related and stress-induced illnesses in employees by nearly 60 percent — which also resulted in a 29 percent decrease in absenteeism for health issues.

- ✔ **MetLife,** one of the largest providers of employee benefits, offers retirement education seminars in various companies. The workshops are free and are presented by Certified Financial Planners, offering advice and instruction on financing retirement for employees of all ages. At the end of the seminar, close to half of the attendees choose to take advantage of the opportunity to meet with a retirement specialist. Assuming an active role in helping employees plan for the future shows a company's concern for all aspects of employees' lives.

- ✔ **Fidelity Investments** offers financial web-based seminars that allow employees to participate from their offices or homes. Fidelity has found that of all attendees at its seminars, half make some kind of change to their retirement goals within a couple weeks. A focus on education, and making it simple for employees to revise their financial goals and plans, has made such seminars successful in the workplace.

Chapter 3

How Recognition Drives Employee Engagement

*T*here are a lot of things that impact employee engagement, but if you only focused on *one* thing that could impact it the most, it would be employee recognition. According to employee engagement research conducted by the Aberdeen Group, "By acknowledging an employee's positive behaviors and demonstrating appreciation for employee contributions, that individual worker will continue those behaviors, stay engaged with the company, and feel motivated to perform." Sixty percent of Best-in-Class organizations (defined as those in the top 20 percent of aggregate performers in the Aberdeen Group report) stated that employee recognition is extremely valuable for driving individual performance. And the *Harvard Business Review* cited "recognition given for high performance" as the most impactful driver of employee engagement.

In this chapter, I discuss what recognition is, why it is important, and how it drives employee engagement. I also offer effective strategies you can use to create a culture of recognition to promote employee engagement. I expand on several of these topics in subsequent chapters in this book.

Embracing This Fact: You Get What You Reward

It seems that not a month goes by without the emergence of some new surefire management fad "guaranteed" to increase employee performance, improve morale, and cure whatever ails your organization. Truth be told, executives and managers quickly embrace and then quickly discard most of these fads — much to the chagrin of the employees who feel like Ping-Pong balls bounced from one new management approach to the next.

There are, however, certain basic truths in management that you can always rely on. One of these basic principles, sometimes referred to as the Greatest Management Principle in the World, is that you get what you reward. We know from extensive research that consequences shape all performance and desired behavior, and that one of the most powerful ways to enhance employee performance is by providing thanks, recognition, and praise for that performance. If you notice, recognize, or reward a specific behavior — for instance, if you thank someone for his or her help on a project — that person will be most likely to repeat that behavior and help you on a future project. I discuss the principles of effective recognition further in Chapter 5.

Given that positive reinforcement is one of the most validated principles in management and psychology, it's surprising how few managers use it on a regular basis. It's common sense but far from common practice in business today. Yet it needs to become common practice if your organization is to thrive, let alone survive.

Everyone likes to be recognized and appreciated. But how many managers consider appreciating others to be a major function of their jobs today? Indeed, how many managers are expected by their organizations to recognize their employees when they do good work? Very few, I would venture.

At a time when employees are being asked to do more than ever before, to make suggestions for continuous improvement, to handle problems quickly, to serve the organization's customers, and to act independently in the best interests of the company, the resources and support for helping them do so are at an all-time low. Therefore, now more than ever, employees need to be told by their managers that their efforts are appreciated, especially when they have done a good job.

The widespread lack of effective rewards and recognition programs at a time when those are most needed is particularly ironic because the behaviors that tend to motivate employees the most tend to take very little time and money to implement. It doesn't take a huge bonus check, a trip to the Bahamas, or a lavish annual awards banquet to get the best out of people. It often just takes a little time, thoughtfulness, and energy to notice what the employee did well and thank him or her for it and to get others to do the same.

Employee recognition is critical to driving engagement and improving organization performance. Although organizations realize the benefits of recognition, they often have a difficult time understanding the steps necessary to design and implement a successful recognition program. To increase employee engagement and achieve a competitive advantage, leading organizations look to a culture of recognition. These organizations are seeking to be more strategic about recognition and investing in ways that will help to drive results.

Helping Your Employees Excel

"Why do people do what they do?" is a question that has fascinated and bewildered mankind since the dawn of time. At the most basic level, unmet needs drive people's actions: When you're hungry, you eat; if you're thirsty, you drink; if you're tired, you sleep. However, once people get their most basic physical needs met, their attention turns to meeting higher-level needs, such as a desire for being valued or belonging to or achieving something meaningful in life. Given the fact that most people spend almost one-third of their adult lives at work, it should be no surprise that they often look to the workplace — and to those with and for whom they work — to help satisfy that list of higher-level needs. Recognition tops that list.

Motivation is the internal human energy that prompts a person to satisfy his or her unmet needs. And while all people have the same basic needs, their priorities are in a state of constant flux. Moreover, each individual has his or her own set of needs. One person might be most motivated to spend more time with his family, another to obtain a pay increase, and another might crave more responsibility and do whatever it takes to get it.

By its very nature, motivation is intrinsic — you can't motivate others; you can only provide an environment that is more conducive for them to be motivated. True, you can at times force others to do what you want, but such motivation is apt to be short-lived and last only as long as direct force or a threat exists. When the coercion stops, so, too, does the person's motivation — and the desired behavior. In fact, the traditional emphasis on coercion has given rise to misconceptions about motivation. One such misconception is exemplified by this old joke: If you tell someone what you'll give him for doing something, that's called an incentive; if you tell someone to do something or else he'll get fired, that's called motivation.

A new way to motivate: What managers can do

Every employee wants to be magnificent. Every employee starts a new job excited about doing his or her best. Yet for many employees, the initial excitement of the job quickly wears off, and their motivation dissipates.

I believe this outcome is the direct result of how managers treat their employees on a daily basis. Show me an unmotivated employee, and I'll show you a manager who has failed to help that employee achieve his or her full potential on the job. This section outlines recent changes in what employees expect in the workplace and explains how managers can more effectively help to motivate today's employees.

No more command-and-control

In recent decades, the use of coercion, fear, and the threat of punishment has become increasingly ineffective for motivating employees. Employees have more of a choice about where they work and more control over their discretionary energy at work — that is, they choose whether to be engaged or not.

Managers increasingly expect employees to use their best judgment at work; to make decisions on their own or to be proactive in solving problems; and to not just do what they are told to do. Moreover, today's employees increasingly want to be given more authority and greater autonomy in using that authority. They want to be trusted to do the work they are hired to do and to do that work to the best of their abilities.

The role of managers has thus shifted from an authoritative command-and-control, my-way-or-the-highway style — which has been the predominant style of management since the Industrial Revolution. Now effective managers are those who act more like coaches, colleagues, counselors, and even cheerleaders for their employees.

Managers need to create a new partnership with employees to help employees reach their own goals, as well as the goals of the organization. The effective use of recognition and rewards is the primary means for creating a supportive work environment in which employees can be — and are — highly motivated and engaged, assuring the success of your organization.

Creating an environment conducive to motivation

Another major change in the workplace is that motivation is no longer the sole province of the manager. While managers still play a critical motivational role, so do team leaders and peers, upper management, and human resources departments . . . even customers. Informal influence and leadership plays a bigger role than ever today.

Regardless of who provides the immediate consequences, it's up to managers to establish a supportive environment in which people can perform at their best and in which each and every individual in the organization can be motivated and engaged. In fact, creating such an environment is perhaps the most important role of managing today.

The key element in shaping a more motivating and engaging work environment is the management of consequences, particularly positive consequences.

The benefits of recognition

Rewards and recognition are tools that any manager or leader can use in any organization to help realize enormous business benefits. In some cases, these benefits directly correlate to recognition; that is, as recognition goes up, so too do the following benefits:

- **Improved morale:** One of the more immediate effects of increased recognition is improved morale. When employees are recognized for doing good work, they feel special and, consequently, happier and more satisfied with their employers.

- **Enhanced productivity:** Employees who feel good about their jobs tend to perform at a higher level; the performance itself becomes a further motivator for wanting to continue to do a good job.

- **Increased competitiveness:** When companies recognize and reward performance that is aligned with the organization's key objectives, the organization becomes more successful, more competitive, and more efficient in reaching its goals.

- **Higher revenue and profit:** Any organization that wants to make money and be profitable will find that recognizing progress in those areas encourages employees to work harder to make money and realize *greater* profits for the company.

Another benefit of using recognition is that it has an inverse relationship to the negative elements of stress and employee turnover; that is, as recognition increases, stress and turnover decrease. Chances are, as you commit to recognizing your employees, you'll see the following:

- **Decreased stress:** There's a fine line between stress and excitement. Recognition helps to make work more fun and exciting, increasing the likelihood that employees will rise to the challenge when needed, rather than feel out-of-control and swamped by their work.

- **Decreased absenteeism:** When employees are thanked and valued for the work they do, they begin to look forward to the time they spend on the job. Absenteeism declines.

- **Decreased turnover:** A study by the Gallup Organization in which 2 million workers at 700 companies were interviewed revealed that the number one factor affecting the length of an employee's tenure at a company was the quality of that employee's relationship with his or her immediate supervisor. More recognition equals better relationships, which equals decreased turnover and increased tenure.

✔ **Lower costs related to turnover:** When employees are happy to come to work and are excited about, and focused on doing their best work, the need for — and costs of — interviewing, hiring, and training new employees all decline.

Figure 3-1 shows this effect of recognition, increasing positive outcomes and decreasing negative ones.

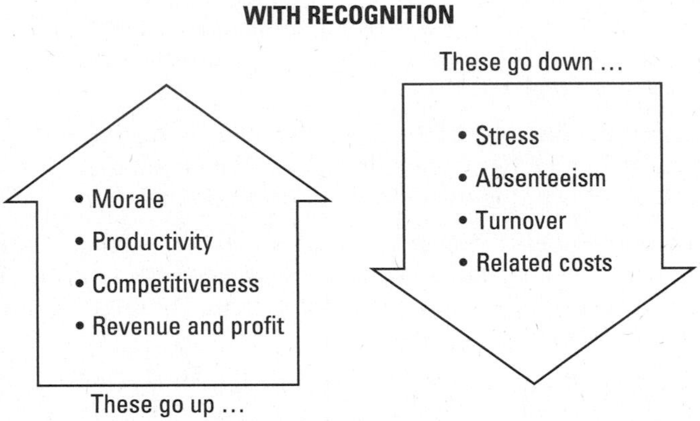

WITH RECOGNITION

Figure 3-1:
Increased recognition increases positive outcomes and decreases unwanted outcomes.

These go down ...

• Stress
• Absenteeism
• Turnover
• Related costs

• Morale
• Productivity
• Competitiveness
• Revenue and profit

These go up ...

©John Wiley & Sons, Inc.

Seeing How Recognition Drives Engagement

To successfully grow employee engagement in your organization, you must make recognition a part of the work environment. Although that's a new concept for some companies, many organizations are getting on board. Case in point: 95 percent of organizations surveyed in the Aberdeen Group's Employee Engagement research reported that they feel employee recognition will improve overall employee engagement. It's not as simple as just *feeling* something, though. Despite best intentions, many organizations still grope their way around employee recognition, wonder how they can build a business case for it, and are unsure of what they need to do to successfully implement recognition. Just ahead, I give you ways to understand (and present) the importance of recognition, as well as best practices for designing an effective recognition program.

The business imperative

In today's competitive economy, organizations must not only identify top talent but also retain their current staff. Employees who feel disengaged from their work environments are likely to look for new opportunities. According to a survey by the Aberdeen Group that involved 1,300 business leaders, improving employee engagement is among the top five business challenges companies currently face.

Fortunately, improving employee engagement is completely achievable (hence this book). You can improve engagement simply by making employee recognition a priority and actively appreciating employee contributions.

If you do not show your employees that you appreciate them on a consistent basis, they will leave. Robert Half International, the staffing firm, has found that the number one reason employees leave their jobs is limited recognition for the job they do. As a result, many companies are investing more in recognition. In fact, 58 percent of the Aberdeen Group's Best-in-Class organizations have implemented a formal recognition program.

Recognition works because it engages employees through a wide variety of methods, ranging from simple interpersonal behaviors and intangibles (like involvement, delegation, and visibility) to activities (such as events, celebrations, team outings, and prizes and awards). Seventy-two percent of organizations with formal recognition programs are satisfied with their employees' level of engagement, according to the Aberdeen Group, compared to 54 percent of organizations that lack a formal recognition program. When you invest in strategic employee recognition, the engagement levels of employees in your organization improve.

Peer-to-peer recognition is also gaining momentum as an effective engagement strategy. Forty-three percent of organizations with formal recognition programs use peer-to-peer recognition tools — such as notecards or and e-cards — compared to only 27 percent of organizations that have no formal recognition program. You can find more on peer-to-peer recognition in Chapter 9.

Creating the recognition-engagement link

How, then, can you link your recognition to engagement behaviors? The link occurs on several levels: first, through the specific *desired behaviors*; second, through the specific *desired results*; and third, through the *specific desired "end state,"* or environmental culture you'd most like to be known for. Table 3-1 provides examples of these kinds of connections.

Table 3-1	Ways to Link Recognition to Engagement Behaviors: Examples
Desired "Engaged" Behaviors	**Potential Recognition Activity to Deploy**
Understanding corporate mission	Recognize examples of work that tie into the mission, using photos, videos, and stories
Understanding professional expectations	Support question-asking; create quizzes and contests about job descriptions
Providing input on workplace matters	Solicit and thank employees regularly for input; make sure upper management is present during key discussions and meetings
Making suggestions	Actively solicit and recognize ideas and allow employees the autonomy to try them; trumpet successes and "successful failures"
Engaging in teamwork and collaboration	Recognize team progress; celebrate milestones and final achievements
Taking initiative	Recognize proactivity and those who ask questions; support extra efforts by allowing flextime and more resources
Doing high-quality work and providing high-quality service	Recognize the attainment of quality standards, error reductions, high or rising client satisfaction scores, and positive customer feedback
Engaging in problem-solving	Recognize creative group processes, brainstorming, and innovative solutions
Bonding with managers and learning about one another	Encourage face time and interactions between employees and managers
Connecting with others	Celebrate successes; enable networking by offering open access to others; encourage or host town hall meetings
Learning and developing skills	Host games and friendly competitions that are based on workplace and professional skills
Engaging in career development	Offer workshops, mentorship programs, time off; and/or funding so that employees can attend seminars
Pursuing career paths	Give employees job variety, opportunities, and opportunities to take on new positions and work challenges
Showing excitement and having fun	Host celebrations and parties

Secondly, you want to make sure you're recognizing the desired results for your organization to be successful and competitive. Although this mandate seems fairly straightforward, it can actually be quite complex. An easy trap to fall into is inadvertently recognizing the wrong things and consequently incentivizing the behavior that's opposite of what you're going for! Most companies, for example, need profitable sales, but they often end up settling for sales revenue of *any* type rather than recognizing only the sales that are actually profitable. Table 3-2 lists outcomes that companies commonly want and identifies what you should (and shouldn't) recognize to achieve that outcome.

Table 3-2	Recognizing the Results you Really Want	
If You Want . . .	*Then Recognize . . .*	*Not . . .*
Profits	Profitable sales	Any sales revenue
Teamwork	Collaboration	Internal competition
Quality	Process improvement	Inspection
Effective training	Skills used on the job	Training time
High performance	Results achieved	Seniority
Problem-solving	Problems found and solved	Problem hiding
Knowledge-sharing	Organizational expertise	Individual expertise
Leadership	Quality of leadership behaviors and decisions	A manager's title or position alone
Creativity	Creative ideas	Conformity
Aiming high	Meeting stretch goals	Over-performance
Safety	Safe behavior	Reported accidents
Cost containment	Reduced spending	Keeping within budget
Customer service	Customer loyalty	Lack of complaints

Lastly, you should recognize desired *end states* — that is, the type of organization and culture you want to be known for, which is a growing factor in attracting and retaining desired talent. So if you want to have a fun place to work, you should do things that employees consider fun on an ongoing basis (like bringing in free food, hosting celebrations, and sponsoring gaming activities, contests, and challenges). Likewise, if you want to be known as a collaborative company, an innovative company, a charitable or green/sustainable company, or even a good talent development company, engage in and recognize activities and behaviors that reinforce that that end state.

Avoiding demotivators

Finally, can we please stop *demotivating* employees? It pains me to see organizations struggle to help make employees more engaged when what they really need to first do is eliminate elements that demotivate their employees. Here's a list of common organizational demotivators that you should strive to get rid of in your company:

- **Organizational politics:** An environment in which competition for power, influence, resources, and promotions is based on subjective and hidden criteria.

- **Unclear expectations:** Unclear, confusing, and contradictory goals, objectives, and standards make it impossible for employees to ever feel secure and confident in their work and accomplishments.

- **Unnecessary rules:** Rules are necessary, but too many of them are demotivating.

- **Poorly designed work:** Poorly engineered work gets in the way of satisfying internal and external customers and frustrates employees.

- **Unproductive meetings:** Employees often leave meetings looking exhausted, battered, and bored — and for good reason.

- **Lack of follow-up:** Most employees could write a book about the latest and greatest programs that died on the vine.

- **Constant change:** Change is necessary, but in some organizations, it seems as if change is arbitrary and capricious.

- **Internal competition:** The healthiest organizations compete against their competition, not against themselves.

- **Dishonesty:** Employees hate being lied to.

- **Hypocrisy:** How can you trust leaders who say one thing and do another?

- **Withholding information:** This is lying by omission. Refer to *dishonesty* just a couple of items up to see why this is demotivating.

- **Unfairness:** Some organizations are full of policies and practices that are perceived as inequitable.

- **Discouraging responses:** Negative responses to employees ideas and suggestions, such as "It won't work," "You can't do that here," and "That's not feasible" are obvious demotivators.

- **Criticism:** Some work environments make employees feel that they are guilty until proven innocent.

- ✔ **Capacity underutilization:** Many people feel that the capabilities they were hired for aren't being used.

- ✔ **Tolerating poor performance:** One poor performer can cause everyone to look (and feel) bad.

- ✔ **Being taken for granted:** Many employees quietly do a good job and are systematically ignored.

- ✔ **Management invisibility:** It is amazing how many employees wouldn't even recognize the division vice president, much less the CEO.

- ✔ **Over-control:** Most employees are willing to be empowered, but few managers are willing to give them the authority to be empowered.

- ✔ **Takeaways:** Reversing a benefit or policy that employees have valued is a perceived loss for employees.

- ✔ **Being forced to do poor quality work:** Some work rules don't allow quality-conscious employees to take pride in the work they do.

Creating a Culture of Recognition

Only 17 percent of organizations have standardized rewards and recognition programs, according to the Aberdeen Group, but for you to successfully ingrain recognition into your company's culture, you need to reach every individual. Organizations that truly create a culture of recognition that drives engagement understand what recognition is, who to include, and how to communicate it.

What distinguishes these companies from others is their ability to define a recognition strategy and then implement that strategy by obtaining executive and management buy-in, aligning recognition and reward programs with business objectives, integrating recognition and rewards, and leveraging social recognition. In this section, I discuss these implementation strategies. For a full discussion of creating a culture of recognition, head to Chapter 8.

Obtaining buy-in from executives and managers

Over the past decade, the relationship between employer and employee has grown strained. Rather than motivating and encouraging top talent, many organizations ignore employee recognition and engagement, especially during difficult economic times. Today, a mere 37 percent of organizations have a clearly defined engagement strategy in place, and only 15 percent of those strategies extend throughout the entire organization. Without a way to engage employees, organizations risk losing top talent and jeopardize organizational growth and success. To overcome this challenge, organizations must focus on creating a culture of recognition.

Despite the benefits of employee recognition, many organizations find it difficult to gain support and articulate the value of these programs to the business. The greatest barrier to employee recognition programs is the lack of senior executive buy-in. A lot of organizations still struggle to implement and maintain recognition programs, but the truth is, these programs really aren't as complex or time-consuming as many managers and execs might fear. Although they agree that employee recognition is important in theory, many managers are too busy with too many other pressing things they feel are more important. To change this paradigm, executives need to start thinking of recognition not as a resource-drain but as a competitive edge.

Research by the Aberdeen Group found that only 14 percent of organizations provide managers with the necessary tools for rewards and recognition, and the national Society for Human Resource Management has reported that 81 percent of organizations provide no training to managers on the topic of employee recognition.

Executives and managers play a critical role in successful recognition initiatives. When managers have the right information, tools, and resources to help manage and optimize their talent, they are able to not only improve recognition, but also drive business outcomes such as engagement, performance, and productivity. I go into greater depth about the topic of executive buy-in in Chapter 15.

Aligning recognition programs with business priorities

To be most effective, recognition programs must also be aligned with business priorities. Management should teach employees how to put organizational priorities into action. They should also work to ensure that they reward behavior that drives business results. These programs are also useful because they help managers recognize and initiate conversations around the right behaviors — a skill that does not always come naturally.

FedEx — delivering integrated world-class rewards and recognition

The FedEx Corporation, headquartered in Memphis, Tennessee, is loved both by its employees (it's made *Fortune Magazine*'s list of "The 100 Best Companies to Work For in America" more than once) and by its customers (on *Fortune*'s Most Admired Company in America list and its Most Admired Company in the World list). The company has over 300,000 full-time employees and earned more than $45 billion in revenues in the most recent year's reporting.

Helping drive FedEx's market success are the company's integrated rewards and recognition programs and activities, which systematically reinforce desired performance and business results for the organization.

A slowing economy, combined with the aftereffects of the 9/11 terrorist attacks, caused many airlines (FedEx Express is one of the nation's largest airlines) to enact massive layoffs. Bucking the trend and the pressure, FedEx Express tightened its belt rather than lay off any employees. It also continued its recognition programs in the face of belt-tightening — a decision that has encouraged employees to work all the harder to help the company meet its goals.

The FedEx Express approach to business is based on the values of people, service, and profit: If you take care of the people, they in turn will deliver the service that customers love, which in turn will drive the profits that you put right back into the people. Applying this philosophy has made FedEx truly a company to be admired.

To begin with, FedEx Express (the largest of the FedEx Corporation's family of companies) has an extensive program of rewards and recognition, including these formal awards:

- ✔ **Bravo Zulu.** The term *Bravo Zulu* comes from military terminology meaning "well done." Any employee who makes an outstanding effort or who has a great accomplishment to celebrate is eligible to receive Bravo-Zulus ("BZs"). Every manager is authorized to give this award, and employees can recommend their coworkers to management as well. Historically, a financial award (cash bonuses under $100, theatre tickets, dinner gift certificates, and so on) accompanies the award, but because of the recent cost-saving initiatives, people are on the lookout for low- or no-cost creative ways to give Bravo Zulus. For example, management has found that a well-written, personalized Bravo Zulu letter that's presented in front of a person's work group is often just as meaningful as getting cash.

- ✔ **Five Star Award.** This is an annual performance award of excellence given to employees who have attained the ultimate level of achievement during the past year. The recipients, especially selected by senior management, also receive a reward of cash or stock options.

- ✔ **Golden Falcon.** This award is given to employees who have been the object of complimentary customer reports to the company or who have demonstrated exceptional performance achievement or unselfish acts that enhance customer service. An example would be the courier with an undeliverable, misaddressed package who goes the extra mile to deliver it in a timely manner.

(continued)

(continued)

✔ **Humanitarian Award.** This is given to employees who promote human welfare, particularly in life-threatening situations. One employee received it for rescuing a man from a burning car in an expressway accident.

While FedEx Express takes great pride in its formal recognition programs, it also strongly supports the efforts of managers and employees to participate in informal recognition. Here are just a few examples of how managers recognize employees informally:

✔ One manager found a certain chocolate bar that just happens to look like the back of a ULD (unit load device). When she sees a really well-loaded ULD, she'll take a quick photo of it. In the next group meeting, she passes around the photos of the well-loaded ULD and rewards with chocolate bars those who packed them.

✔ Every morning, one manager (who can carry a tune!) sings to the employees as they are sorting packages.

✔ At another station, the work team chipped in and bought a boom box. Each employee gets to be "DJ For A Day." Not only do employees get a chance to tease one another about their taste in music, but they get to know each other better, too.

✔ Workers selected as employees of the month receive a copy of the notice placed on the company's wall of fame, with another copy FedEx'd to their homes. When they arrive home from work that day, both they and their families have the good news to share.

Integrating recognition and rewards programs

Companies are realizing the importance of recognition to engagement and are increasingly seeking to better formalize and institutionalize recognition. According to a recent employee engagement survey by the Aberdeen Group, 67 percent of its Best-in-Class organizations have a formal recognition program in place, compared to 58 percent of Best-in-Class organizations just a few years earlier.

Only 19 percent of organizations fully integrate reward and recognition programs, however. To fully engage employees, organizations must integrate the two. In fact, organizations that integrate recognition and rewards well are nearly twice as satisfied with these programs, versus companies that keep them separate (87 percent versus 45 percent, respectively). Sixty-eight percent of organizations that integrate recognition and rewards can also better link engagement to profitability.

Leveraging social recognition

Communication is key to a successful employee recognition program and must be authentic between employers and employees to build trust. Although 40 percent of organizations understand that stronger communication and collaboration are at the heart of employee recognition, identifying the right communication channels can be challenging.

One powerful tool for communicating recognition is social media, especially when facilitating peer-to-peer recognition. Websites such as Facebook, Twitter, Pinterest, and LinkedIn are all good options. Some organizations tweet praise for an employee using a company hashtag, while others post e-cards and postcards on employees' Facebook pages. Another option is to use your internal social network, where you can recognize folks among their coworkers. According to the Aberdeen Group, 42 percent of Best-in-Class organizations use external social networking sites, compared to 34 percent of the other companies surveyed. Thirty-five percent of Best-in-Class organizations use internal networking sites compared to 22 percent of other companies.

Organizations such as KPMG, Deloitte, and PricewaterhouseCooper know social recognition is a key driver for employee engagement and performance because it allows people to connect, collaborate, and recognize each other in real time. Additionally, 37 percent of Best-in-Class organizations the Aberdeen Group surveyed stated that social recognition tools align with business goals, compared to 25 percent of the other companies surveyed.

Wells Fargo has an electronic peer-to-peer praise program called E-wards that allows any employee to recognize any other employee for doing a great job. It's made up of three parts:

- ✔ E-cards are online thank-you cards that anyone can send to anyone else, with a copy going to a recognition mailbox for tracking purposes. Those being thanked are entered into a quarterly drawing for prizes. In the first year alone, Wells Fargo employees used 1,600 e-cards.

- ✔ E-wards are used to praise consistent performance over time based on five values of the organization (leadership, "e-novation," teams, entrepreneurship, and customer service). The electronic award goes to the nominee's manager for approval. The award recipient then gets a certificate with the details of the achievement and a scratch-off ticket for a gift worth $50 to $250. In its first year, 900 e-wards were distributed in the organization.

- ✔ Ride the Wave is a once-a-year celebration for select recipients of the e-card or e-wards recognition. Senior managers review nominations of all winners, select the 70 most impressive achievements, and invite them to attend a three-day, off-site special event with a guest of their choice. The event combines professional development with fun and includes even more recognition.

A Quick Look at How You Can Leverage Recognition Technology

Technology plays a pivotal role in helping organizations consistently recognize employee contributions. Currently, most organizations are leveraging existing talent management technologies, such as performance management, learning management, and employee self-service providers, to improve engagement. As the employee recognition market matures, organizations need to consider solutions that specialize in linking recognition to organizational performance by offering capabilities like e-cards and online recognition tracking. Currently, only 25 percent of organizations are leveraging online tools that track rewards and recognition progress against stated performance goals.

In this section, I outline the elements of recognition technology that have the most impact on engagement by reinforcing desired performance goals of the organization and connecting employees to the organization's mission and values, which together drive the business aspects of the organization. You can find a complete discussion of technology and online recognition systems in Chapter 12.

Reinforcing desired performance goals

Being able to track the effectiveness of engagement and recognition efforts can help organizations better align engagement with business objectives and improve performance. Research by the Aberdeen Group found that Best-in-Class organizations have a significant advantage in being able to measure these activities. Forty-six percent of Best-in-Class organizations can measure the success of employee engagement efforts compared to 25 percent of other companies surveyed. Forty-three percent of Best-in-Class organizations have access to metrics on recognition efforts compared to only 18 percent of other companies surveyed.

Unfortunately, despite a high demand for better data, analytics in human capital management remains incredibly complex and complicated. Few human resources professionals and technology providers have been able to simplify the process in a way that enables organizations to collect data, assemble it into useful information, and deliver reports to senior leaders. Recognition is no exception.

Connecting employees to the organization's mission and values

Recognition is most effective at driving employee engagement when it directly links employees to the mission and core values of the organization. Most organizations, for example, are looking to drive behaviors that reinforce their core values. Some organizations may wish to showcase events while others prefer personalized messaging. Since recognition is ideally aligned with an organization's culture, any technology solutions need to be customizable to reflect the company values and overall mission.

Looking Forward, Staying Ahead

When you're able to better harness the power of employee recognition, you'll be well on your way to driving a greater degree of employee engagement and shaping a more motivated workplace. Experiment, learn, and build on your successes. Stop whatever's not working and try something different. If you systematically improve, you'll create a workplace where individual and organizational goals will be aligned and people will be excited about their jobs, enjoy their coworkers, and want to do the best job possible each and every day. Not only will this give your organization a competitive advantage, but it will also make you proud to be a leader.

Your job, however, will not be done. To sustain the advances you've made to increase employee engagement, you must also align desired behaviors and performance with your company's hiring, orientation, and training systems, and with the use of traditional incentives such as raises and promotions. When this happens, you will then have truly created a culture of recognition that reinforces desired behavior, performance, and engagement in a self-sustaining way. You will have created the kind of environment we all dream of working in — an environment that puts people first and rewards and recognizes their contributions to customers, coworkers, and the organization.

Recognition works. When managers recognize their employees' efforts, employees will respond by giving their best efforts — they will be engaged.

Part II
The Fundamentals of Employee Recognition

Top Five Ways to Engage and Retain Contingent Workers

✔ **Offer "temp-to-hire" programs.** These look first to hire full-time employees from within the pool of current temporary workers who are known to the company before opening the position up to the public.

✔ **Give them repeat business!** Contingent workers have to be wary of longer-term projects with larger employees. Even though such projects provide needed and often well-deserved financial rewards, they also can provide a false security that takes the worker away from the pulse of the market and its ever-changing needs and priorities.

✔ **Assign projects that enhance their skills, increase their visibility, or solidify their reputation.** For employers, such projects can help attract the most talented workers who are eager to be on the cutting edge of market needs. For employees, these projects keep them at the forefront of relevant skills.

✔ **Give them access to or pay the fees for business services.** Examples of such services include MyBizOffice (`http://www.mybizoffice.com`) or concierge services that can provide useful time-saving services for the contingent employee.

✔ **Communicate!** Provide ongoing communication from periodic meetings and inclusion in communications that all full-time employees receive.

Find out more about fundamental recognition principles at `www.dummies.com/extras/recognizingandengagingemployees`.

In this part . . .

- Effectively recognize and engage your nontraditional staff members and colleagues, such as virtual employees, contractors, and global partners around the world

- Identify the three types of employee recognition (formal, informal, and day-today), and discover the ins and outs of each

- Examine the gap between what managers think motivates employees and what actually does — and then figure out what you can do to close it

- Uncover why some managers successfully use recognition on a regular basis, while others are resistant

- Learn how you can convert low-use managers into high-use ones

Chapter 4

The Importance of Employee Recognition Today

• •

In This Chapter

▶ Uncovering the link between performance and recognition

▶ Overcoming change and uncertainty with recognition

▶ Recognizing remote workers around the globe

• •

*I*t is the best of times, it is the worst of times. The state of morale in the workplace is somewhat grim today. Some 40 percent of employees report that their jobs are very or extremely stressful, and 56 percent say they are somewhat or completely dissatisfied with their jobs. An overwhelming number of employees — 85 percent — report being overworked and under-appreciated.

At the same time, today's employees have much to be excited about. Forty percent work remotely, an arrangement that allows them new levels of freedom and autonomy in their lives and greatly reduces the time and expense spent commuting. They're able to more freely apply themselves at work, and they can be creative in how they approach problems and where they obtain help and answers — a sharp contrast to previous eras when employees had little freedom or autonomy and were more subject to the whims of their managers.

Today's employees thus have different recognition needs than the employees of even ten years ago. In this chapter, I explain what these differences are, why they've come about, and how you as a manager can meet them. But before I dive into that, I set the stage by exploring the benefits of recognition in general.

The Benefits of Recognition

Employees have always liked being recognized when they do good work, but today, they don't just *hope* it may happen; they expect it. In my research, I've found that 99.4 percent of today's employees expect to be recognized when they do good work, while research by Maritz Motivation has found that only 12 percent of employees strongly agree that they are consistently recognized in ways that are important to them, and nearly three times as many (34 percent) disagree or strongly disagree that they are recognized in ways that are meaningful to them. In addition, Maritz has found that employees who do receive recognition where they work are

- ✔ 5 times more likely to feel valued
- ✔ 6 times more likely to recommend the company as a place to work
- ✔ 7 times more likely to stay with the company
- ✔ 11 times more likely to feel completely committed to the company

And according to research conducted by TowersWatson, committed employees deliver 57 percent more effort than uncommitted ones. Add to that the true cost of employee turnover (which studies from the Society for Human Resource Management place at 1.5 times an employee's annual salary), and the numbers quickly become significant in terms of the actual cost of replacing employees — as well as lost opportunity when experienced employees leave and take all the knowledge they've learned with them.

Using recognition is far from frivolous; it can make or break any organization and the managers in it. People are the competitive edge of any organization, and treating employees right has never been more important. Jeffrey Pfeffer, a Stanford Business School professor, recently concluded, "Companies that manage people right will outperform companies that don't by 30 to 40 percent."

One of the most powerful tools in a business's arsenal for increasing motivation is recognition. Recognition is a significant driver of employee engagement, and having engaged, satisfied employees leads to increased customer satisfaction, greater customer loyalty and profitability, and thus enhanced bottom-line success for the organization. Watson Wyatt's WorkUSA Report found that organizations with highly engaged employees enjoy 25 percent higher employee productivity and a lower turnover risk and attract top talent more easily than those without engaged employees. And a study by the Office of the Auditor General of British Columbia concluded that "recognition has been shown to motivate staff, increase morale, productivity, and employee retention, and decrease stress and absenteeism."

Towers Watson has found that ". . . companies with high employee engagement had a 19 percent increase in operating income and a 28 percent increase in earnings per share. In contrast, companies with poor employee engagement scores had declining operating incomes and an 11 percent drop in earnings per share." And the Corporate Executive Board, in its study "Driving Employee Performance and Retention Through Engagement," found that recognition was one of the top methods for increasing employee retention.

People do not commit 40, 50, or 60 hours a week or more out of their lives to just show up at work. They want to make a difference in their work — and to be appreciated for doing so. Further evidence points to the power of recognition:

✔ In recent surveys of American workers, 63 percent of the respondents agreed that most people would like more recognition for their work, and the same percentage ranked "a pat on the back" as a meaningful incentive.

✔ Robert Half International, the nationwide staffing firm, conducted a survey of why people leave their jobs and found the number one reason to be "limited praise and recognition for the work they do."

✔ According to the People, Pay, and Performance study by the American Productivity Center in Houston, if the reward is cash, 5 to 8 percent of an employee's salary must be given to change behavior, as compared to only about 4 percent of the employee's salary if the reward is not cash.

Positive reinforcement really does work, and anyone can learn to reward and recognize effectively and thereby benefit from using recognition.

The Recognition and Performance Link

Recognition and performance are closely linked: Recognition has a measurable and positive impact on job performance. As employee performance increases in response to recognition, managers tend to provide additional recognition, creating a self-perpetuating cycle of recognition and performance (more about that cycle in Chapter 7). In my doctoral study, I found evidence to support the link between the use of recognition and enhanced performance in at least three different ways.

First, managers in my doctoral study broadly agreed with the notion that the use of recognition led to enhanced employee performance in many ways, as they expressed in these statements (the parentheses indicate the percentage of managers in the study who agreed with each statement):

✔ Recognizing employees helps me better motivate them. (91 percent)

✔ Providing nonmonetary recognition to my employees when they do good work helps to increase their performance. (84 percent)

✔ Recognizing employees provides them with practical feedback. (84 percent)

✔ Recognizing my employees for good work makes it easier to get the work done. (80 percent)

✔ Recognizing employees helps them to be more productive. (78 percent)

✔ Providing nonmonetary recognition helps me to achieve my personal goals. (69 percent)

✔ Providing nonmonetary recognition helps me to achieve my job goals. (60 percent)

Second, 73 percent of managers in the study reported that they received the results they expected either immediately or soon after using recognition, and 99 percent said they felt they would eventually obtain the desired results.

Third, of the employees who reported to the managers in this study, 78 percent said that it was either very important or extremely important to be recognized by their managers when they do good work. Employees expected recognition to occur "immediately" (20 percent), "soon thereafter" (53 percent), or "sometime later" (19 percent).

It's true: Recognition really does help managers obtain desired results and performance!

The Significance of Recognition Today

Today's employees and managers find themselves in a unique point in history. In response to the recent malaise in the U.S. and world economy (the Great Recession), companies spent a number of years focusing on survival by downsizing staff, payroll, and benefits to keep the companies afloat. They tasked fewer employees with doing more work. These tactics kept many organizations alive in the short term but at a significant cost to employees in the long term.

Although employee productivity increased in the short term (I think employees were scared about being on the next layoff list!), after months and even years of tight budgets and short staff, many of the employees that remained became jaded and burned out, and productivity has since plummeted.

One company that managed to do more than just survive the Great Recession and to get its employees engaged at higher levels is Zappos.com. The company's CEO Tony Hsieh revolutionized selling shoes online by creating an employee culture built on valuing its people and striving to make them happy. He's succeeded on multiple levels, including reaching $1 billion in sales in just eight years. Customers and employees alike rave about the company's superior service. Every year, management invites staff to submit 100 to 500 words describing what the Zappo's Culture means to them. The text is published — unedited — as *The Zappos Culture Book* and is used as a manual to show prospective employees and orient new ones. "At Zappos, our belief is that if you get the culture right, most of the other stuff — like great customer service or building a great long-term brand, or passionate employees and customers — will happen naturally on its own," wrote Hsieh in a blog post on the topic.

More and more companies are realizing that their employees are truly their competitive edge in driving a successful business. As business guru Peter F. Drucker has written, "Developing talent is business's most important task — the sine qua non of competition in a knowledge economy."

Key Workforce Trends Impacting Employee Motivation Today

The world is changing in new and dramatic ways that affect every employee. In this section, I examine five of the major trends that are shaping today's workforce and pushing managers worldwide to recognize and engage their employees in new ways. These trends are not simply on a short-term cycle, but part of a longer term fundamental shift in the way that people think about work and interact with their employers and each other. To be effective at recognition, it's imperative for employers to understand today's workforce trends.

Attracting and retaining talent: The growing shortage of skilled workers

The Great Recession of the late 2000s caused millions of workers to lose their jobs, leaving an overabundance of unemployed, highly skilled workers. However, as economic growth now gathers pace, talent shortages in certain industries appear almost as acute as before the recent economic collapse. And in some areas of health care, computer science, and IT, the shortage never actually disappeared — those remain highly challenging environments for hiring, motivating, and retaining key talent still today. The new operation reality for businesses of all types and sizes is that the best educated and skilled technical and professional employees are in greater demand, harder to find, and harder to keep, and will command a premium to switch or relocate to new jobs.

The allure of working part time

More than 18 million people choose to work part time, according to the U.S. Bureau of Labor Statistics. About 61 percent of these part-timers have some college education. Women represent two thirds of the part-time workforce, which they increasingly seek in their prime earning years to balance work and family responsibilities. "Professional moms would be thrilled to lower their hours to spend more time with their children, and they don't mind giving up benefits to achieve that work/life balance, " reports Alison Doyle, an About.com job search and employment subject matter expert. "Other part-time labor sources include near-retirees and older workers who don't want to retire or are unable to retire but don't want to commit to full-time positions." And in a study by Corporate Voices for Working Families, a Washington, DC-based research firm, researchers found that engagement was 55 percent higher for hourly workers with flexibility than for those without, while turnover was half.

To meet this shortage of skilled workers, managers need to get more creative in hiring and motivating workers. For example, hiring a greater percentage of part-time employees can help companies tap into the new demographics of single-parent workers, retirees, and students.

Likewise, companies and each of their managers must be skilled at keeping employees — especially those with the requisite skills and experience. Executives and managers have to make organizational changes to prevent treating nontraditional workers (for example, part-timers, Millennials, and contingent workers) as second-class employees. Employers must better adapt to the motivation preferences of these new categories of workers and recognize their employees in ways the employees prefer when they perform well.

They're special: Millennials are changing the rules at work

Millennials, the youngest generation of workers, born roughly between 1980 and 2000, are redefining the workplace. The following list outlines some of their key values and attributes:

- ✔ **They're globalized and tech-savvy.** They're used to being connected to people across the globe and having access to information at all times. They're comfortable interacting with many cultures, especially online.

- ✔ **They're used to having blurred (or nonexistent) borders between work and personal time.** They are comfortable working during personal time and doing personal stuff during work hours. It all balances out to them.

✔ **They care about the world.** They want to work for companies that are socially responsible, ethical, and honest.

✔ **They're hardworking and expert multitaskers.** They are comfortable managing many goals at once, quickly progressing to the next action item on each.

✔ **They think very highly of themselves and believe they deserve to have a job that challenges, appreciates, and engages them.** They expect their job to fully engage and use their skills and knowledge.

✔ **They are highly interactive and thrive on constant feedback.** They expect daily praise and feedback and believe they deserve recognition and rewards when they achieve desired results.

Although Millennials may appear high-maintenance to some managers, the key to getting the most from them is to play to their strengths and channel their energy. If you give younger employees a reason to get excited, they show an extraordinary work ethic and passion to get the work done — and to have fun in the process. Take time to get to know your Millennial employees, ask their opinions, involve them in decisions (especially those that affect them and their work), create socializing opportunities at work (and during off hours), and focus on learning and development opportunities for them. I share more about how best to motivate the Millennials in Chapter 16.

Everyone's his own boss: The rise of the contingent worker

One of the most important workforce trends of the past two decades has been the rise of a new breed of contingent workers (consultants, freelancers, contractors, "micropreneurs," and temporary, "permanent" temporary, and part-time employees). In the United States alone, contingent workers make up about 20 percent of the labor force, a number that is expected to grow to 30 percent to 50 percent of the workforce.

Many of these folks are professionals who were dislodged from salaried careers as a consequence of business restructuring and economic upheaval. Instead of waiting for new opportunities to come to them, they started up their own businesses, providing services to clients on a project-by-project basis.

These contingent workers need to always have an eye on the next project and the next employer, even as they are immersed in a current project; networking becomes a lifeline, not just a social endeavor; and marketing services need to become second nature. They also worry about things traditional employees often take for granted: employee benefits, vacation time, and finances for retirement, for example.

As a manager, you have to understand and manage a contingent workforce that may be spread across various states, countries, and time zones. Your organization's ability to attract needed talent, maximize the motivation of such talent, and access that talent over uneven periods of work becomes paramount.

If contingent workers must follow the work rather than the company, how do you retain the critical talent and competence that drives your organization's competitive advantage? How do you protect the knowledge and intellectual property that can slip out the door when you lose these workers at the end of a contract? How do you go about accessing the talent you need across the globe, juggling myriad legal, financial, and regulatory issues across jurisdictions? How can you find, let alone manage and motivate, such talent? The strategies to attract, motivate, and retain contingent workers can be as varied as the workers themselves. You can offer them the following:

- ✔ An orientation that allows them to understand the mission of the organization and how the work they're doing ties to that mission

- ✔ Ongoing communication from periodic meetings and inclusion in communications so that they feel fully informed

- ✔ Training that develops their skills in conjunction with the skills your organization needs

- ✔ Business services and support for helping to complete assigned work.

- ✔ Invitations to join staff for department or companywide meetings, team-building activities, and celebrations

- ✔ Opportunities to get to know them and learn their names, their abilities and aspirations, and what motivates them

- ✔ Praise when they do good work for you and the company

- ✔ Temp-to-hire programs that look first to hire full-time employees from within the pool of current temporary workers before opening a vacancy up to the public

- ✔ Assignments that enhance their skills, increase their visibility, or solidify their reputation

Assignments that help to stretch a contingent worker can be a win–win for the worker and your organization. For employers, such projects help attract the most talented workers who are eager to be on the cutting edge of market needs; for employees, these projects keep them at the forefront of relevant skills.

- ✔ Repeat business!

You will never receive first-class performance from a contingent employee who feels that he or she is treated as a second-class citizen!

We're all connected: The evolving role of virtual employees

With the changing nature of work today, more organizations have to adapt to new circumstances for recognizing employee performance. Increasingly, employees are working more independently in their jobs, given that many organizations feature decentralized operations — meaning as a manager, you may not work in the same building (or even state) as some of your employees. Global companies increasingly expect executives to oversee staff in remote, and often overseas, locations. Some companies don't even have a bricks-and-mortar office at all.

Telecommuting, flexible working hours, and job sharing define the workplace of today. *Futurework: Trends and Challenges for Work in the 21st Century,* a Department of Labor report, found that roughly 1 in 10 workers fits into an alternative work arrangement, with nearly 80 percent of employers offering some form of nontraditional staffing arrangements. And some 47 percent of employees today now do some amount of telecommuting.

While it's tough for some managers or business owners to welcome the option of allowing employees to work remotely, remember that employees need to be treated as though they are responsible, trustworthy people. Most employees perform better if they feel empowered and trusted.

Making sure a virtual employee stays motivated, happy, and productive is the key to ensuring the success of a virtual workplace. To do so in a virtual environment, you have to be more conscious and deliberate about recognition because there are fewer spontaneous opportunities to acknowledge an employee's hard work and accomplishments.

So how can you best recognize performance when you don't have physical contact with your employees for weeks or months at a time? It comes down to creativity and foresight. Consider these examples:

> ✔ Barbara Green, office manager for Buckingham, Doolittle and Burroughs in Canton, Ohio, shares this example of "virtual applause": "We sent an e-mail to our entire staff asking everyone to applaud the great efforts of our office services department at 4 p.m. at their desks. Members of that department work throughout the building and are rarely in one place at the same time, so this was a terrific way for each staff member to receive the benefit of the praising at exactly the same time and in the same way."

✔ Noticing that most client letters of appreciation were never shared with home-based employees, Cruise.com, headquartered in Ft. Lauderdale, Florida, created the Friday Fan Mail e-Bulletin, which recognizes excellence in service. Every week, agents forward e-mails or letters to the HR department, where they are compiled and sent out in an e-bulletin to all employees. Once a month, the agents who have submitted customer e-mails participate in a drawing for a $25 gift certificate.

Managers must take a proactive role in fostering a sense of teamwork by involving virtual workers in all team meetings that affect their work, using any means available: telephone conferencing, e-mail, chat rooms, and so on. Be sure to include some form of recognition in each meeting.

Verbal ways to recognize employees from a distance include the following:

✔ Make recognition a part of any communication you have with your virtual employees, including conference calls, web chats, e-mail, and virtual meetings.

✔ Have the payroll department include fax-back forms with all employee paychecks to obtain feedback on how things are going. Discuss issues that were raised in your virtual meetings.

✔ Ask employees to submit questions or concerns. Take those issues submitted seriously and get back to the employees quickly to answer questions and resolve concerns.

Employees at other locations and those who telecommute from their homes already feel like second-class citizens. They imagine they are the last to hear about changes and news in the organization. Be empathetic with employees who do not work full time at the main office, and, when possible, duplicate any form of communication, recognition, or celebration that is done at the central office. But think it through: With any reward and recognition program, managers must be sure to recognize and reward the behavior they desire with things that are valued and meaningful to their employees — not themselves. This is especially true when designing a virtual reward and recognition program because being a virtual employee brings in a new set of issues that need to be identified and addressed. I outline some of these issues in the next section.

The world is getting smaller: The impact of globalization

U.S. companies continue to expand their operations globally at breakneck speed. In the process of going global, one of the most significant challenges organizations face is learning how to motivate, recognize, and reward people of all cultures. The key to success rests in understanding the cultural attitudes and business practices of other countries. Companies that foster cultural sensitivity to help workers from varying backgrounds feel comfortable can increase employee productivity and job satisfaction.

In America, most companies use individual public recognition, rewards, ceremonies, and bonuses to recognize accomplishments. Employee-of-the-month awards, gift certificates, time off, and other incentives are also used to motivate and reward employees. As organizations cross borders, however, they are learning that what motivates their American employees may not work for their employees in Latin America, Asia, Europe, or Africa. Worse, an action that is favored in the United States may be inappropriate elsewhere and inadvertently offend the recipients.

In Germany, for example, business is serious and workers are conservative and very private. Rather than an energizing force, public ceremony and recognition of accomplishments tend to embarrass the German worker. Other cultures look at the American focus on praise and recognition as a weakness. "Why are Americans so insecure about themselves?" an Asian businessman might ask. "Why do they have to be reassured about everyday activities they were hired to do?"

Managers in U.S. corporations that employ international workers must overcome the assumption that American views and business practices are universally held. "In the United States, we've made a mistake thinking that because we're U.S.–based, what's good for us is good for everybody around the world," says Carol Kaplan, manager of global compensation and benefits at Applied Materials, Inc. "What happens then is that we export programs that aren't culturally sound and then end up creating animosities toward corporate headquarters."

In fact, from one country to the next, the list of differences is significant: perceptions of time; future orientation; business focus on profit; and view of relationships. In the U.S., for example, change is often viewed positively, seen as progress, and strongly linked to future success. In cultures of Europe and Asia that are steeped in history and tradition, however, great pride is taken in doing things the same way previous generations have done. Countries such as France and India value stability, continuity, and tradition — factors that are not as highly valued in typical U.S. businesses.

Sensitivity to local attitudes and customs, cultural expectations, economics, political situations, and the history of the countries in which businesses are operating is critical to creating a successful global rewards and recognition program. U.S. companies cannot transfer American customs and business practices into the global market and expect them to be successful.

Incentive Trends in Today's Workplace

Everyone likes to be recognized for doing a good job; smart managers and business owners have known this fact for years, and they have successfully used it to motivate employees and enhance their performance. But now more than ever, the use of recognition is a critical ingredient in the success of an organization. In this section, I outline five major trends related to incentives that have influenced the importance of recognition in today's work environment.

The decline of traditional incentives

In recent years, traditional incentives, such as money and promotions, have lost their power to shape desired employee behavior. According to an article in *Compensation and Benefits Review:*

- ✔ Eighty-one percent of workers claim they would not receive any reward for any increases in productivity.

- ✔ Sixty percent of managers report that their compensation will not increase if their performance improves.

- ✔ Only 3 percent of base salary separates average from outstanding employees.

Clearly, the traditional system of rewards in business is in crisis if it fails to differentiate and encourage high performance on such a widespread basis. Part of the problem stems from a past over-dependence on financial rewards to the exclusion of other potential reinforcers. In the words of Peter Drucker, "Economic incentives are becoming rights rather than rewards. Merit raises are always introduced as rewards for exceptional performance. In no time at all, they become a right. To deny a merit raise or to grant only a small one becomes punishment. The increasing demand for material rewards is rapidly destroying their usefulness as incentives and managerial tools."

And it gets worse. Material rewards such as cash have, in some cases, actually been found to have a *demotivating* effect on employees. As Cecil Hill, corporate manager of improvement programs at Hughes Aircraft Company in Los Angeles explains:

> I found certain aspects of the cash awards approach would be counter-productive at Hughes Aircraft. For example, cash awards would reduce teamwork as employees concentrated primarily on individual cash gains. We also found that United Airlines had dropped its longtime cash awards system because of litigation problems. Other companies pointed out a negative boomerang effect whenever ideas were turned down, while many firms reported an ongoing problem with timely response, and

others noted disagreements on determining dollar amounts and conflicts regarding what constitute 'a part of normal job performance.'

We have also found instances where pay for certain types of intellectual performance tends to denigrate the performance and remove it from the intellectual achievement category, which elicits pride and satisfaction, and reduces it to a more mundane pay-for-performance concept. In short, cash awards seemed to have an overall demotivating effect.

In addition, organizations today are less able to offer their high achievers incentives such as promotions. Because of increasing competition in the global marketplace, most organizations have been forced into extensive internal changes manifested by downsizing, cost-cutting, and the flattening and elimination of numerous levels of hierarchy. These changes have greatly reduced the number of positions available for employee promotions. In a survey reported in the *Washington Post,* 43 percent of respondents from 700 organizations indicated they are able to offer fewer opportunities for advancement in years to come. As Harvard's Rosabeth Moss Kanter observed, "In this time of corporate hierarchy-shrinking and organizational layer-removal, companies cannot afford the old-fashioned system in which promotion was the primary means of recognizing performance. Greater accessibility to rewards — at all levels — is a necessity when employees stay in place longer, and recognition is an important part of this."

The rise of nontraditional incentives

Nonmonetary incentives have actually come to rank higher in importance for most employees than traditional organizational rewards such as cash and promotions. In multiple studies dating back to the 1940s, employees have consistently ranked items such as "full appreciation for work done," "feeling 'in' on things," and "interesting work" as being more important to them than more traditional incentives such as good wages, job security, or promotion and growth opportunities. In a more recent survey of workers conducted by the Society of Incentive Travel Executives Foundation, 63 percent of the respondents ranked even a pat on the back as a meaningful incentive. In another study, 68 percent of respondents said it was important to believe that others appreciated their work, and 67 percent agreed that most people need appreciation for their work.

To illustrate the power of positive reinforcement, Daniel Boyle, vice president and treasurer of Diamond Fiber Products, Inc., in Thorndike, Massachusetts (now Cascades Diamond, Inc.), described the impact that the award of a "100 Club" nylon and cotton jacket had on one employee:

> You might think this is a trivial thing, but it means a lot to the people who earn a jacket. A teller at a local bank told me once that a woman came in and proudly modeled her baby blue 100 Club jacket for bank

customers and employees. She said, "My employer gave me this for doing a good job. It's the first time in the 18 years I've been there they've recognized the things I do every day." During those years she had earned hundreds of thousands of dollars in wages, which had paid for cars, a home mortgage, food, other essentials, vacations, college educations. In her mind, she had provided a service for her earnings. The money wasn't recognition for her work, but the 100 Club jacket was.

Think of the impact recognition could have had on this employee if it was used on a daily basis, instead of only once in her 18 years of service to the company!

This shift in desired incentives is further demonstrated by Beverly Kaye and Sharon Jordan-Evans' recent study of the reasons why employees stay with a particular company. Listed in priority order — starting with the most important — the top-ten reasons employees stay are

1. Career growth, learning, and development

2. Exciting, challenging work

3. Meaningful work, making a difference, and making a contribution

4. Great people

5. Being part of a team

6. Good boss

7. Recognition for work well done

8. Autonomy, sense of control over one's work

9. Flexible work hours and dress code

10. Fair pay and benefits

Note that the traditional incentives of fair pay and benefits are last on the list. Pay and benefits are a foundation upon which managers need to build, but they are not the main reason why employees are loyal to their organizations — far from it. A survey of executives by staffing company Robert Half International confirms the importance of recognition in employee retention. That survey found the number one reason employees leave organizations today is "limited recognition and praise" for the work they do. This response ranked higher than compensation, limited authority, personality conflicts, and all other responses.

The increased use of variable compensation

There's an emerging trend in employee compensation today toward *variable compensation systems* in which base salaries are frozen and merit increases are paid only on a bonus basis, or in accordance with specific performance targets. While variable compensation makes a lot of sense intuitively because it ties pay and performance tightly together, employees can become demotivated when they don't meet their targets and therefore don't get their bonuses. This effect becomes even more pronounced when achieving their targets are outside of their control.

Because of their risk, variable compensation systems place pressure on organizations to find ways other than traditional pay to reinforce desired behavior (even if the employee falls short of a goal). Informal rewards can help accommodate this need for new reinforcers, and they are perfectly compatible with variable compensation systems.

The increased need for empowered employees

Increasingly, employees are expected to be self-directed and empowered. Whether they are in different locations (or on different shifts) than their managers, have flexible work hours, or telecommute, today's employees are expected to act independently and in the best interests of the organization, with less direct management supervision than in the past. As Joseph Maciariello and Calvin Kirby observed in their book *Management Control Systems: Using Adaptive Systems to Attain Control* (Prentice Hall), the challenge for managers is to build adaptability into the controls of an organization, thus providing workers with more flexibility and freedom to innovate while managers still direct their activities toward the common purpose of the organization. Recognition and rewards are tools of engagement that managers and workers alike can use to reinforce desired behavior and performance in their work environments.

As the speed of work has increased and technology has allowed the workforce to become more dispersed, the need to connect with employees on a timely basis to validate the quality of their work has increased. The increased use of recognition is an effective strategy for meeting this need.

The increased amount of change and uncertainty

Businesses of all types and sizes are experiencing change, and they are experiencing it at a faster and faster rate than ever before. The nature of effective rewards and recognition is changing as well. As management professor Henry Mintzberg of McDill University in Montreal, Canada, has observed, when operating in dynamic, changing work environments today, management must use more flexible, less formalized *coordinating mechanisms,* that is, ways to monitor and manage the work being done. The result is a reduction in the reliance on formal management controls.

Informal — and therefore more flexible — systems work better for organizations during times of constant change, whether the need is to stabilize operations or to better or more quickly meet changing market demands. As Maciariello and Kirby explain, "The association between the informal and formal changes with the degree of uncertainty. As stability and predictability increase, the use of formal systems increases. In times of major change, the informal system should be the dominant management system. The formal system, that is, the policies and procedures that applied to the past products and customers, may actually be . . . a potential barrier."

The use of informal rewards provides just the right combination of relevance, immediacy, and individual value. Considering that a reported 33 percent of managers would rather work in another organization where they could receive better recognition, this issue is critical to shaping motivation and performance in today's fast-moving organizations. It is also critical to an organization's ability to thrive, let alone survive, in the future.

Although employees value recognition and appreciation highly, the impact goes far beyond workforce contentment. Recognition can also increase a company's revenues while decreasing its costs — a potent combination in any business. The consistent use of recognition not only results in a higher level of productivity and performance from employees, but the organization also develops a reputation as an "employer of choice," making it easier to attract new employees.

In addition, employees who are treated well inevitably treat their customers better. Chances are you'll never get employees to treat customers better than they are being treated themselves! As J.W. Marriott put it, "At Marriott, we know that if we treat our employees correctly, they'll treat the customers right. And if the customers are treated right, they'll come back."

The Bottom-Line Impact of Recognition

A question remains, however, for many managers: "Will recognition enhance the profitability of my organization? If I spend the time, the energy, and/ or the money to do more recognition, will there be a payback in over- all earnings to the firm that is greater than the resources I put into it?" Again, the answer is an unequivocal yes. For example, the Medill School at Northwestern University identified a direct financial link between engaged, motivated employees and client satisfaction and the profitability of firms. In a study reported in *Harvard Business Review*, Sears Roebuck was likewise able to establish that every 5 percent rise in employee satisfaction caused a 3 percent increase in customer satisfaction and a 1 percent increase in profitability.

The anecdotal evidence is also amply available:

- Pegasus Personal Fitness Centers asked employees to make a list of the rewards they wanted, up to a $25 value, to be given if they achieved per- formance goals. The company reports that this practice helped double sales in a six-year period.

- Oil giant Amoco offered employees a variety of gifts and contests. One plant saved $18.8 million in two years from such efforts.

- Amtech threw "Victory Parties" for its employees and credits the tech- nique with helping to obtain a phenomenal 8900 percent growth in rev- enue over a five-year period.

- WordPerfect Corporation offered a Hawaiian vacation challenge, and motivated employees responded by doubling revenues in a single year.

- American Express used a "Great Performers" poster campaign to help increase net income 500 percent in 11 years, with a return on investment of 28 percent.

- American Airlines's AAchievers points-for-merchandise rewards awarded employees points for suggestions they made to save money, fix problems, and so on. Cost savings that resulted from employee sugges- tions allowed the company to purchase a new airplane.

- Boardroom, Inc., created the "I-Power" program to recognize and reward every employee who submitted two suggestions per week, resulting in a five-fold increase in the company's revenues in just three years.

Overwhelming evidence in recent years proves that recognizing employees when they do good work is not just the right thing to do, but it also is the smart thing to do if you are interested in obtaining results.

The business case for the benefits of recognition and rewards is substantial, and you can use that data to systematically make your case for a rewards and recognition program in your organization.

Towers Watson compared high employee engagement organizations with low employee engagement organizations over a 12-month period. Table 4-1 outlines the dramatic financial impact the study revealed.

Table 4-1	High Employee Engagement Organizations versus Low Employee Engagement Organizations	
Factor	*High Employee Engagement Organizations*	*Low Employee Engagement Organizations*
Operating income	+19.2 percent	−32.7 percent
Net income growth	+13.7 percent	−3.8 percent
Earnings per share growth rate	+27.8 percent	−11.2 percent

Towers Watson also found that the financial returns of *Fortune*'s 100 Best Places to Work were 233 percent higher over a six-year period as compared with overall market returns of the S&P 500. Companies with higher employee satisfaction scores — driven in large part by feeling valued for the work they do — have been shown to have a 700 percent higher shareholder return, and a recent study reported in *Incentive* showed a direct correlation between the perceived use of recognition in organizations and the profitability of those firms.

It's no wonder recognition has become a strategic imperative on the part of so many organizations today. The individual, organizational, and financial benefits of using positive employee recognition to systematically increase employee engagement is substantial for any organization's success today.

Chapter 5

The Principles of Employee Recognition

. . . .

In This Chapter

▶ Looking at the three types of recognition

▶ Identifying the kind of motivation your employees like

▶ Using motivators to help your employees reach their potential

. . . .

*R*esearch suggests that, to get results from their employees, managers today need to consider a range of tools that only a few years ago may have been considered too fuzzy, abstract, and ill-defined to be taken seriously. Although the best managers may have always been skilled at providing recognition to employees, organizations today need *every* manager to be rewards-and-recognition savvy and to create the kind of workplace in which we all would like to work. In this chapter, I outline why recognition packs such a punch and explain how you can leverage its power for the greatest good.

Fundamentals of Employee Recognition

Recognition is a positive consequence you provide to a person for a desired behavior or result. Recognition can take the form of acknowledgement, approval, or an expression of gratitude. It means appreciating someone for something he or she has done for you, your group, or your organization. Recognition also can come in the form of asking for an opinion, involving employees in a decision, or encouraging them in their careers. You can give recognition as an employee strives to achieve a certain goal or behavior or after he or she has completed it. Used properly, recognition takes on an almost magical quality.

Getting familiar with the three core principles

Wanting to recognize your employees is a good first step, but you have to embark on a deliberate effort to understand and implement the principles that comprise the foundation of employee recognition. Without comprehending certain key concepts, your attempts at recognition could easily go astray. These three concepts should inform and offer context for all of your recognition efforts:

✔ **You get what you reward.** The most proven principle of management and motivation known to mankind (we're talking about evidence from hundreds of studies) is the simple and commonsense notion that you get what you reward. That is, the behaviors and performance that you notice, inspect, recognize, appreciate, reward, incentivize, or acknowledge will be repeated by those you acknowledged and perhaps others as well who noticed or heard what happened.

✔ **If you are serious about performance, get serious about recognition.** Although most organizations are serious about performance, their mission, and their goals and purpose, they often do not take the topic of recognition as seriously. That is, they offer recognition in a rote way, without evaluating whether it is aligned with desired performance or even effectively working.

If you simply set up a recognition program because other companies have them, without performing a systematic analysis of what your employees most want and then identifying how you can offer those things when your employees perform well, your recognition program is likely to have little, if any, impact on your stated goals.

✔ **All behavior is a function of its consequences.** This is fundamental reinforcement theory first made popular by management theorist B. F. Skinner, who said, "To any possible consequence, there are three possible responses: a positive response or consequence, a negative response or consequence, or no response or consequence." In fact, it could even be said that all behavior is driven by its consequences. Behaviors that result in a positive consequence tend to be repeated; behaviors that result in a negative consequence tend to stop. When an action has no consequence, there is no impact on the behavior. You can't just hope for your employees to change or make passive-aggressive commentary; you have to actively provide immediate, positive consequences for the behaviors you'd like to continue.

Looking at the three types of recognition

Employee recognition can be broken down into the following three types:

- ✔ **Formal recognition:** A structured or planned program of recognition for desired performance. Examples include president's awards, years-of-service awards, and employee-of-the-month awards. This recognition can be significant and symbolic, given the public forum in which it is typically presented. The challenges of formal recognition are that it isn't very timely and typically is given to only a very small number of employees.

- ✔ **Informal recognition:** A spontaneous gesture of sincere thanks for desired behavior or performance. Examples include a pass-around trophy that acknowledges exceptional customer service and bringing in donuts or a pizza to celebrate a department success. These forms of recognition are increasingly more important to today's employees than formal recognition but can be hard to track and difficult to consistently apply across the organization.

- ✔ **Day-to-day recognition:** Daily feedback about positive employee performance. Examples include dropping by to tell someone "good job" on an assignment and a simple thank you in person or in front of others for a job well done. In many ways, this is the ultimate form of recognition; it's where the rubber meets the road in creating a results-oriented culture of recognition for your organization. On the other hand, it can be difficult to measure, track, and keep fresh.

All these forms of recognition offer value, and every manager should strive to use them all as they manage others to maximize results and variety.

Making Recognition Meaningful

Recognition can have a powerful impact on the management and motivation of employees, groups, and organizations. It can turn everyday work into a very positive experience and has the power to inspire, nurture, and even create! But not all recognition is equally as powerful; it must mean something to the people upon whom you bestow it. This section explains how you do that.

Turning recognition into a priority

As important as recognition is, I find that one of the great challenges is getting people to take the topic seriously. Because recognition sounds so easy to do, people often feel that they must already be doing it! Unfortunately, more times than not, that is not the case. I often find myself telling managers, "Yes, I *know* you *can* do recognition. My bigger concern is *will* you do so?" I discuss this topic in depth in Chapter 7.

One way to reinforce your commitment to meaningful recognition is to lead by example. Model the behavior you expect others to follow. Having top managers practice employee recognition sets the tone for all managers and sends the message, "If I can make time to do this, no one else in the organization has an excuse not to." The publisher of the *Washington Post* is said to give handwritten notes to reporters he feels have written excellent articles. Similarly, one bank president gold-plates quarters a roll at a time to pass out to individual employees when their performance merits special acknowledgment. Likewise, all supervisors at Busch Gardens in Tampa, Florida, are provided tokens with the words "Thank you" on them to use as an on-the-spot form of recognition.

Identifying the kind of recognition your employees appreciate

Before you can recognize your employees in ways that are effective, you first have to understand your employees themselves. Find out what they want; don't assume you know. By unilaterally deciding what to do or what to give employees who perform well, you run the risk of missing the opportunity to turn recognition into a motivational tool. Instead, involve employees in determining what would best reward or recognize them for doing good work. Here are some suggestions:

- On an employee's first day at work, ask the new employee to jot down on an index card a few items that most motivate him or her.

- In a group meeting, go around the room and ask all attendees to share two things that motivate them.

- Pass around a copy of my book *1501 Ways to Reward Employees* (Workman Publishing Company) and ask employees to initial in the margin any ideas they especially like. Then when an employee performs well, you can select something you already know he or she will find motivating.

Realize that one type of recognition no longer fits all. Paying even above-market rates or having a few traditional (and predictable) recognition activities or a single great formal recognition program is no longer enough. Update formal recognition programs to make them exciting and relevant. Johnson & Johnson surveyed employees and found that some of the organization's traditional awards were not considered recognition by over half the employees. So the organization made adjustments that were most meaningful to their employees. In short, you've got to experiment, learn, and discuss recognition ideas and activities on an ongoing basis.

Don't confuse recognition with reward. *Recognition* is the activity of acknowledging an employee for a job well done, and a *reward* is money, or an item or an experience with monetary value that is provided for desired performance. Harvard Business School professor and management consultant Rosabeth Moss Kanter defines a reward as "something special — a special gain for special achievements, a treat for doing something above-and-beyond."

Key attributes of effective recognition

Not all recognition is created equal. Although you can be creative in your efforts to you develop and implement a recognition programs, you should take into account the nine attributes I describe in this section if you want your efforts to be successful. Doing so will help you get more out of your recognition efforts.

It is contingent on a desired behavior or activity

The term *contingency* refers to how closely the recognition relates to the behavior you recognize. If you give *contingent recognition*, you give recognition only when an employee exhibits a desired behavior or performs at the desired level — for example, when an employee successfully handles a difficult customer request or completes a project on time. *Noncontingent recognition* is generalized; that is, it doesn't correspond to a particular achievement or level of performance. An example of noncontingent recognition is holding a company picnic for all employees or celebrating an employee's birthday. The employee didn't do anything special to receive the recognition that was provided.

As you think about kinds of recognition policies you can put into place, keep in mind that contingent recognition — recognition in response to a significant achievement — is more effective than noncontingent recognition. Avoid using recognition simply to be nice, because you want your employees to like you, or because you feel guilty. Instead, link recognition to the performance objectives, values, and behaviors that will have the greatest impact on your continued success. In this way, your recognition efforts will become self-fulfilling, reinforcing desired behaviors and actions so that they occur again and again.

It is timely

Recognition is the most meaningful when it is given as soon as possible after the desired behavior or action. In fact, the timelier you are in recognizing a desired behavior, the greater the reinforcement of that behavior and the sooner your employee will repeat it. I like to say that when the thought crosses your mind that someone did a good job, act on that thought! Don't assume the employee knows he or she did a good job or that the employee was just doing the work he or she is being paid for. Be proactive in closing the gap between what was done and when it was noticed. If the employee achieved something significant, you might do or say something quickly to acknowledge the achievement and then come back to the matter when you can to offer a more significant form of recognition, such as a thoughtful gift or organized formal celebration.

Recognition loses meaning (or can even alienate the recipient) when it is not timely, so saving up individual recognition for an annual performance appraisal or rewards banquet can be counterproductive. And certainly don't save up a bunch of thank you's to deliver all at once. Delaying recognition weakens its effect. The connection or reinforcement is not as clearly made; the opportunity for providing impact and meaning is missed. If you are truly on the same wavelength as the employee, you'll want to amplify the successes when those occur!

It is specific

When giving recognition, avoid using generalities. Instead, be specific about why the recognition is deserved. Stating exactly what the recognition is for serves two purposes: First, you make clear to the individual exactly what you appreciate about what he or she did, which, in turn, helps increase the chances of the behavior or results being repeated. Second, it shows the recipient that you've paid attention to what he or she has done and you're not simply offering empty praise or paying lip service. Remember, specifics add credibility to any praise. It's your evidence as to why the person truly did do a great job!

It is frequent

Positive reinforcement is most effective in shaping desired behavior when you give it frequently, at least until the behavior becomes established. For recognition to reinforce performance, the recognition itself has to be systematic. You want to catch the person doing the desired behavior as much as possible — initially, every time you see or hear about it. After the behavior becomes more like a habit, you can back off the reinforcement. And in the long-term, research indicates that it is actually the unpredictable reinforcement that becomes the strongest reinforcer. That is to say, once you have the momentum of excellent behavior being truly engrained, keeping it going takes much less effort. Always consider frequency when you design a rewards and recognition program.

A question I often get is whether you can ever over-do recognition. That is, does it cheapen praise if it is used too frequently? I've found this is seldom the case — especially if each instance of praise and recognition has the attributes described in this section. There also should be some variance for circumstances. For example, if you are in a new relationship, as is the case with a new hire, err on the side of providing more recognition than less. Again, in addition to providing needed direction, it helps you build a positive, trusting relationship more quickly.

A good way to help ensure that you're giving recognition often is to plan regular events designed to recognize achievements. Organizations typically provide nonmonetary recognition on a formal yet infrequent basis around specific events — celebrating a record sales quarter, for example. If you want to institutionalize nonmonetary recognition, you can adapt this same idea: For example, take time to debrief projects when they are done to specifically call out things that went well, things learned, and problems averted. Or, you can take the idea further by making recognition a daily part of your management practices: give daily feedback on performance, offer personal one-on-one praise, and make frequent use of thank you notes, for example. For information on how impactful praise can be, refer to the later section "The Power of Praise."

It can be formal or informal

Formal recognition is one that stems from a planned and agreed-upon program of incentives. Examples of formal rewards include employee nominations for innovation or cost-saving suggestions or attendance awards. An informal recognition is more spontaneous and flexible, often stemming from the relationship between the parties involved. Examples of informal recognition include a personal word of thanks for a job well done or recognition in a staff meeting for excellent customer service. Of course, formal and informal are not mutually exclusive; provide both types of recognition to maximize impact.

It's said that formality leads to a pattern of defined behaviors — that is, a formal recognition program can amplify those core behaviors that most impact the organization's success — whereas informality leads to a pattern of interacting roles because informality stems from the personal relationship of the parties involved.

Although everyone likes a spontaneous personal word of thanks, formal praise offers a different form of validation for a job well done, and because it is often done in front of others, including those above you in the organization, it tends to be more highly valued by recipients.

It occurs in the proper setting and context

You can recognize an employee privately or in front of some or all company personnel. Recognition can be presented impersonally — for instance by mail — or it can be very personal, even anecdotal and emotional. Before deciding which setting is best, keep these things in mind:

✔ Take into account your employee's personal nature. Shy individuals (perhaps 20 percent of the population), for example, usually prefer private and less formal displays of gratitude.

✔ Regardless of the size of the audience, most employees prefer recognition that is presented with a personal touch.

The significance of the provider matters

We know that, in general, employees most value recognition from those they hold in high esteem. This can be their manager, of course, but it can also be someone higher in the organization. Who then should provide the recognition? The answer will vary with the circumstances, but as an achievement grows in its reach, consider having someone higher in the organization call it out. Sometimes, you can take the guesswork out of it and ask the employee being recognized who they would most prefer to be recognized by.

It has value to the recipient

Good recognition must be meaningful to the recipient. If your recognition takes the form of something the employee doesn't value or want (for example, giving a plaque or certificate to someone who already has dozens), you're more likely to demotivate the individual rather than make him or her feel valued and important.

Recognition is more meaningful when the form it takes is highly valued by the recipient. One individual may value rewards that relate to his or her job (a specialized work tool, a software upgrade, or an educational opportunity, for example) while another individual may value rewards that relate to his or her personal life and can be shared with others. Such rewards may include dinner out with a significant other, a weekend get-away, a barbecue set, or tickets to a sporting event. Customize rewards and recognition for the recipient. (Check out the earlier section "Identifying the kind of recognition your employees appreciate" for suggestions on finding out what your employees value.)

Consider whether the recipient would most value tangible recognition, intangible recognition, or both. Tangible recognition might be a trophy or plaque, while intangible or symbolic recognition includes ceremonies, public announcements, time off, or the gift of more responsibility, more work space, or the ability to work from home more frequently.

It doesn't have to cost money

One of the most amazing and delightful ironies about recognition is that the most powerful forms of it tend to cost little or nothing. While money is, of course, a top motivator for all of us (and it is nice to receive gifts and merchandise, especially in response to having done a good job), simple, sincere words and actions often have the most impact on how people feel about what they do, whom they work for, and where they work.

Asking an employee for his or her opinion, involving him in a decision, granting her permission to pursue an idea, or supporting him when a mistake is made can resonate most deeply, because it illustrates your trust and respect for that employee. In fact, probably the very best form of recognition is a simple thanks for having done a good job.

Using Motivators to Help Employees Do Their Best

The focus of management used to be on "renting" employee behavior; in some work environments, staff was even referred to as "hired hands." Today, it's not good enough to simply rent the behavior you want from employees; you've got to find a way to tap into their hearts and minds and to elicit their best efforts. You have to make employees feel valued so that they *want* to do their best work on a daily basis and to consistently act in the best interests of the organization. If you truly want your company to be competitive in today's fast-moving, global marketplace, you need to obtain extraordinary results from ordinary people. You can get such results from your employees by focusing your attention on how you treat them. For the best results, pay employees fairly, but treat them superbly.

Identifying key motivators

Getting people to perform at their best is the function of what management theorist Frederick Herzberg calls *motivators* — those items that drive employees to do their best work. So what kinds of things motivate employees? Here are a few:

- ✔ Feeling that they are making a contribution
- ✔ Having a manager who offers praise when they do a good job
- ✔ Having the respect of their peers and colleagues

✔ Being involved and informed about what is going on in the company

✔ Having meaningful, interesting work

✔ Having growth and development opportunities

Since money is a basic need, don't you sometimes have to pay people well first, *before* these factors become motivating to employees? This question came up at a conference keynote presentation I was giving, and I was delighted when another member of the audience stood up and said, "Not necessarily! I found that by using positive reinforcement, I was able to increase the level of performance of my employees, which led to increased sales revenues, which ultimately made it *possible* to pay people better." In other words, nonmonetary incentives became the catalyst for improving employee productivity, enabling *everyone* to gain financially in the process.

The power of a simple "thanks"

Recognition starts with a thank you. And sometimes that's all it takes. Most employees don't just need to be thanked, they *expect* to be thanked for something they've done. Even affirmation from coworkers can change employees' attitude and give them a greater sense of contentment.

Employees expect the thank you to come immediately or soon after their good performance. Waiting too long to express appreciation shows indifference and reinforces the impression that the thanks is an afterthought.

Employees need to feel as though their efforts are well spent, even if the results are small or subtle. If they feel as though they're consistently giving their all, only to hear it's not enough, the time will soon come when their motivation wanes and their interest in doing a good job falters. Focusing on accomplishments gives your employees the encouragement they might need to keep moving forward in a difficult time. Small wins can lead to bigger wins.

Busting the money myth: Why cash isn't enough

Most people work so that they can pay their bills. However, most people don't come to work just for money.

Now, I'm not saying money isn't important; clearly it is. We all need money to pay our bills and live in the manner to which we are accustomed. I'm also not saying money has no motivational value; clearly it does. Just how much of a motivation money is varies over a person's life. If you're about to buy a new home, have some unexpected medical bills, or have children in college, you're probably more keenly aware of your monetary needs and are much more motivated by cash than you were when you were in, say, high school.

Despite cash's fundamental importance in most employees' lives, it's not the only (or even necessarily the most powerful) motivator. Understanding why is key if you want to keep your employees engaged. (To discover what truly motivates employees, head to the earlier section "Using Motivators to Help Employees Do Their Best.")

A paycheck is not recognition

The salary you pay employees is *compensation*. Compensation is a function of your company's compensation philosophy and policies, its market, and geographic considerations.

According to Herzberg, a fair salary is considered a *hygiene factor* — something all employees need to do the job they were hired to do. Other hygiene factors include adequate workspace, sufficient lighting, and a comfortable environment. Hygiene factors enable employees to do their jobs at the basic level, but they don't necessarily motivate them to perform their jobs at the highest level possible. You have to go beyond the hygiene factors to truly motivate your employees. In short, you can't count compensation as recognition; recognition is what you offer employees *above and beyond compensation* to get the best effort from them.

As long as your employees' hygiene factors are intact and they are able to comfortably keep up with their monthly bills, you can take them to the next level so they are doing their best, using the motivators I outline in the earlier section "Using Motivators to Help Employees Do Their Best."

Be careful that you do not simply acquiesce to those individuals who constantly ask for more money. Why? Because you want to reinforce results, not requests. This point is a critical one: You will never get the best effort from employees just by paying them more. Employees who only want more money will never be satisfied with what they are paid; their expectations will always rise with each salary increase, and because there will likely be a limit to what they can be paid, they then will be dissatisfied.

The cons of cash rewards

Monetary rewards such as merit increases, bonuses, and the like are important, but seldom are they today's employees' only motivators for making their best efforts on the job. A study by Maritz Research, a division of Maritz, Inc., based in Fenton, Missouri, revealed the following anomalies about cash rewards:

✔ Rewards that are strictly monetary are not as effective as noncash-based items. Because they tend to be less personal, the opportunity to develop and grow interpersonal relationships is hindered.

✔ Monetary rewards do little to establish a link between the behavior and the incentive. Instead of furthering company values, they diminish them and promote a culture of unnecessary spending.

✔ In most organizations, performance reviews — and corresponding salary increases — occur only once a year (even less if salaries are frozen), whereas the things that motivate people are typically activities that have happened recently within the immediate work group. To motivate today's employees, managers need to recognize and reward achievements and progress toward goals on a more frequent, even daily, basis. Especially important is thanking employees when they do good work.

If money isn't a top motivator, then why is it all my employees talk about?

A question employers often ask me is, "If money isn't a top motivator, then why is it all I seem to hear about from my employees?" I've had a chance to examine this question firsthand in several companies and have discovered three possible explanations:

✔ In companies where people are doing jobs they don't enjoy and the managers never show their appreciation, employees conclude, "If this is what it's like to work here, at least they had better pay me well." In other words, in the absence of recognition, money becomes a form of psychological reparation for enduring a miserable job — sort of like combat pay in the military, that increased differential in compensation for those that are putting themselves in harm's way.

✔ In organizations in which managers use *only* money to thank people — for example, bonuses for completing projects, on-the-spot cash for desired behavior, or an extra percentage in the employees' annual salary increase — the message that the managers are sending, albeit unintentionally, is that cash is the *only* medium of gratitude. In other words, managers have *trained* employees to expect cash as the only true form of thanks.

✔ In almost any organization, some employees define their worth to the organization in terms of what they are paid. Higher pay indicates higher worth, lower pay indicates lower worth. This correlation may or may not be true, but it's definitely true for those that believe it.

A common misconception exists about the use of rewards and recognition to motivate employees: that it costs companies too much money — or more money than is readily available. But rewards, recognition, and praise do not need to be lavish or expensive to be effective. In fact, today's employees report that the most motivating and meaningful forms of recognition typically cost little or nothing at all!

Although money is important to almost everybody, it is certainly not the only motivator. Today's employees value many other things where they work, and surprisingly, some of the top motivators, such as praise, involvement, and support, have the least financial cost.

You can't always control compensation

Another way to look at the relation between money and motivation is that most of us cannot influence what employees earn, but there are a lot of things we can do to influence how excited and motivated they are about their jobs on a daily basis. Management's daily interactions with employees can do one of two things: They can either promote trust and respect between managers and employees, or they can erode it. Not much of a choice when you think about it, is it?

Treating employees well is of paramount importance if you want them to come to work energized and committed, and to bring their best thinking and initiative with them.

The Power of Praise

There's an old Greek proverb that says, "Many know how to flatter, few understand how to give praise." In the workplace, going beyond flattery to master praise is an important and powerful way to keep your employees engaged. Praise is priceless, and yet it costs nothing. Consider this: In a survey on workplace incentives, Gerald Graham of Wichita State University found that the number one incentive, according to workers, was personal praise from a manager for doing a good job, yet 58 percent of employees said they seldom if ever received such praise.

High-quality praise simply communicates (1) I saw what you did, (2) I appreciate it, (3) here's why it's important, and (4) here's how it makes me feel. You can praise an individual employee one-on-one, directly, or in front of others. You can even praise someone who is not around, knowing that your remarks will more than likely make their way back to the person.

Four types of praise

In my research, I've found that simple praise for employees who do good work represents four of the top categories of motivators. This praise falls into four types:

- **Personal praise:** Face-to-face thanks and acknowledgement for a job well done is instantaneous and fresh and can be done pretty much anywhere, even in the hallway or parking lot.

- **Written praise:** Written note or formal letter of thanks offers recognition that is a tad more lasting in that the written communication can be shared with others or saved for future perusal.

- **Electronic praise:** Personal thanks and acknowledgment via e-mail or voice mail is another spontaneous form of praise that you can do quickly as you review e-mail messages or as you leave positive voice mails for deserving employees during your drive home from work.

- **Public praise:** Recognition in front of one or more other people, in a public forum such as a meeting or a broad form of communication such as a newsletter or newspaper, again amplifies the recognition. More people get to hear about it, many of whom might subsequently offer their own additional congratulations to the employee for a job well done.

At first glance, these forms of praise may all seem the same, but I've learned that this is not the case. Each of these dimensions is mutually exclusive and provides a different value and meaning to an employee than the other forms offered. Being praised to one's face means something different from receiving an e-mail or note or being praised before others. Each is a form of recognition, but each carries different meaning to the person who receives it.

At meetings, allocate some time for recognition of outstanding effort or the sharing of success stories. End meetings on a high note, especially meetings whose agendas are laden with less-than-happy line items; it's a great way to remind employees that even in down times good things are still happening.

Elements of a good praising

Although giving effective praise may seem like common sense, a lot of people have never learned how to do it. I suggest an acronym — *ASAP* — to remember the essential elements of a good praising. Praise should be as *soon*, as *sincere*, as *specific*, as *personal*, as *positive*, and as *proactive* as possible.

As soon as possible

Timing is critical. To be most effective, the thank-you should come soon after the achievement or desired activity has occurred. If you wait too long to thank a person, the gesture loses its significance, and your employee assumes that other things are more important to you than taking a few minutes with him or her.

As sincere as possible

Your praise should be based on a true appreciation of and excitement about the other person's successes; otherwise, your thanks may come across as a manipulative tactic — for instance, a ploy used only when you want an employee to work late. As the saying goes, "People don't care how much you know, until they know how much you care."

As specific as possible

Avoid generalities in favor of details of the achievement. Compliments that are too broad tend to seem insincere. Specifics give credibility to your praise. Say what the employee did and why her effort was of value. For instance, "Thanks for staying late to finish those calculations I needed. It was critical for my meeting this morning."

As personal as possible

The most effective forms of recognition are the most personal ones. They show that recognition is important enough for you to put aside everything else you have to do and focus on the other person. Because we all have limited time, the things you do yourself indicate that they have a high value to you. Recognition by way of a quick e-mail or voice-mail message is certainly appreciated, but praise in person means much more to others, when you are able to do it.

As positive as possible

When you say something like, "You did a great job on this report, but there were quite a few typos," the *but* erases all that came before. Save the corrective feedback for the next similar assignment. Separate constructive criticism from your acts of praise.

As proactive as possible

Praise progress toward desired goals. Don't wait for perfect performance; praise improvements and behavior that are approximately right. You will get the results you want sooner as you develop a success momentum with the employee.

Chapter 6

The Manager's Role in Recognizing Employees

In This Chapter

▶ Closing the gap between what managers think is motivating and what actually is motivating

▶ Implementing immediate recognition

▶ Demonstrating the value of recognition

*I*t's difficult to overstate the impact a manager has on his or her employees. As Jim Moultrup of the Management Perspectives Group once said, "Continuous, supportive communication from managers, supervisors, and associates is too often underemphasized. It is a major, major motivator."

As I explain in Chapter 4, recognition works. The principles of positive reinforcement and the use of recognition and rewards to reinforce desired behavior and performance are some of the most thoroughly proven concepts known in management today. In a survey of American workers, for example, 63 percent of respondents ranked "a pat on the back" as a meaningful incentive. And research conducted by leadership experts Jim Kouzes and Barry Posner found that 98 percent of respondents indicated that getting encouragement helps them perform at a higher level.

At work, the recognition that means the most to employees is that which comes from their immediate managers. Studies have validated this fact: An employee's manager is the most important person in his or her work life; hence, most employees feel that "if you have a good manager, you have a good job." When employees identify the traits of the best manager they ever had, it is common for them to list items such as "trusted and respected me," "challenged me to do my best," and "made me feel special." Likewise, the phrase "people leave managers, not companies" pretty much sums up what study after study has proven: The number one reason employees leave an organization is because of a poor manager. In this chapter, I explore the critical role that managers have in shaping relationships with employees in positive and productive ways through recognition.

Closing the Perception Gap between Managers and Employees

Ask any manager what he thinks his employees want from their jobs, and you'll probably get a list of items that is heavy on financial incentives, such as increased pay, bonuses, promotions, and so forth. But ask any *employee* what he really wants from his job, and you'll likely get a very different answer. In a series of studies originally conducted by Lawrence Lindahl in the late 1940s (and subsequently repeated with similar findings by Kenneth Kovach in the 1980s and myself in the 1990s), what managers believed that their employees most wanted from their jobs was in sharp contrast to what the employees themselves reported as being most desirable. Each group was asked to rank the importance of various elements of their jobs and work environments. As the rankings from Lindahl's study indicate (see Table 6-1), a significant discrepancy existed between the two groups' perceptions.

Table 6-1	What Motivates Employees?	
	Manager Rankings of Employees	**Employee Rankings of Themselves**
Full appreciation for work done	8	1
Feeling "in" on things	10	2
Sympathetic help on personal problems	9	3
Job security	2	4
Good wages	1	5
Interesting work	5	6
Promotion/Growth opportunities	3	7
Personal loyalty to workers	6	8
Good working conditions	4	9
Tactful disciplining	7	10

Managers thought the traditional job incentives of good wages, job security, and promotion/growth opportunities (each of which has a financial cost) were the things employees most wanted from their jobs. Employees, however, ranked full appreciation for work done, feeling "in" on things, and sympathetic help on personal problems highest in their rankings — ironically, items that have no direct financial cost and that require only a small amount of awareness, thoughtfulness, and time on the part of managers. This gap in perceptions between managers and their employees has persisted to this day. As a manager who is implementing recognition, your role is to close that gap.

What managers believe that their employees most want from their jobs often differs considerably from what employees themselves report as being most desirable.

Probably the best way to close or eliminate this perception gap is to *start with your employees:* Get to know them and what motivates them. Doing so will show your employees you have an interest in them and their success. For example, take new hires out to lunch or coffee on their first day of work and ask them questions such as these:

- ✔ "There are a lot of places you could have worked in this community. What was it about this job and company that most attracted you?"

- ✔ "What type of work do you like best? Are you a 'lone wolf' who likes to work independently, or do you prefer to be a part of a team and work closely with others?"

- ✔ "If a special project or assignment came up, would that entice you?"

- ✔ "What do you hope to learn in this job? What skills do you hope to develop?"

- ✔ "Where do you want to be five years from now?"

- ✔ "What do you do on the weekends? What hobbies do you have?"

- ✔ "What's your family situation? Do you have any children? What are their names and ages?"

The more you know about someone's motivators, the better you are able to inspire that person to do a good job. This isn't about manipulating employees to get them to work harder; rather, effective managers help their employees on their career journeys so that the employees are more willing to help the managers in return.

Getting to know your employees shouldn't stop after they first start their jobs. Take time to check in with them on a periodic basis, perhaps in one-on-one meetings.

In a company I worked for, all managers were asked to hold one-on-one meetings with each of their employees; each of these meetings was to last about 20 minutes and occur at least once every two weeks. The meeting's agenda was based on what the employee most wanted to talk about. If the manager forgot this focus and launched into something he or she wanted to discuss, the meeting was rescheduled to discuss the employee's agenda items. Initially, employees used the time to ask questions about assigned work and projects, but as the meetings progressed, the topics did as well, hitting on career paths, strategy and advice about developing better working relationships with others, and sometimes even role-playing difficult discussions. Employees universally reported that they looked forward to these one-on-one meetings with their managers and that the time spent in the meetings was some of the most valued time in their jobs!

Top Motivating Techniques Reported by Employees

In a study of 65 potential workplace motivators by Professor Gerald Graham of Wichita State University, all five of the top employee-ranked items took the form of a nonmonetary form of recognition. Of these five top-ranked items, three required little or no financial resources and very little time to successfully implement. The top-ranked item, "Manager personally congratulates employees who do a good job," had the highest ranked impact, even though almost 60 percent of respondents said their managers seldom if ever provided such a thanks. For the second-highest ranked employee motivator, "Manager writes personal notes for good performance," 76 percent of respondents reported seldom if ever receiving such notes from their managers.

Table 6-2 lists the top employee-ranked motivators in Graham's study and indicates the motivational impact of each item and frequency of its use.

Table 6-2	Top Five Motivating Techniques, Based on Employee Responses	
Technique	*Motivational Impact (Ranked Highest to Lowest)*	**Frequency of Manager Use (%)*
Manager personally congratulates employees who do a good job	1st	42%
Manager writes personal notes for good performance	2nd	24%
Organization uses performance as the major basis for promotion	3rd	22%

Technique	Motivational Impact (Ranked Highest to Lowest)	*Frequency of Manager Use (%)
Manager publicly recognizes employees for good performance	4th	19%
Manager holds morale-building meetings to celebrate successes	5th	8%

*Percentage of respondents who say their manager or organization typically use these techniques.

Simple techniques, such as including employees who directly report to you on your weekly to-do list and checking their names off when they have met or exceeded their job responsibilities and received recognition for doing so, can go a long way toward making employee recognition both simple and doable.

In addition to these surprising findings, Dr. Graham found two common characteristics among the top motivating incentives in his study. The most motivating incentives to employees are ones that are manager-initiated and based on performance:

- ✔ **Manager initiated:** Motivation is very personal, and it is influenced most by those with whom employees work closely — starting with their immediate manager or supervisor. Motivation happens within the context of their relationships. As a manager recognizes an employee for doing good work, he strengthens both their relationship as well as the employee's desire to further do good work.

- ✔ **Based on performance:** People feel most valued when they are recognized for doing the job they signed up to do or for going above and beyond what is expected of them to act in the organization's best interests. People who perform well feel good about themselves, which further increases their motivation.

Graham found that the type of reward most preferred by employees was personalized, "spur-of-the-moment recognition from their direct supervisors," yet as he writes in his conclusion, "It appears that the techniques that have the greatest motivational impact are practiced the least even though they are easier and less expensive to use."

Implementing and Leveraging Recognition for Greatest Impact

Employee motivation is very personal and is influenced most by those with whom employees work closely — starting with their immediate managers or supervisors. Relationships — and the interactions that occur within relationships — provide the context for motivation. Certain relationships, especially those that are important to us (like the ones we have with managers) or that involve people we hold in high esteem (like the relationship we may have with a mentor), are especially impactful. As a manager and therefore someone who is important to the employee, you have the power to be a motivating influence simply by virtue of being in the manager-employee relationship.

As the preceding section makes clear, the most motivating incentives for employees are those that are 1) manager-initiated rather than organization-initiated, and 2) contingent on performance. As a manager, you need to take personal responsibility for recognizing your employees, and then you need to keep at it on a daily basis. The best way to do this is to make a plan — one that includes easy ideas you can implement immediately, as well as a long-term strategy that helps you both improve your motivation skill set and make recognizing your employees a habit.

Individual recognition techniques for immediate application

Try to recognize employees every day — not every employee every day, but every day someone. You should have no trouble doing this if you remain on the lookout for things your employees have done well.

As you get started on recognizing individual employees right away, remember that the key is to keep it simple. Your efforts should be deliberate, but they don't have to be elaborate. You can try some of these easy-to-implement ideas today:

- ✔ **Take a few moments at the end of the day to reflect on whose performance you've noticed.** Write thank-you notes for those individual employees and leave the notes on their desks as you exit the office for the day.

- ✔ **Manage by wandering around.** Get out of your office to see, meet, and speak with employees about their work. Chances are you'll begin to notice more things to recognize. Take different routes in and out of the premises to make sure you informally cross paths with all of your employees.

✓ **Greet individual employees by name and with eye contact.** Take a few minutes to see how they are doing. Be sincere.

✓ **When you read your mail, look for positive items to share with others or at all-department meetings.** Take time at the beginning or end of meetings to share positive news, such as letters from customers or to ask whether any team members would like to recognize or praise another team member.

✓ **Make an effort to meet with employees you don't see or speak with very often.** Take a break together, have coffee, or enjoy an off-site lunch.

✓ **Act on good news!** Catch people doing something right and thank them for it in the moment.

✓ **Take time to listen when employees need to talk.** Be responsive to people, not just to problems. Many managers get so laser-focused on solving problems that they miss handling their employees' needs and emotions in the situation.

✓ **Remember the 4:1 rule:** Every time you criticize or correct someone, plan to praise or thank that same person at least four times going forward. In other words, strive to find positive things to notice about employees' work so you don't fall into the habit of being quick to react to mistakes they have made.

✓ **Think of mistakes as opportunities for learning.** Help employees learn from their mistakes by discussing the situation, what lessons were learned, and how they would handle a similar situation in the future. Avoid criticizing employees for making mistakes, especially in front of others. Be quick to thank and compliment others and slow to criticize and judge them.

A good rule is to praise publicly and reprimand privately.

✓ **Spread positive gossip!** Tell others what you are pleased about and who is responsible. Be quick to give credit for work your employees do.

✓ **Take time to celebrate individual or group milestones, desired behavior, and achievements!** Bring in some refreshments and host a spontaneous celebration to honor an individual or team achievement.

Taking your recognition efforts to the next level

To create a successful habit of recognizing your employees, you should match the recognition to the person, the achievement, and your budget.

Match the recognition to the person

When it comes to effective recognition, one size does not fit all! You need to customize your recognition for each of your employees. Whereas some employees may prefer recognition in private, others would prefer it in public, and others may not have a preference. Will a thank-you do? How about occasional on-the-spot forms of thanks, a gift card or free lunch, a coupon for ice cream, a small gift, and so on? Does the employee want his peers to be aware of his good performance?

To find out the type of praise and recognition each of your employee's prefers and to determine how you can deliver the praise in meaningful ways, you need to know each employee's preferences and personality. Use strategies to keep recognition top-of-mind with your employees. As I mention in numerous places in this book, have one-on-one conversations with each of your employees, or look for opportunities to call out successes you see in all aspects of your job (online, in meetings, and in casual conversations). You might also want to have a reminder system linked to your calendar, or set up a buddy system with another manager whereby you remind and prompt each other on the topic. This is about personal, daily awareness.

After you find out what works for each individual employee, establish an action plan that fits that employee's needs. If you try to fit all employees into a single category, you'll end up meeting the needs of only some members of the group.

Match the reward to the achievement

Match the reward to the achievement. Small forms of recognition should accompany small behaviors — someone helping you out on a work assignment, for example. Use larger forms of recognition for greater achievements. An employee who finished an important, months-long project would merit a public thanks in front of everyone in the department, a formal letter for the employee's personnel file, or a chance for the employee to have his or her choice of next assignment. Which of these forms of recognition you use depends on that employee's personal preferences, as explained in the preceding section.

Use other leaders in your organization to help you recognize employees who are deserving; ask your manager to thank one of your employees, for example. Doing so shows the employee that others higher in the organization know who they are and are aware of the contribution they are making.

Match the reward to your budget

You need to know the budget, items, or programs available for employee recognition in your organization, and then you need to make the most of the resources at your disposal.

You can do a *lot* of recognition with little or no budget: Recognizing employees in a public forum, having thank-you cards on hand for employees to use to recognize one another, and instituting a program that reinforces the company's core values are options that don't need to cost much. (For additional low-cost but meaningful kinds of recognition, head to the nearby sidebar "It's not the cost; it's the thought that counts.") If you have *some* budget for employee recognition, you can do even more to thank and surprise deserving employees with thoughtful gestures and mementos of their efforts.

It's not the cost; it's the thought that counts

In my work with myriad companies over the years, I've collect several low-cost ways to recognize employees for their contributions:

Giving a personal thank

Giving thank-you notes

Sending praise via e-mail

Leaving a message of praise on voice mail

Giving praise in a public way

Using a pass-around trophy

Making time available to spend with a manager or company president

Having the employee's car washed by a manager or executive of the employee's choice

Assigning employee parking spaces

Reading positive letters from customers aloud at staff meetings

Making reference to employees' contributions in the company newsletter

Featuring employees in the community newspaper

Naming days in an employee's honor

Having a Wall of Fame to display photos of achievers

Creating a team project scrapbook to display in the company lobby

Giving certificates of appreciation

Celebrating with balloons and computer banners

Packing lunches for employees

Loaning your car to an employee

Creating a personalized or fun award (Golden Banana, Spirit of Fred, Order of the Extended Neck, and so on)

Providing time off (an extra break, a long lunch, a three-day weekend, and so on)

Performing a least-favored or menial task for an employee (a "Dump a Dog" program)

Having a victory celebration

Providing "performance passes" that enable employees to use a lending library for books and audios

Handing out coupons that let employees bring their pets to work

Featuring employees in company ads

Deputizing a "Confetti Committee" to hold spontaneous celebrations

Baking cookies, distributing candy, making ice cream floats for employees

Cooking and serving a meal for employees (barbeque, breakfast, and so on)

Offering a management challenge (that is, if the goal is met, the manager must perform some action — shaving his head, dressing in a crazy outfit, and so on.)

Don't be limited to only what your organization makes available to recognize employees. I've found many managers will dip into their own pockets to cover the cost of a pizza, a gift card, or a personal gift for a deserving employee!

Seeing How Recognition Impacts Your Workforce

When it comes to the money your bosses are investing in recognition, your role is two-fold: to demonstrate the value of the recognition and to execute cost-effective recognition properly. Effective recognition programs at the individual and team levels can require a substantial investment of time and money. Even though the best recognition is free, the time and effort involved still costs money. Consider, for example, an organization with 100 managers who each spend an average of two hours and $25 a week on recognition. If the *fully burdened cost* (hourly wage plus the cost of benefits) of each manager is $50 an hour, the time that the supervisors devote to their recognition efforts alone costs the company approximately $650,000 per year.

And that's just the beginning. Say that this company has ten teams, each with ten employees, and each team spends one hour per person (at a fully burdened cost of $25 per hour) and $30 a week on recognition-related activities. That works out to an additional $140,000 per year in real costs to the company.

The grand total of dollars spent on this very simple approach to individual and team recognition is close to $800,000 in time alone! And this is before you factor in the costs of any organizational recognition tools or merchandise.

If you were the CEO of this company, wouldn't you want to know what benefits the organization was getting for this significant investment of company resources? A smart CEO, of course, would have no problem with the $800,000 expenditure, provided he or she was confident that the program was an investment that would produce in excess of that cost.

Unfortunately, poor recognition can easily turn a huge investment into a huge expense with low return and major morale consequences for the organization. When recognition is executed properly, however, the benefits — improved performance, desired results, and reinforcement of company goals and values, to name just a few — far exceed the time and money spent on recognition.

As a manager, you need to be aware that you should recognize employees for behaviors and results that will drive maximum benefit for the organization. Read on for more.

Improving employee performance

Recognition geared at improving performance should be goal-oriented. Goal-oriented recognition is targeted at helping an organization achieve a desired outcome. People do things largely for the positive consequences they anticipate. Major motivators of both individual and group performance comes in the form of the following:

⯌ **Contingent promises,** better known as *incentives*

⯌ **After-the-fact recognition,** called *positive reinforcers*

When used appropriately, these forms of recognition can lead to desired behaviors or results. Your role as a manager is to make sure that you make the connection between desired performance and the employees that made that performance happen.

At Emery Air Freight, now a part of Consolidated Freightways, managers used positive reinforcement to dramatically reduce the company's costs of doing business. Emery was losing a lot of money because its containers were not fully loaded when shipped. Workers knew that they were supposed to ship fully loaded containers; the performance expectations had been communicated to them many times. However, while workers reported that their containers were fully loaded 90 percent of the time, a review found that the containers were actually fully loaded only 45 percent of the time. Through the use of positive reinforcement and feedback on performance (primarily just praise from management!), the percentage of full containers increased from 45 percent to 95 percent, saving the company millions of dollars. In a similar type of praise-for-performance program, Weyerhaeuser Paper Company increased the productivity of logging trucks from 60 percent to more than 90 percent.

How can you best identify and improve results? By following a process in which you pinpoint specifics, list possible solutions, evaluate options, prioritize next steps, and recognize progress and success.

Step 1: Pinpoint specifics

Isolate the problem or opportunity by using the following questions to think about and more precisely identify a particular problem area or opportunity where you can take initiative. As you read each question, visualize your workplace and the way things are currently done there:

⯌ How long has the situation existed? Is it getting worse or better?

⯌ Who is affected by the existing situation? Do they want to change things?

⯌ What costs are incurred by the problem? What opportunities are lost?

⯌ What will be the consequence if the situation is not changed?

⯌ On a scale of 1 to 10 (1 = highest), how urgent is the situation?

Step 2: List possible solutions

After you clearly identify the problem, brainstorm with others to come up with options for ways to correct the situation. Briefly explain the nature of the problem or improvement you are addressing and the starting point you have identified.

If you have already decided on a course of action, the group's role is to provide feedback, offering ideas about ways to improve the solution, to streamline it, to sell it, and so on. If you have not yet identified a course of action, the group will engage in a four-minute brainstorming session to generate suggestions for you. Take notes on the ideas and honor each idea by writing it down.

Step 3: Evaluate options

Now narrow down the options you've created. One way to do this is to create a "force field analysis," a process first suggested by Kurt Lewin for weighing the factors that are helping or hindering the action you wish to implement.

Simply make two lists about each option. Label the first list as "Helping Forces," that is, those factors that will make your efforts easier. Examples of helping forces may be your own initiative and resources, job know-how, a supportive boss, peers willing to help, alignment with an organizational initiative, a friend outside the organization to discuss the situation with you, and so on.

Label the second list "Hindering Forces." Hindering forces are the factors that will make your efforts harder. Examples of hindering forces are length of time the situation has existed, limited resources (money, staff, and/or time), negative attitudes of others, existing organization policies, the difficulty of change, and so on.

For each factor, draw an arrow the length of which indicates the strength of the factor (a longer arrow means a stronger factor), as shown in Figure 6-1. Then ask yourself, What could be done to strengthen the helping forces and weaken or eliminate the hindering forces?

Step 4: Prioritize next steps

List the steps needed to correct or improve the situation; then prioritize those steps to create an action plan for moving forward. What do you want to be different based on the action you take? What specifically will be improved, how, by whom, and by when? Each step should show exactly what you will do (for example, conduct a trial run, secure permission, get so-and-so's support, write up a proposal, and so forth).

Should I Provide More Recognition to My Staff?
(+/− on 1 to 5 Scale)

	HELPING FORCES		HINDERING FORCES	
Figure 6-1: Use Lewin's force field analysis to narrow down your options and find the best ones.	+4	My employees seem to like and want more recognition	I'm pretty busy and focused on my job and its priorities	−4
	+5	My organization wants me to use more recognition	I'm not sure how to provide recognition well to employees	−2
	+4	Would help with employee morale and retention	Recognizing others doesn't come easy to me	−2
	+18			−11

©John Wiley & Sons, Inc.

Step 5: Recognize progress and success

When progress is made against the goal by individuals or the team as a whole, do something to recognize that progress. The recognition you provide will not only make those who have worked on the problem or project feel valued and validate their efforts, but it will also help drive future efforts from both those who have been recognized or others who saw or heard about the recognition that was given.

Reinforcing company goals and values

Although recognizing employees is certainly a nice thing to do, for maximum impact, you must tie the recognition to your organization's goals and values. If your organization has taken the time and effort to clearly establish its core mission, values, and strategies, then the rewards and recognition you or other managers give should clearly and systematically reinforce the behaviors and results that reinforce the company's goals and values.

To recognize employees for their actions and behaviors that contribute to achieving company goals, identify the organizational goal they helped achieve and describe how their actions helped do so. Before long, employees will start to understand that embracing and acting in accordance with the company's mission and goals is what it takes to get recognized. In this way, systematically acknowledging employee efforts that move the organization toward achieving its objectives fosters employee support of those goals and, in turn, brings them closer to full realization.

Before recognition can help move an organization toward achieving its goals, employees must be thoroughly aware of those goals.

Validating employees' goals

As a manager, you should meet regularly with employees to check on their progress toward the performance goals you and they have set up and to discuss ways you can best support them in achieving those goals. In addition, you should identify the kinds of recognition and rewards that motivate your employees to try to attain these goals.

If the employees' goals are aligned with company goals, however, you create an environment in which employees actively work toward the company's success rather than just doing their jobs. Encourage employees to think outside the box to find new and innovative ways to participate in the company's success. For example, managers can help employees establish goals that are linked to finding new cost-savings measures or to better ways of conducting an existing practice or procedure. Having the organization's end goals in sight and empowering employees to be creative and to develop their own skills and abilities enables you to tap into a tremendous reserve of energy, ideas, and initiative.

As you think about ways to use recognition to reinforce and validate your employees' goals, keep in mind that the best way to keep your employees focused on their goals is to give them feedback on their progress so that they clearly know how they are doing.

Traditionally, performance reviews occur once, maybe twice, a year. More frequent reviews of employees' performance and efforts to achieve set goals lets them know where they stand before the work is completed. With proper guidance during the course of the year, many unintentional mistakes or behaviors can be averted. More frequent review sessions should concentrate on existing goals — of the employee and of the organization — and should include discussions about the employee's future and development opportunities.

Creating an optimal work environment

By applying the principles and ideas included in this chapter, you will be well on your way to shaping a more motivating workplace. If you keep at it, you will soon have employees who are dedicated to their (and your) success and a work environment in which people are excited about their jobs, enjoy their coworkers, and want to do the best work possible each and every day.

Five important lessons for managers to better recognize their employees

1. Start with your employees: Get to know them, their preferences, and their career aspirations.

2. Make sure job expectations are clear and that your employees have the tools necessary to succeed.

3. Establish a plan to check in with your employees to see how they're progressing toward their goals.

4. Look for and act on opportunities to recognize employees when they do good work. Try to do this as a matter of habit.

5. Celebrate successes as they occur. As your employees make progress or achieve their goals, recognize them by doing something they value.

Not only will this kind of work environment give your organization a competitive advantage, but it will also make you proud to be a leader in a culture of recognition. You will have created the kind of work environment we all dream of: one that puts people first, and rewards and recognizes their contributions to their customers, coworkers, and organizations.

Of course, your job won't be done. To sustain the results you've achieved, you will need to keep at it over time. Remember, motivation is a moving target and requires an ongoing, consistent focus.

Chapter 7

Getting Managers to Recognize Employees

*E*mployees expect to be recognized when they do good work. Dozens of studies and surveys support this statement, and almost any employee is likely to confirm it. Thanking employees for doing good work increases the likelihood that they will want to continue that high quality of work for you and your organization, and it serves as a catalyst for getting others to perform better as well. For these reasons alone, you would think that almost every manager in today's organizations would use recognition as standard operating procedure. But that's not true. In fact, the opposite is most often the case.

In this chapter, I discuss why certain managers don't use recognition as much as they should (while others embrace it), how to help the holdouts convert, and how others across the organization can get managers to buy into the importance of recognition.

The $64,000 Question—Why Do So Few Managers Recognize Employees?

During my three-year doctoral study at the Peter F. Drucker Graduate Management School of the Claremont Graduate University, I sought to answer a simple question: Why is it that so few managers recognize employees when they do good work? Moreover, I wanted to determine what factors either encourage or inhibit the use of employee recognition by managers. In this section I share my findings.

Highlighting the characteristics of high-use managers

I studied managers from 34 organizations, representing 7 industries (healthcare, financial services, insurance, hospitality/restaurant/retail, information technology, manufacturing, and government). During my study, I looked at 140 different variables that ranged from individual factors (such as awareness, skills, and demographics) to organizational factors (such as age, size, and culture). The results surprised me.

For example, some managers had programs, tools, and budgets for recognizing their employees but still not did not engage in recognition, while other managers who didn't have any of those elements available to them still made recognition happen. Why? If availability of resources didn't seem to be a factor, what was? I discovered that most of the *high-use managers* (managers who most frequently use recognition) shared the following characteristics:

- ✔ **Feel personal responsibility for recognition:** High-use managers not only internalize the importance of recognition, but they also take ownership for implementing it. They don't pass the buck or sit by passively and wait for someone else to do it; they see it as their obligation to execute recognition to help create the motivational environment for their work group.

  The top reason given by managers who frequently recognize employees is that they feel it is their responsibility as a manager to make recognition happen, to create the motivational environment for the employees they manage.

- ✔ **Possess skills and confidence:** High-use managers in the study had the interpersonal skills and confidence to use recognition, got better at using it, and continued to use it over time. Low-use managers did not know how to effectively provide recognition and felt strongly that its use would lead to undesired outcomes. However, if low-use managers get effective training in recognition, they are much more likely to recognize their employees.

- ✔ **Had received reinforcement for using recognition:** High-use managers were reinforced for using recognition (most notably by their employees), suggesting that the more recognition a manager gives, the more likely that he or she will be thanked by recipients — and the more likely the behavior will become a habit. Organizations interested in creating a recognition culture should thus consider vehicles for employees to recognize their managers at different levels of the organization (more on the cycle of recognition later in the chapter).

- ✔ **Tend to be younger:** Younger managers (those under 50) were more likely to use recognition than older managers (those over 50) who had worked many years in the same job or for the same organization and were more likely to feel that recognition was not an important behavior to practice. In fact, age was the only highly significant demographic factor that differentiated the group of high-use managers from the group of low-use managers; other demographic factors such as gender, ethnicity, nationality, and educational level had no significant impact (positive or negative) on the giving of recognition.

Older managers may be reluctant to use recognition and thus need additional evidence, convincing, and encouragement to do so.

✔ **Had role models:** High-use managers were significantly more likely to have had parents who used recognition, although neither high-use nor low-use managers reported that their own managers recognized them. While there's little we can do about the upbringing of those with whom we work, it is encouraging to know that high-use managers recognize their employees despite not receiving similar recognition from their own managers. This suggests that a culture of recognition can be built from the bottom up and not just from the top down.

Looking at additional factors that influence giving recognition

In addition to uncovering common personal characteristics among high-use managers in my study, I discovered other elements that impact whether a manager participates in recognition. Uncovering these factors (such as time, fear of not being fair, and the current competitive environment) was just as surprising to me as the characteristics. Read on as I share the findings with you.

Limited time

High-use managers in the study did not see time as a major constraint; instead they ranked it as a positive factor in that recognizing an employee for doing good work takes so little time — you can do a great praising in just a few seconds. For example, thank someone in passing in the hallway or start a meeting by sharing a positive letter from a client or customer.

Low-use managers, however, cited "limited time" as one of the main reasons why they didn't use recognition. They felt they were too busy to take the time to thank others for the work they'd done. It seems that a lack of time is not a true obstacle to giving recognition, but only an excuse for those managers who don't want to give it.

Recognition inequities

Most managers are concerned about the possibility of overlooking deserving employees when people are singled out for recognition. Evidence from my study indicates, however, that concern over leaving someone out when using recognition is more of an *excuse* for low-use managers and more of a *consideration* for high-use managers. For example, a manager may have had an experience in which he or she overlooked someone who should have been recognized. Low-use managers use this as a reason not to recognize employees (for example, concluding they would only recognize the entire department together going forward so as not to risk leaving someone out again), whereas high-use managers take into account this consideration, learn from instances in which recognition didn't go as planned, and are careful not to exclude anybody who deserves recognition in the future.

Another type of inequity that concerns managers is when they do something for their people that they were proud about, but their efforts are not well-received. Take, for example, the manager that took it upon himself to purchase coffee mugs customized with the team name for all members of his team when they completed their stated objectives in working together. It was a thoughtful gesture, but the reaction of the group was, "We saved the company all this money and this is what we get for our efforts?" The manager was a bit taken aback, but instead of reacting negatively to a well-intentioned idea, he was smart enough to approach the instance as a learning opportunity and instead asked the group what a more meaningful form of thanks for their efforts would have been. Using setbacks as opportunities for growth is another mark of a committed, high-use manager.

Competitive pressures

As the amount of change, pressure, and market constraints of an industry or business increases, so, too, does the need for a concerted effort to enhance employee recognition. When times are tight, many managers focus more on the mechanics of the business, like pricing and discounts, product offerings, and operation efficiencies, and spend less time on thanking, encouraging, or supporting their employees. For employees in high-demand positions (technical and minimum-wage employees, for example), the need for recognition also increases as an effective strategy for holding onto talent.

Thus, it's often in times of stress and change — when managers are least likely to be able to use recognition — that they most need to use it. And if they are in a competitive industry in which they have a difficult time finding candidates to hire and keep, using recognition to create a positive work culture goes a long way in making employees feel valued for their efforts and thus more likely to stay with the company and even to recommend the organization as a great place to work for others that they know.

Programs, tools, and budget

In my study, I discovered that managers' working relationships and circumstances more greatly influenced their practice of recognition than the quality of existing recognition programs and tools. Organizational culture, programs, and tools can help facilitate recognition, but they don't seem to be prerequisites for its use. In other words, a manager who believes in recognition makes it happen regardless of the programs, tools, or budget available to him or her. And on the flip side, an organization that provides recognition programs and tools shouldn't expect that just having those available will be enough; instead, upper management needs to sell managers on the importance of recognition, teach managers what recognition looks like, strongly encourage them to participate, and hold them accountable if they do not.

Available budget was also not a prerequisite for the effective use of recognition. Not only is money not the top motivator for today's employees, but spending money on recognition tools and programs or having a budget for recognition is not a prerequisite to having managers use recognition. High-use managers find ways to recognize employees regardless of whether they have a budget or resources set aside for that purpose. Of course, once they are truly persuaded of its importance, executives are more likely to make programs, tools, and budget for recognition available to managers, which those managers then will be more likely to use.

How behaviors become self-perpetuating: Cycles of recognition

In my doctoral program study, I also found that individual managers perpetuated their own use (or nonuse) of recognition. That is, managers who were high-users tended to have a positive experience with the behavior, which made them more likely to use recognition with those they managed. High-use managers received reinforcement for the use of recognition by (in order of most to least importance) their employees, themselves, other colleagues, suppliers, and their own managers. They also obtained the results they desired in using recognition, which included increased employee performance and morale. Based on this success, they were more likely to use the behavior again and again to the point that it became a daily part of their behavioral repertoire as managers (see Figure 7-1). Plus, the more they used recognition, the better they got at delivering it.

Low-use managers, on the other hand, did not have a positive experience with the use of recognition, avoided the behavior as much as possible, and thus had little or no chance of being reinforced for the behavior. They didn't derive any benefits from their use of recognition, and their concerns and fears about recognition became excuses for not doing it. The result: Because the behavior was not a priority, they enhanced neither their skills nor their confidence, a negative cycle started, and they further avoided recognition altogether, as Figure 7-2 shows.

These findings further reinforce that a positive personal experience is more important than the ready availability of programs, tools, budget, or other resources when it comes to triggering a positive cycle of recognition for any manager.

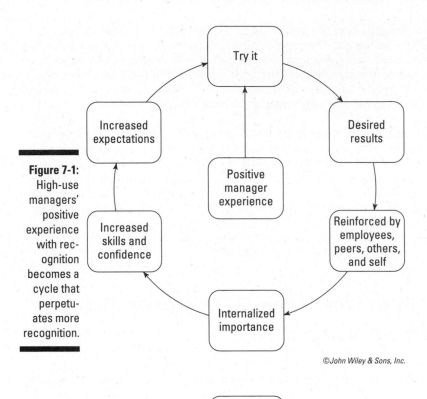

Figure 7-1:
High-use managers' positive experience with rec-ognition becomes a cycle that perpetu-ates more recognition.

©John Wiley & Sons, Inc.

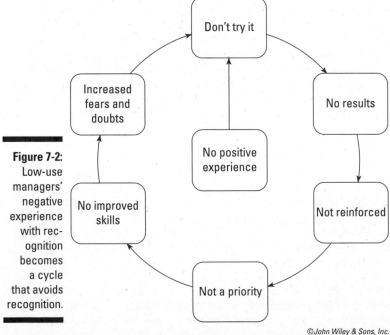

Figure 7-2:
Low-use managers' negative experience with rec-ognition becomes a cycle that avoids recognition.

©John Wiley & Sons, Inc.

Converting Low-Use Managers into High-Use Managers

Given the differences between a high-use and low-use manager, the next matter is figuring out how to convert a low-use manager into a high-use manager. Can a low-use manager ever become a high-use manager? And if so, will the change last? How can you raise managers' awareness of recognition and its benefits, help them learn the relevant skills to use recognition, and encourage them to take the first step and make an ongoing effort to recognize others?

Taking a ride on the cycle of success

By creating a cycle of behavior and response that leads to the escalating use of recognition on the part of managers, as Figure 7-3 illustrates, it may be possible to initiate a low-use manager at any point of the cycle, converting him or her into a high-use manager.

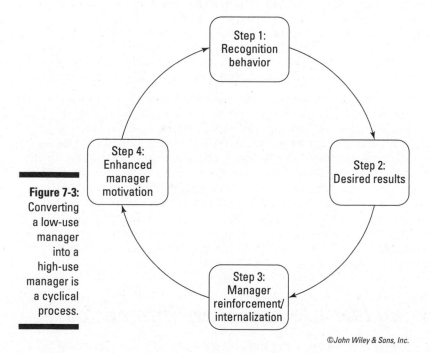

Figure 7-3: Converting a low-use manager into a high-use manager is a cyclical process.

©John Wiley & Sons, Inc.

The cycle includes these four steps:

- 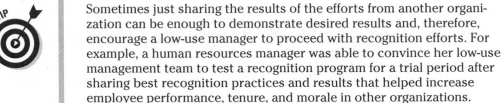 **Step 1 — Recognition behavior:** This step involves the actual act of recognizing someone, in any way. For example, managers reflect on their day prior to leaving work to think about who made a difference, finished a project, helped a coworker, or delighted a customer, and then they do something about it — write a note or send an e-mail to thank those individuals, for example.

- **Step 2 — Desired results:** This step refers to the impact the recognition has and whether it's the impact the manager wanted. If the recognition yields the positive results the manager was aiming for, the manager is more likely to do it again.

 Sometimes just sharing the results of the efforts from another organization can be enough to demonstrate desired results and, therefore, encourage a low-use manager to proceed with recognition efforts. For example, a human resources manager was able to convince her low-use management team to test a recognition program for a trial period after sharing best recognition practices and results that helped increase employee performance, tenure, and morale in other organizations.

- **Step 3 — Manager reinforcement/internalization:** Thanking managers when they use recognition reinforces the behavior and makes it more likely that they will continue to recognize others as they internalize the connection between the behavior and the acknowledgement received. For example, by thanking a low-use department manager for introducing her to a key client when he visited the office, one employee made client introductions a routine part of every client visit to the office.

- **Step 4 — Enhanced manager motivation**: As the desired behavior is consistently recognized and internalized by the manager, it impacts the manager's ongoing motivation and becomes more habitual. The manager's behavior can become further enhanced and locked in by the organization raising awareness about the topic of recognition, explaining why it's important to the organization's success, and communicating the expectation that all managers consistently engage in employee recognition. For example, by bringing in an outside authority to address all managers at a quarterly meeting, one company was able to simultaneously raise the awareness of the importance of recognition with the expectation that all managers practice it more often. Tying recognition to performance metrics also can significantly impact the legitimacy of the practice.

Spurring low-use managers into action

 The trick to starting this cycle lies in finding a catalyst — an event or trigger mechanism that will help low-use managers personally experience recognition in a positive, meaningful way, such as the following:

- ✔ Having an executive request that all managers start doing more employee recognition, tracking that behavior, and periodically reporting out findings to the group.

- ✔ Making it a policy or practice to start all meetings with some type of recognition.

- ✔ Connecting the low-use manager with another manager who is a recognition advocate so that the recognition advocate can share why she uses recognition, how she uses it, and the results she has obtained from using it.

- ✔ Seeing an admired leader in the organization recognize someone.

- ✔ Receiving personal feedback and coaching from someone on the company's recognition or training team, or from human resources.

- ✔ Reading an article that lends immediate credibility to the behavior and persuades the individual to act differently. The business press frequently references studies and statistics about what motivates employees and how the most effective styles of motivation change over time. Selecting articles and other references that include this kind of information can help make the case for individual managers and persuade them to give recognition a try.

When converting managers who seldom use recognition into managers who often use recognition, small successes work best. A seemingly small step has the potential to make a profound difference and start the person on a journey toward using recognition more regularly.

I was working with one government agency whose human resources director was frustrated by the inaction she encountered from the managers on the topic of recognition. Finally, she announced, "That's it. I want every manager to get out of their office *this afternoon* and recognize employees in their area for something they've done well." And so the managers who had previously dragged their feet got out of their offices and looked for things their employees had done that warranted being recognized. The effort was a success. In fact, one group of employees was so grateful for the recognition that they purchased a thank you card for the manager, and everyone signed it in appreciation. For the first time, that manager saw that recognition does have a direct impact on employees.

Simple techniques may be most effective — placing a stack of thank you cards on a manager's desk and getting her commitment to write a few notes to deserving employees at the end each day, or having her list her direct reports on her weekly to-do list and checking off each employee after she "catches" that employee "doing something right" and recognizing him for it.

Techniques such as these can go a long way toward making recognition simple and doable. Managers need to personally experience the behavior and its potential and then systematically build upon its use and subsequent successes. When they are convinced of the value of recognition, tools, resources, and encouragement can make identifying recognition opportunities and delivering the actual recognition routine.

Calling All Employees: Getting Managers to Give More Recognition

After presentations on the topic of recognition, I often have individuals tell me, "These concepts are great — I wish I could get my manager to thank and appreciate me more!" To which I often reply, "When was the last time you praised your manager?" This response often catches people by surprise, as if a manager doesn't or shouldn't need thanks or praise, or that it's not an employee's place to give it. Nothing could be further from the truth.

All people need to be appreciated for the jobs they're trying their best to do, and managers are people, too. "But," an occasional employee protests, "that's why they get the big bucks!" Being in a position that pays more money doesn't change a person's basic needs. Managers, regardless of how much money they make, need to be valued as much as everybody else.

Praising up

You may have a manager who just reacts to mistakes — it's a common tendency. If you wait for your manager to become enlightened on his own about how to treat people better in the workplace, you may find yourself in for a long wait unless you find some way to offer help and encouragement that will enlighten him. So why not try what I call *praising up*? *Praising up* can be an effective strategy for getting your manager to focus on the positive things you (and others) do.

Praising up isn't about being a sycophant and offering an abundance of vague, flowery flattery. The guidelines for effective praise hold for managers just as they do for any employee. You need to be timely, sincere, and specific in selecting when, what, and how you thank your manager. Better yet, you can make focusing on the positive a routine part of your relationship with your manager.

More times than not, when you initiate these kinds of positive interactions, your manager will look for occasions to acknowledge you and your work in the future.

A friend of mine who is the general manager for a printing company recently told me that a new employee said to him during her first week on the job, "Once a week, I'm going to come into your office and tell you about all the great things I've been doing. You're going to agree with me. I'm going to do this because I need to hear that you appreciate my efforts in order to keep charged up to do my best work." My friend agreed to the arrangement, and at the end of one of their fifth review session, the employee announced, "You're getting good at this!" My friend had to agree. Until those interactions, he had never taken the time to thank or appreciate his employees much before, but he came to realize that not only were these opportunities for recognition important to his employee; they were times he enjoyed as well.

Think of the things your manager does that you appreciate and make a point to thank him or her for doing those things. And if you want to encourage certain behavior from your manager, act to recognize that behavior when you see it, as well. Remember, you get what you reward. A fundamental characteristic of human nature is to give others what we receive. This works equally well with managers as it does with any employee.

Tried and true tactics for getting praise

I recently read an article that discussed strategies for asking your manager for more money to improve your financial outlook. I think being able to ask your manager for praise to improve your emotional outlook is just as important. After all, if your heart isn't in your job because you aren't appreciated enough (the plight of most people), it doesn't matter how much you're paid to stay in the job.

All employees need to be praised and recognized for doing a good job. All employees need to know that the time and effort they spend on their work makes a difference and that they are making a contribution at work. If you rely solely on your manager to take the initiative in appreciating you for doing a good job, you may end up getting less praise than you want and — given today's time and energy constraints — almost certainly less than you need to continue working at a high level.

When you don't get recognition or praise, you start to feel abused and burnt out in your job. Instead of their jobs energizing and exciting them, unappreciated employees tend to be drained by their jobs. They can even come to feel like victims, as if they don't deserve appreciation and are incapable of ever doing well enough to be thanked and valued for their contribution.

Fortunately, no one needs to feel like a victim when it comes to praise. If you want more praise from your manager, try the strategies I cover in this section.

Model the behavior

One way to subtly influence the behavior of another person is to treat that person as you'd like them to treat you. You might, for example, say to your manager, "Gary, yesterday when we had a key client in the office, I really appreciate the way you took time to explain my role on the project to him. It made me feel valued and glad to be on your team. Thanks for doing that." A typical manager might respond with, "Oh, I didn't realize that was so important to you" and then — human nature being what it is — Gary will almost inevitably be a little more on the watch for similar instances to acknowledge your efforts.

Ask for the praise

Many people feel awkward about asking for praise. They feel that they shouldn't have to ask for it and that asking for praise diminishes its value. I disagree on both accounts: If the activity is important to you, you *should* ask for acknowledgment, and asking for praise is not just for an ego boost; it serves a practical function as well. It helps you ensure that you know specifically what you did well so that you may be more apt to repeat it.

You can bring up the topic in a general way by saying, "Mary, I've never told you, but it really means a lot to me when you give me specific feedback about projects I do after they are finished. I learn from your comments, and if you liked my work, hearing what you liked about it not only makes me feel good, but it also reinforces those aspects of the job that I am doing well so I can be sure to continue doing those things." After all, no one is a mind reader, and getting praise makes it easier to better focus future efforts for any performer.

Plan for recognition

Include praise and recognition along with all the other important elements of getting a task accomplished. When planning a project, for example, you can also plan for the type of praise, recognition, or celebration that will occur if the project is completed within the schedule and budget as planned. You could announce, "If this team accomplishes its objective, it will be significant to the organization and we will present our finished work to upper management together as a team."

In fact, determining during the planning stages the recognition that will happen at the end of a project creates an added draw and incentive for getting the job done.

Stay authentic

How do you keep from seeming like you are being egotistical or simply currying your boss's favor? Be honest and direct and emphasize the positive and practical aspects of receiving immediate and specific feedback about your performance. As the saying goes, "Feedback is the breakfast of champions!" Don't be afraid to seek an adequate serving! As I've stated, a fundamental principle of all human behavior is that you get what you reward. When you get sincere, specific praise from your manager, you want to continue to perform and to do so at higher levels.

Combating Six Common Excuses of Low-Use Managers

Organizations must meet low-use managers at their own level if they are going to make recognition a personal, practical, and positive experience. As someone who is trying to get managers on board with recognition, you have to overcome misperceptions and constraints; remove objections and obstacles; and confront excuses. As drawn from my doctoral research, following are the six leading excuses low-use managers give for not using recognition and what you can do to combat them.

"I'm unsure how best to recognize my employees"

The top reason given by managers who seldom recognize employees is that they are unsure how best to recognize their employees.

Most low-use managers have a blind spot about recognition. They aren't sure what to do, when to do it, how to do it well, and so on. The topic thus becomes a difficult one for them. These managers need to know specifically what recognition looks like because the behavior does not come naturally to them. They also need to have an increased awareness of the importance of recognition, to be trained in the skills of recognition, to be provided with individual feedback, and to be shown positive examples and techniques that they can actually *do*, no matter their time and resource constraints. To make sure they are on the right track, managers should discuss potential recognition strategies with their staff and seek feedback on their own recognition behaviors.

One great example of figuring out how best to recognize employees comes from BankBoston (now a part Bank of America), where managers give employees a blank index card on their first day of work and ask them to make a list of the things that motivate them. The manager ends up with an individualized motivation checklist for every employee.

"I don't feel providing recognition is an important part of my job"

Yes, managers aren't hired to recognize employees per se; they're hired to perform specific functions of the organization, from sales to operations. But recognition can help them be successful in their jobs and achieve their goals, as well as the goals of the department and the organization.

Organizations need to make their expectations about recognition clear: that providing recognition is not an optional activity, but rather, an integral part of the organization's strategies, specifically tied to achieving the company's goals. Supervisors need to evaluate their managers on the success of their efforts at providing recognition in a frequent and meaningful way. Supervisors and executives should make recognition a real, important part of the ongoing planning of organizational, team, and individual goal setting, and not suffer the fate of "management by announcement," in which an initiative is announced once and then never heard of again.

When I worked in human resources for a large financial corporation, a manager came to our department for help. Specifically, he wanted us to motivate his employees who he felt were not doing adequate work. He was a bit disappointed when we suggested that perhaps motivating his employees was *his* job. The fact of the matter is, if you are a manager today, your first and foremost job is the motivation of your team. Without that, it's unlikely you'll have much success with anything else you try to achieve.

Following are some examples illustrating how various companies have made recognition a part of a manager's job:

- ✓ A vice president at AAA of Southern California personally wrote notes of thanks to individuals in field offices, demonstrating to all managers under him that, if he made it a point to recognize employees in his job, everyone working for him needed to do so as well.

- ✓ At the Walt Disney Company, all managers are specifically evaluated on their ability to recognize and encourage their employees. They're expected to ask their employees how they, the managers, can better support them and to talk with their employees about their futures with the organization.

- ✓ When one of his line managers would share an employee achievement, a plant manager at AlliedSignal, an industrial chemicals plant in Moncure, North Carolina, would suggest possible forms of recognition that the line manager could consider to help to celebrate the achievement.

"I don't have the time to recognize my employees"

As I indicate early on in this chapter, high-use managers actually rate time as a facilitator for conducting recognition because some of the best forms of recognition (personal or written praise, public recognition, and positive voicemail or e-mail messages) require very little time to initiate and accomplish. Thus, the reaction by low-recognition users of not having enough time is often no more than an excuse for not doing the behavior. Such excuses can be countered with techniques that can be readily applied, even by busy managers. Consider these examples:

 ✔ **When you hear good news, act on it by sharing or amplifying it to others.** Pass it on, print it out, or add additional praise whenever possible!

 ✔ **As you hear or learn of positive items and good news, collect them to share at staff meetings.** If you share these events at the start of the meeting, you begin the meeting on a positive note.

 A manager at ESPN told me the first item on the agenda of *every* staff meeting she has with her group is naming five things that are going well. Sometimes listing the five things is easy to do, sometimes it's harder, but the meeting participants don't go to the next item until it's done. She believes that this is the foundation for her team's ongoing success in working together.

 ✔ **Manage by wandering around.** Doing so gives you a chance to connect with staff in an informal way, increases your visibility, and lets you see how things are going. I recommend scheduling specific times on your calendar to make sure you do this.

 ✔ **Keep some simple tools handy that you can use to recognize people in the moment.** All managers and supervisors at Busch Gardens in Tampa, Florida, are provided tokens inscribed with the words "Thank you" to use as an on-the-spot form of recognition for any employee caught demonstrating one of the organization's core values.

I interviewed a manager at Maritz, Inc., Sandy Hackenwerth, who was widely regarded in that organization as an excellent role model for using recognition. I asked her how she did it, and she replied, "Do you know how, when you go to a meeting and there's initially wasted time while everyone waits for others to show up? I always bring note cards with me to jot thank you notes to others. Or when there is a company announcement about promotions? I always jot each of those newly promoted a quick e-mail. It doesn't take that long, but it means a lot to them, and they thank me for doing it. If you have a constant focus on recognition, it's easy to find time to recognize others."

"I'm afraid I might leave somebody out"

Another common concern of managers is the possibility of leaving out someone who is deserving of recognition. Whereas high-use managers translate this concern into a greater commitment to recognize *everyone* who deserves it, low-use managers take this concern and interpret it as an excuse for not recognizing employees at all.

One great way of encouraging the low-use managers to overcome this concern is to suggest that, before commending the team in public for completing a project successfully, they check with you or another team leader to see whether they have all the names of those who assisted with a project. Also remind them that if, at any time, someone deserving is left out, it is perfectly acceptable to simply apologize and make amends as appropriate.

I recently attended an awards presentation at which the presenter and top manager personally checked to see that all award recipients were present so that the names of those who were absent would not be called (otherwise, they would miss their recognition). The presenter later recognized the absent individuals in person.

Don't wait until the end of meetings to recognize people; you could run out of time! One corporation specifically invited top-performing employees to a meeting at headquarters, telling them they would be publicly recognized at the meeting, only to have time run out at the end of the meeting, which resulted in numerous honorees not being mentioned at all.

"Employees didn't value the recognition I gave in the past"

Instead of being put off by what might not have worked in the past, low-use managers should make a fresh start and seek to find out what forms of recognition their employees most value. Managers can talk with employees one-on-one or have a group discussion about potential rewards and incentives, or they can ask each participant to bring two suggested motivators to the next staff meeting to share with the group.

By involving employees in decisions that affect them and their jobs, managers increase the employees' commitment and buy-in. They also increase the likelihood that their recognition efforts will be successful. For example, a manager at Hyatt Hotels Corporation asked her employees at a staff meeting what ideas they had for increasing recognition. One of the employees suggested that the department rotate the responsibility for recognition throughout the group so that each week one person would be responsible for finding an individual or group achievement and then recognizing it in some way of their own choosing. Creativity flourished; recognition skyrocketed.

"My organization doesn't facilitate or support recognition efforts"

Although recognition efforts can flourish even in the absence of formal organizational support, such support can help managers maintain their commitment. Information, training, tools, budget, and programs that reinforce recognition activities should be made available on an ongoing basis — even if all managers do not use these resources. Doing so supports recognition efforts and reinforces the organization's expectation that every manager take seriously his or her responsibility to provide recognition.

If your organization doesn't support recognition, all is not lost! You can apply the techniques and strategies I discuss in this book in your own workgroup and sphere of influence, taking time with your own group to discuss, plan, and practice recognition. You can also be an advocate of the topic to your manager, passing on useful examples and techniques to others you work with and suggesting that the company consider doing more to value its employees. Or you could focus on some simple strategies for getting started.

Each morning's plant-wide meeting at AlliedSignal used to be a giant forum for a "blame game," where the focus was on mistakes and problems the plant was having. Then the company changed the way it started these morning meetings. At the beginning of the meetings, employees were given a chance to publicly exchange thanks and acknowledgements with other employees. With this simple change, a very different positive energy started to emerge, and the negativity stopped.

Using and Advocating for Recognition, No Matter What Your Position

Upper level executives aren't the only people who can and should work to get managers to adopt recognition practices. In fact, even though you may not have official power to make others use recognition, you can still do a lot to make your workplace one that practices recognition. In this section, I share insights and lessons about how everyone in your organization can contribute to a recognition culture (I examine this topic further in Chapter 8).

Recognizing employees is one of the most important things a manager can do to build morale and enhance performance in today's fast-moving, competitive workplaces. It is also essential to an organization's ability to both attract and retain talent and to get the most out of the investment being made in that talent.

What managers can do

If you are a manager, giving recognition is well within your abilities. Successful implementation depends far more on your internal sense of competence and your simple commitment to try it than on formal organizational efforts, programs, tools, and resources. Opportunities to recognize your employees and make recognition part of your behavioral repertoire are all around you on a daily basis; they can even extend to how you delegate assignments.

Managers can't control their age or their upbringing, but they can become aware of their biases, overcome beliefs that hamper their effectiveness, and learn new behaviors that will help them — and the organizations for which they work — be successful.

Managers who don't currently recognize their employees need to make employee recognition a part of their daily behavioral repertoire. Those who do offer recognition to their employees can continue their efforts to invest in and improve their recognition.

Following are two examples of companies that strive to improve upon their already robust recognition efforts:

- ✔ **At Walt Disney World**, managers meet monthly to discuss how they can do more to recognize their employees. Although they already have hundreds of recognition tools, programs, and activities in place, they don't rest on their laurels. Instead, they constantly try to do even more because they know that recognition drives everything that makes their organization a success.

- ✔ **At American Express**, all managers are taught a concept they call "link and label," in which every manager who provides a development opportunity to an employee is asked to explain why he thought the project would be a good fit for the employee, what the employee can expect to learn from it, and how it will lead to other opportunities and responsibilities. The policy turns project assignments into opportunities for seamless recognition.

What HR professionals can do

If you are a human resources professional, you need to be a leading advocate for the importance and use of recognition in your organization on an ongoing basis. Here are some suggestions:

- ✔ Ask managers to use and discuss recognition behaviors, activities, tools, and programs with those who report to them.

- ✔ Establish a cross-functional recognition task force to deal with recognition recommendations and strategies for the organization.

- ✔ Using the ideas I outline earlier in this chapter, develop ways of targeting low-recognition managers for individualized attention.

At BankBoston (now a part of Bank of America), a member of the recognition committee had the task of calling on those managers who did not use the organization's programs to explain and update them, often inviting them to discuss the use and impact of the programs with other managers who were more active users. A similar strategy was used at Florida Hospital. An HR representative systematically met (individually or in small groups) with all managers who scored below average on employee recognition on the organization's engagement survey. The conversations served as a catalyst to engage the managers and create a plan for them to do more recognition.

What executives can do

If you are an executive, realize that you set the tone for what everyone else in your organization feels is important. What you notice, they notice; what you model, they model. Determine what actions you need employees in your organization to take and value those that have done so, helping to lead the charge with your own actions.

A general manager at Xerox Corporation saves time at the end of each of his management team meetings to go around the group and ask each manager present to share one thing he or she had done since the group was last together to recognize a person on his or her staff. Not only does the energy level rise during this portion of the team meetings, but managers also take notes on each other's ideas and then use those ideas themselves. As a result, they've become a self-learning organization on the topic of employee recognition.

What consultants can do

If you are a consultant who works in employee motivation, you can do a number of things to promote recognition:

- ✔ Assess and articulate remedies for improved employee recognition efforts.

- ✔ Explain and defend those recommendations to both upper and middle management.

- ✔ Help managers and executives tie recognition to desired performance as much as possible and to link recognition to the strategic objectives of the organization.

Based on quantitative improvements in the employee recognition scores that were obtained from his pre- and post-assessments, one consultant was able to show significant progress toward the organization's goals of increasing recognition, decreasing turnover, and moving the organization closer to becoming an "employer of choice" in its industry.

Part III
Implementing Recognition throughout the Organization

Top Five Things to Remember When You're New to Recognition

- ✔ **Start in your immediate sphere of influence.** Start with the people to whom you're the closest: your direct reports (or supervisors, for that matter), or even the colleagues you work with the most. Because you already know them and have a good rapport, you're probably more likely to know what they deserve recognition for and to give the recognition in a sincere manner.

- ✔ **Do just one thing differently.** It's far better to focus on one thing, do it well, and do it consistently than to try to do a dozen things that never go beyond the initial intention. After you achieve some success and momentum, you can always build on a successful practice.

- ✔ **Ask employees what motivates them.** Motivational preferences differ from person to person, and for the same person over time.

- ✔ **Instead of dwelling on what you can't do, focus on the hundreds of things you can do.** Anyone can, for example, write a simple thank-you note expressing heartfelt appreciation for a job well done. Also, if your organization has recognition tools you can use, take advantage of those. If your company has recognition programs you can nominate people for, do that as well.

- ✔ **Don't expect perfection.** There is no perfect way of doing recognition, and any new behavior or change will be awkward at first. Instead, try out some small things, learn from what works, and then seek to improve.

Find out more about employee recognition and engagement in my online Cheat Sheet at www.dummies.com/cheatsheet/recognizingandengaging employees.

In this part . . .

✔ Determine which of the various methods of training would work for your managers and executives, and design your strategy for making sure your upper ranks are prepared to launch a wide-scale recognition effort successfully

✔ Identify simple and easy ideas to recognize individuals that you can try immediately

✔ Understand the nuances of recognizing teams as a whole, as well as each team member — and know how to prevent common mistakes

✔ Bring individual and team recognition together as part of a larger, strategic organizational recognition effort that can make a company-wide difference

Chapter 8

Creating a Culture of Recognition

- -

In This Chapter

▶ Gaining buy-in and sponsorship

▶ Using reports to measure and track recognition

▶ Training managers to recognize

- -

A recognition culture is one in which individuals and teams (regardless of rank, title, expertise, or tenure) freely and readily recognize and celebrate one another's successes and contributions. In such a work culture, individuals trust and respect each other and are excited about everyone's success in the organization.

You can raise managers' levels of awareness about the importance of recognizing employees, and you can have them practice their interpersonal skills so they can increase their ability and comfort level with the behavior. But what keeps managers acting on their best intentions to frequently recognize employees on an ongoing basis? I'm convinced that the ratio of success increases when managers develop an individualized strategy and support plan to stay committed to the task of recognition.

In this chapter, I discuss the key attributes found in cultures of recognition as identified by Recognition Professionals International (the leading association on the topic that I helped found): manager accountability, leadership sponsorship, measurement and tracking, management training, communications, recognition and rewards, and process improvement.

Management Accountability

Recognition is the leading driver of performance, and managers need to be the leading driver of recognition — especially in the beginning of any recognition program. Therefore, a central element in any culture of recognition is management accountability, that is, the organization's leadership actively owning, believing, and practicing recognition with its employees and others on a frequent basis.

It's important for upper managers and executives to set an example by actively participating in recognition and encouraging their direct reports to do the same. This trickle down approach can start with an executive discussing ideas with his or her direct reports for how he or she can acknowledge, recognize, or celebrate achievements.

As you can see in Figure 8-1, all other elements of the culture-of-recognition model directly influence manager accountability — that is, the actual use of recognition — and manager accountability directly influences the other elements. All these components must exist in a symbiotic relationship if you want to be successful in building (and maintaining) a culture of recognition. Executives must help managers make employee recognition a priority and then, in turn, those managers need to make sure their managers are making it a priority. In the sections just ahead, I discuss these six elements of the culture of recognition model that directly influence manager accountability:

✔ Get managers and executives to buy in and make sure they know what's expected of them

✔ Measure, track, and report recognition usage for ongoing feedback and improvement

✔ Give managers training on effective recognition so that they understand why it's important and how to best make it happen

✔ Communicate frequently and give consistent reminders

✔ Ensure recognition and rewards are easy to use and meaningful

✔ Coordinate process improvements and regular reviews to improve

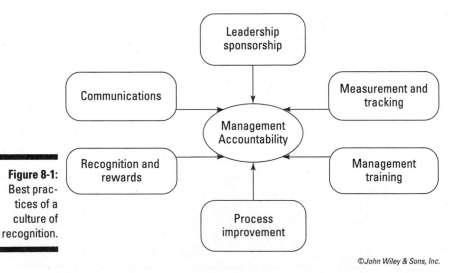

Figure 8-1: Best practices of a culture of recognition.

©John Wiley & Sons, Inc.

Leadership Sponsorship: Getting Buy-In from Upper Management

A successful recognition and rewards program requires active support and advocacy by upper management. At the very least, executives should understand, value, and participate in their organization's recognition initiative in several ways:

- ✔ Through participation in an executive leadership briefing to establish buy-in, and to review program objectives, program design, and rollout
- ✔ By taking a role in helping to launch the recognition initiative and their ongoing communication about the program
- ✔ In their expectations related to how they can actively support recognition in their own daily work practices.

Getting the upper echelon to support recognition efforts is essential. Without buy-in from the top levels of the organization, you may never be able to truly integrate your recognition efforts into the organization's culture. When senior management recognizes employees regularly, they demonstrate a commitment to it, thereby inspiring and setting the tone for middle managers and everyone else in the company. I cover strategies for how best to sell the idea of recognition to upper management in Chapter 15.

After you get buy-in, executives need to help set expectations for all managers to meet. With executive support, you can require managers to recognize their employees (and others throughout the company). Don't simply suggest or encourage managers to participate; make it mandatory. Without this pressure and obligation from above, many managers will never take the topic seriously — especially at the start of the program.

Ultimately, senior leadership needs to take ownership and personally buy into the topic, not just provide budget approval. This kind of commitment only happens when you truly get their personal, emotional commitment and not just their policy and budgetary sign-off. Senior leadership will need to have a visible and meaningful presence in the recognition program for it to work.

One way executives and recognition advocates can help managers truly adopt recognition as part of the organization's culture is by clearly demonstrating how recognition helps managers reach their goals and how it positively impacts their employees and the company's overall performance.

Although executives can perpetuate a culture of recognition through sponsorship, according to national Society for Human Resource Management, some 52 percent of organizations don't have leadership sponsorship of their recognition programs, which is a shame, because executive-level leadership and commitment to recognition is critical to the success of your recognition program. It sets the standard for engagement and drives employee participation. Even though executives' schedule demands might make finding time to focus on employee engagement and recognition difficult, it's still critical that you get them to try: Organizations with a highly engaged executive team typically have better employee involvement at all levels.

People often view sponsorship and support as meaning that executives are involved strictly in strategy, planning, policies, procedures, administrative, accountability, and budgetary support. However, to successfully drive a culture of recognition, upper management needs to go beyond just supporting the administration of recognition. Upper managers need to actively take ownership for recognition practices and programs, using recognition themselves. Having top managers practice employee recognition sets the tone for the behavior of all managers in the organization and symbolically says, "If I can make time to do this, no one else in the organization has an excuse not to." Executives in today's most successful and innovative organizations thus initiate actions that demonstrate their commitment to valuing their employees in a very hands-on manner.

Measurement and Tracking: Assessing Your Recognition Program's Progress

An old management maxim says, "If you can't measure it, you can't manage it." Recognition is no exception. People do what gets measured. Nothing makes managers actually use recognition more than knowing they're being measured on the behavior. In addition to including it in their performance reviews and compensation plans, you can institute standard monthly reporting that shows managers their recognition usage — as well as that of their direct reports. In some cases, you may even want to review these reports with their bosses, as well. Today's technology helps to make this objective more viable, as discussed in Chapter 12.

You can use analytics to make better decisions about recognition use, coaching, and budget — which is music to most executives' ears! Read on for the details.

Setting goals and a recognition baseline

Justifying the time, effort, and expense of any recognition program means demonstrating its impact, which requires that you determine a baseline and then show progress toward your goals. What to measure, how to measure, and how the results relate to the business strategy are critical in determining progress; therefore, defining program objectives and measures is one of the first and most important steps to implementing any successful recognition and rewards program. You must establish key performance indicators, track program performance, and measure progress toward your goals and objectives on an ongoing basis. This is quite an opportunity, given the national Society for Human Resource Management reports that 36 percent of organizations don't systematically measure or track the use of recognition in their organizations.

Your employee recognition efforts should ideally directly support the organization's business objectives. After you determine the program goals, you have to figure out what key behavioral metrics to use to measure those goals. Program measurement then starts with setting a baseline for all measures that have been set. A few examples of standard reports for a typical online recognition program include the following:

- **Award points deposited:** Displays the number of award points received by participants by business unit, location, division, cost center, and so on

- **Budget usage:** Provides summary and detail budget usage information

- **Enrollment:** Displays enrollment information for all participants

- **Nomination activity**: Provides nomination activity for all recognition given and received

By systematically measuring relevant objectives, you can better make behavioral and program changes to attain desired program objectives more effectively. For maximum understanding and maximum ability to make changes, make sure that all participants have access to reports that show both their recognition activity and how those activities impact their job success. Program administrators can also track the used and unused portion of the available budget as another measure of success against targeted activity goals.

Getting feedback reports

Reports are vital to your tracking and examination of your desired recognition activities. They let managers monitor how everyone is using recognition to best impact employee attitudes and performance levels, and administrators have access to summaries to track program activity and budget usage for their entire business unit. You can pull reports, using various parameters, including date, cost center, location, and type of activity. Most online recognition programs allow you to easily export reports into several formats that typically fall into one of the following three categories:

- ✔ **Pull reports:** Designated managers and administrators with the appropriate user rights and security level would have access to these online reports.

- ✔ **Push reports:** These reports are automatically generated and can be sent by e-mail with an Excel attachment on a predefined, recurring schedule to one or multiple organization users. This method is especially handy in the early stages of your program to get managers used to and focused on the level of their own recognition activity. Plus they can compare their efforts to that of other managers. To protect confidentiality, all reports are accessible to users based on predefined permission levels over a secure web interface.

- ✔ **Administrative reports:** The organization can be provided with comprehensive report options and program management reports, and dashboards (visual representations of the data for easier tracking) can be customized to meet the organization's specific needs. For example, you can set up the dashboard to show program utilization, key performance indicators, culture trends, and budget. The next section has more details.

Using dashboards

Participant dashboards present information about the recognition program to users as a snapshot, and participants can then drill down for more information. Dashboards typically include top promotions, points earned, news feeds, social recognition feeds, promotion leaderboards, activity recap, and even a reward wish list. Administrator dashboards are fully customizable, and they typically include action notifications, a recap of top promotions, points earned by promotion and overall earnings, points redeemed by promotion and overall redemptions, and top participants.

Additionally, managers and administrators with the proper security level have access to the reporting dashboards, which combine a set of gauges and charts that measure key indicators. Most organizations also use a variety of standard and customized tracking and reporting tools, including not only the operational reports that allow you to see transactions and recognition events, but also custom reports, which can be developed to align your organization's strategic initiatives with recognition activity.

You can brand the website and associated dashboards to your organization, using your company's logo, marketing designs, and color scheme. You can also build it to support and reinforce your core values and strategic objectives.

Management Training and Support

The relationship between managers and their employees is the number one driver of employee engagement. Since managers are the link between employees and senior leadership, they have the greatest ability to create a high-recognition, high-performance culture. To support the organization's mission, managers must understand the importance of recognition and how to use it to support business strategies, which means the recognition training that you provide is essential to creating a culture of recognition.

Effective management training on recognition has been demonstrated to increase recognition by at least 50 percent, especially when accompanied with communication that supports the program's use. Managers' ability to effectively reward and recognize achievement has been shown to increase employees' discretionary effort by over 20 percent and their intent to stay by over 30 percent, which results in increased performance and improved retention.

Train managers in both strategic elements (the potential impact of recognition on your company's mission, for example) and in more pragmatic aspects (like program rules and how to use various tools and supporting technologies). Initially, training on the goals of the program and proper use of the recognition software platform educates managers on how to best use the recognition program. As the program goes live, the built-in reporting tools identify adoption/participation rates across the organization, distinguishing top performers, as well as areas of opportunity for improvement, both overall and by individual managers.

In my experience, most organizations that roll out a new recognition program spend excessive time on the mechanics of the program — that is, how to nominate employees for various awards, how points can be redeemed, and so on — and too little time on why recognition is critical to the success of the organization and the responsibility and obligation of every manager to better recognize employees.

Involving heads, hands, and hearts

According to my doctoral research on employee recognition, the number one reason managers cite for not using recognition with their employees is they "don't know how to do it well." This shortfall can be overcome by providing training to managers on the issue, using what I call the Heads, Hands, and Hearts approach.

Heads: Raising manager awareness

In the Heads portion of the training, you need to address the beliefs managers have about recognition in general and about their role in making it happen. Perhaps you've already heard things like, "I'm not sure how to do recognition well," "It's not my job to do recognition," and "Employees will take advantage of me."

To combat these mindsets, provide research about the proven impact recognition has on employee performance, productivity, morale, retention and any of the other specific behaviors and results the organization is trying to obtain from its recognition efforts. Then train managers on the best practices of recognition. Interactive training of this type often covers the topics of the importance of recognition, linking recognition to performance, current recognition best practices, and low- and no-cost recognition solutions.

Hands: Knowing how to recognize right

During the Hands portion of the training, look at the specific skills and behaviors that managers need to use to recognize others well and compare those to each manager's skill level and comfort in performing those behaviors. A manager can become motivated to want to recognize his or her employees but still not understand how best to do that. This portion of the training, then, is a combination of knowing the principles of recognition that I discuss in Chapter 5 and using the recognition tools and programs the organization makes available.

To help make recognition more personal and accessible, try to include in your training success stories from other managers that illustrate how they drove higher levels of performance and participation through increased recognition use with their employees.

Hearts: Developing passion for recognition

The Hearts portion examines the motivation, passion, and emotional energy managers feel about using recognition with their employees. This level of commitment tends to increase as managers see the results they are able to obtain and the impact that recognition has on their employees.

The goal of effective management training should be to change the beliefs about recognition and, since our behaviors stem from our beliefs, increase the amount of recognition that is subsequently used by managers. Some studies show that effective management training increases recognition usage by up to 80 percent and the use of organizational rewards by up to 50 percent, yet, according to the national Society for Human Resource Management, 81 percent of organizations don't provide recognition training to their managers. Why? A host of reasons, from feeling the behavior of recognition is so simple and obvious that no training is needed, to budget and time constraints — and lots more reasons in between.

Choosing a type of training

You can perform recognition training in-person, over the phone, or online. In-person training has the advantage of interaction, discussion, and activities to help bring the concepts to life, while online training offers the benefits of efficiency, accessibility, and consistency of the training message; can reach a wider audience; and can be financially more economical. Video training, including short how-to videos, is also increasingly being used as part of online training. You can also use a hybrid training format: Offer a live online webinar or webcast that's accompanied by a teleconference, for example. Some companies offer customized training geared to the specific needs of their managers (as identified by evaluations) and then supplement those efforts with coaching for particularly at-need managers.

After you decide on the type of training you want to conduct, set a schedule. You can offer trainings as often as once a month, quarterly, or once a year. In the beginning of a new recognition program, you may want to offer more sessions to accommodate all managers and staff, and then, once the training takes hold, you can back off that schedule. Some companies provide quarterly training sessions with experts and guest speakers from the world of recognition and employee engagement, or offer webinars and podcasts to continually update the knowledge of managers and employees on the topic.

To supplement training, online and print resources can be helpful for providing quick answers to questions that managers may have about using the organization's recognition programs. These items can include user guides, FAQs, and additional support resources such as research updates or best practices from inside or outside the organization. Increasingly, employers are also using apps to quiz managers and employees about core concepts in the training. Many companies also use Train the Trainer sessions, which teach a few training facilitators the concepts of the topic so they can then train managers and employees throughout the organization. These sessions are ideal for companies that have a lot of departments or divisions or are geographically dispersed.

Communications: Implementing a System That Works for You

Successful manager participation begins with effective communication, so you'd be well advised to develop and deliver a strategic marketing and communication campaign that includes a variety of media. The goal of your recognition communications is to maintain an ongoing marketing effort, consistently inspiring managers and employees about recognition in general, and your programs specifically. Ultimately, these regular conversations and interactions weave themselves into your company's daily rhythm — and that's one way you can tell that recognition has become part of your culture.

Communication at all levels of the organization is critical for any successful recognition program, and the message you communicate should be consistent with your mission, vision, values, and overall organizational goals. Most importantly, it must resonate with your employees.

Delivery of such a message often includes a mix of mediums: print (brochures, letters to participants, and paycheck insertions); personal communications (meetings or phone calls); electronic collateral (e-mails and banner ads and notifications on the company's intranet, for example); and environmentals (physical posters, banners, and print media that hang in the work environment). As you design a communications plan for your recognition initiative, keep in mind these three main stages: prelaunch, launch, and ongoing communications.

Prelaunch communications

Upper management should give plenty of updates to managers and any relevant employees about the program prelaunch. Communications should focus on the program goals, the recognition team, timelines, and updates. As the launch of the program draws near, you can focus on some prelaunch activities such as developing and distributing a manager's guide to your program. This guide should detail everything your managers need to know about the program. Then follow it up with a series of informational e-mails to managers; these information e-mails will extend beyond the program launch date.

The purpose of the prelaunch communication is threefold: to let managers know what's coming down the pike (and when), to start shaping expectations, and to collect any initial issues, concerns, and questions they may have. Depending on the organization, advance communication can begin up to a year prior to the actual program launch.

You can incorporate information about the importance of your recognition and reward endeavors and provide program overview in your town hall meetings, regular communications, and corporate messaging. Ask senior leadership to make videos and/or attend road shows to promote the program as you lead up to the program launch.

Launch communications

Most organizations conduct a launch event to kick off a new recognition program. If you choose this strategy, make the launch fun — consider a challenge or contest to see which department can get the most people registered onto the new software, for example. After you launch your recognition program and tools, it's best to start manager trainings immediately and use those sessions to communicate to managers and employees.

I worked with one leadership team prior to the launch of a new recognition initiative and challenged them to strategize how they could get every employee registered on the new recognition system on the first day it was available. They held a contest, conducted hourly updates, and awarded prizes for various milestones on the first day. The result? They attained the goal of 100 percent registration in the new recognition program!

Aside from regular training, you may want to consider these tactics to get people excited and involved in your recognition program:

- Identify "recognition champions," whose job will be to trumpet the values and success of the program throughout the organization and serve as ambassadors for the program in the various areas in which they work.

- Host kickoff webinars featuring the organization's CEO or other key executives. This can be an effective way to get the word out about the purpose and expectations of the recognition program.

- Host live events. Although you can make recognition content available through an online portal, live events are what truly create the excitement and buzz.

The importance of these training and review sessions cannot be overstated. Even the best designs and tools will be ineffective without proper understanding of recognition techniques and guidelines and proper use of program tools.

Ongoing communications

Announcing a new recognition initiative or sending out a one-time memo about the value of recognition and your new program is not enough. You have to be persistent with ongoing praise, recognition, and celebration in your communication.

The first 90 days after a recognition program launches are the most critical for creating program awareness, improving employee engagement, and encouraging program registrations. Therefore, you need to make sure that you're delivering essential communication through multiple channels. To really sink into your organization's culture, executives, managers, and recognition champions need to use praise, recognition, and celebration to encourage the organization until the practice of recognition is embedded in your corporate culture.

A successful recognition program must have a strong, diverse communication plan to keep it going. These efforts can include environmentals, such as banners and posters; push notifications, reminding managers and employees by e-mail about aspects of the program (e-mail notifications and alerts are very helpful for keeping people informed and motivated about the program on an ongoing basis); and website communication, such as messages from the CEO or a story-sharing, best-practices feature. To empower employees in the recognition program, you can also encourage social participation, peer-to-peer recognition, and the giving of nonmonetary recognition among all employees. Remember: Because not all employees may have access to the organization's intranet (or may not even be at a physical company location for that matter), a range of communication tools needs to be deployed.

Ask your executives to be the ongoing public face for your program. Ask them to write a quarterly column of support. Provide talking points that they can use during presentations. Challenge them to include a discussion of recognition with their own direct reports as well as part of any major public meeting, such as a conference call or an annual company event. By making recognition easy to understand and execute, you make it easy for them to be included.

During ongoing communications you can generate feedback reports for the program administrators, managers, and executive team so that they can see information on key program indicators on a continuous basis (often right on their dashboards).

Resist the temptation to meet with your executive leaders only once a year about the organization's recognition program and initiative. The better approach is to give recognition a visible profile in your organization on a regular basis. Report on your recognition program's results quarterly. Share quantitative and qualitative examples of recognition at work on a weekly or monthly basis. Recognize your leaders publicly to demonstrate your system in action. The conversation doesn't have to be detailed and extensive; it simply needs to be frequent and visible.

Recognition and Rewards: Making It Easy

To get people to use recognition programs, the programs need to be simple, clear, relevant, and meaningful to recipients. The good news is that an abundance of tools, such as online and mobile apps, are available to help busy managers create personal and meaningful recognition in just a few steps on their computers or mobile devices. Managers can use these tools to set goals and prepare performance reports, invite employees to participate in recognition, create certificates of achievement and notes of congratulations, and schedule recognition efforts (and their reminders) ahead of time.

Computer-based tools may not make life easier for all managers; some managers don't feel comfortable using technology, so introducing recognition apps to them might cause an adverse effect. If any of your managers have a hard time with the tech options, make sure to have alternate options for them to use. Also, I've found that if you use online or electronic praise only, employees can come to miss the personal connection — your dropping by their offices, for example. Make sure you continue to use all the "touch-points" available to connect with others! Online recognition should supplement, but not replace, personal recognition throughout the organization.

I discuss more about online programs in Chapter 12. For now, I take you through how to set up your recognition and rewards program, your reward options, your program participation, and redemption options.

Setting up your program

During the set-up phase of your program, make decisions about the following things:

- **What behaviors and performance you want to drive.** You can drive almost any type of behavior and performance with your recognition program — core values, safety, suggestions, referrals, teamwork, and wellness.

- **Who will participate:** To foster a culture of recognition throughout the organization, employees of all levels and in all work environments should be eligible to participate in the recognition program.

- **How frequently you want recognition to occur.** For example, you can set a goal of 100 percent of employees receiving nonmonetary recognition from management or peers each quarter, and 20 percent of employees receiving recognition with a points or monetary component.

- **How award points are accumulated and redeemed.** Are there sufficient opportunities for employees to earn award points and to care about their accumulation? The more initiatives and behavior goals you incorporate into your recognition system, the more it increases employees' ability to accumulate a meaningful sum of award points to redeem for a reward of their choosing.

- **How you will build awareness and communication**. You might launch the program with an all-hands meeting or simultaneous meetings across the organization, introducing a recognition website and new recognition tools anyone can use.

Determining rewards options

Employees will be more engaged in the recognition program if they have access to an assortment of reward options and are given the power to choose for themselves how they would like to be rewarded. Here are some commonly used reward options:

- ✔ **Name brand merchandise items:** Hundreds of thousands of today's best-selling items.

- ✔ **Custom-branded items:** Selection of ready-to-order organization-branded merchandise items (hats, polo shifts, coffee mugs, umbrellas, and so on).

- ✔ **Prepaid debit cards and virtual debit cards:** Available from most credit card companies.

- ✔ **Travel awards:** Travel certificates available in a variety of denominations.

- ✔ **Points for time off:** A number of specialized organization-supplied benefits or rewards can be included into the program catalog. For example, participants may have the ability to redeem their accumulated points for one day paid time off (PTO). Participants could then use their earned PTO to volunteer with one of the organization's charitable partners for the day.

- ✔ **Charitable donations:** Participants can donate their points to charity. Points may be redeemed for charities of the participant's choosing — this requires some additional vetting of 501(c)(3) charities — or from a list of charities preselected by the organization.

Promoting program participation

People need a reason to participate in the recognition program, and participation rates vary based on the type of program and the frequency of rewards. Here are some suggestions that can foster greater employee participation in your recognition program:

- ✔ **Make the program fun.** People love fun things!

- ✔ **Recognize individuals for engaging in activities.** This is the simplest and most effective way to promote participation.

- ✔ **Make the rewards valuable to your employees.** The program will only be successful if participants see the value of their reward and recognition activity redemptions. Therefore, the kinds of awards that are available is important. For this reason, try to include employee representatives when you're selecting reward options, or provide a wide enough assortment of options to increase the chances that everyone will be able to find something that he or she wants.

What motivates one person may differ greatly from another. Use the demographic data you have to target your redemption communications to create a more personalized experience for your employees. Doing so will increase employee participation and redemption.

Also, for merchandise, I recommend that you price the rewards you offer at face value. Doing this makes the experience more familiar, easier, and generally positive. If you inflate the value of available items, you risk causing frustration for your participants when point values don't equate to actual costs. ("Why is this flat-screen TV three times what I can get it for at Costco?")

✔ **Encourage participation any way you can think of.** The main goal is to be creative! Here are some ideas to get you started:

- *Quizzes:* As part of the initial recognition program, you can build skills with quizzes, webinars, and learning tools focused on the particular incentives.

- *Team competition:* By using fun, team-oriented competitive strategies — basically turning the competition into a friendly game — employees become more engaged in the recognition program and are motivated by both their daily personal progress and their team's progress.

- *Sweepstakes:* In a recognition sweepstakes each employee that gives and receives recognition is entered in a monthly drawing to win a nominal amount of points (100 points for five winners, for example). The winners are then announced and highlighted in a news story that runs across the home page of the company's recognition website. This encourages recognition behavior and allows the organization to magnify the recognition across the organization.

- *Online training:* When employees enter the program website, give them the opportunity to participate in some online training. The training can be fun and simple but also effective in delivering your message.

- *On-the-spot recognition card:* This can be a gift card or it can contain instructions for registering online for the employee recognition platform, thereby accomplishing two key items: 1) it gets the employee to go online and 2) it increases the chances that the employee will use the recognition program again.

Monitoring the frequency with which rewards are redeemed

Another element you have to consider is what is an acceptable frequency of reward redemption. Redemption rates vary widely, but, as the preceding section explains, you can influence redemptions with a combination of contests, promotions that work like games, personalized benefit statements, and attractive rewards. Should employees need award examples or encouragement to redeem their points, you can feature seasonal items on the program website and e-mail reminders highlighting specific examples, such as charity and travel options, or sharing what others have earned with their award points.

Looking at the type of program

The frequency with which rewards are redeemed is influenced by the type of recognition program you offer:

- **In level-based programs,** you give recipients an award based on various levels, and they can immediately select an award from a collection of award items within that level category. These types of programs typically have very high redemption rates.

- **In points-based programs,** recipients can bank their points indefinitely. Many recipients prefer to save their points until they have enough to get something really good (like paid time off, preferred parking spot, role on an executive advisory team, or a perhaps a trip). In these types of programs, it takes more time before employees redeem their points, and your points and rewards management system has to keep track of the accruing points for a longer period — typically 18 months.

Aiming for an optimal redemption rate

When employees can rack up points indefinitely without expiration, ideally reward redemption rates will be approximately 70 percent — that is, about 70 percent of the points in the system are redeemed.

A redemption rate of 65 percent to 75 percent generally shows that recipients are confident in the continuity of the program. Very high redemption rates (well over 70 percent) often indicate that recipients feel a level of uncertainty about the stability of the program — or even the company — and are thus eager to use all their points immediately.

Unusually low redemption rates can also indicate that something's not right: The problem may be with the program, with the reward offering, with the level of funding, or with the work environment. If your redemption rates drop or exceed normal, anticipated ranges, start monitoring, surveying, or asking questions of employees about the program, about the reward items, and about their confidence in the company's commitment to recognition.

One way to spur redemption is to create a wish-list feature in your online rewards selection that allows users to set personal targets for rewards they want to attain and automatically tracks their progress toward those goals with every log in. Once employees accumulate the targeted number of points, they can receive a notice that they've hit their target point total for their desired reward redemption.

Taking a closer look at redemption rates

In programs with substantial *accrual rates* — that is, lots of ways to be recognized, combined with higher recognition frequency, and varied amounts of award point values — you will see higher redemption rates. Here are some key principles of recognition participation metrics you might want to examine:

✔ **Frequency of reward deposit:** The more frequently people are awarded, the more likely they are to save their points.

✔ **Regularity of reward size:** The more the deposits are the same amount, the more likely participants are to save their points.

✔ **Redemption preferences of participants:** Some people like to "shop" regularly, redeeming small amounts of points on a pretty frequent basis; others tend to be savers, holding out for larger rewards by holding onto their points over time.

Most people will only redeem 60 percent to 80 percent of their points at any given time, leaving a balance of 20 percent to 40 percent still in their accounts for the next time they redeem.

Many participants save their rewards in an attempt to reach higher levels of reward categories or denominations. The ability to save and combine reward values drives both initial and repetitive behaviors.

Process Improvement: Reviewing Your Program

Even the best recognition program doesn't stay intact and effective forever. To keep your program fresh and the energy for it high, you need to periodically review what's working well (and what's not), and then make modifications accordingly. You can do reviews as often as doing so makes sense to you — the key is just to set a schedule and stick to it.

Don't wait until something is wrong to do a review. Instead, make your reviews part of your regular program maintenance. Doing so keeps your recognition culture strong. Also reviews are an important part of helping all program participants grow in their recognition abilities. As you and your colleagues use recognition more often, you'll all become more competent and confident in doing so. In turn, your effectiveness will increase, encouraging you to do more recognition until it becomes an ingrained habit.

If you don't stay conscious of your efforts and seek to improve your recognition ability on an individual level, you may lose the spontaneity, freshness, and sincerity of being thankful for an employee's good work. This leads to your recognition becoming mechanical, and employees will likely perceive it as manipulative. In Chapter 9, I discuss in more detail ways to keep individual recognition strategies vibrant.

Organizationally, process improvement has three steps: program review, program analysis, and program modification. Read on to find out more.

Program review

When you conduct a program review, you gather data so that you can analyze what's working and what's not. Taking the time to step back from the program mechanics to reflect allows you to remind yourself of your original program objectives, review your progress to date, and recommend enhancements or course corrections to ensure that program goals are met. Typically, people do reviews frequently in the launch and beginning stages of a new program, and less frequently as time goes on.

Conducting a formal review

You can conduct this review of your recognition program as part of your quarterly or annual account review; doing so is standard business practice and an opportunity for you and others to give feedback on the program itself and your process — and to make any changes, as needed.

These formal reviews show all aspects of program performance, including website activity tracking, types of activities being recognized, top recognizers and recognition recipients, most active business units or departments, budget usage, cost per recognition, and top retailers for reward redemption. These reports let you start determining where opportunities for improvement exist. During these reviews, discuss the level of manager participation, identify any areas for improvement, and determine how participation and effectiveness can be further improved.

Getting weekly or biweekly feedback

Although reviews are meant to cover and analyze all bases, sometimes participants are not as forthcoming in a formal review — or sometimes, the structure doesn't lend itself to anecdotal or more esoteric issues. So in addition to formal reviews, consider establishing regular weekly or biweekly team meetings at the beginning of your recognition program to touch base on any number of things: program schedule, data or technical issues, employee questions, and new ideas, information, or action steps.

Team meetings are just as important for ongoing communication and thorough auditing. These operational meetings give you a chance to discuss any ongoing issues or concerns in the day-to-day management of the program and thus tend to be less formal than reviews.

Gathering feedback at any time

A really easy, quick way to get feedback on a regular basis is through pulse surveys. You can give these short surveys to managers and employees at any time to gather their feedback and insight regarding what can be improved. Pulse surveys always have the same questions, enabling you to compare apples to apples and thus get a reliable read on the pulse of your employees. These surveys give real-time status reports and keep everyone up-to-date on the ongoing performance of the recognition program.

Program analysis

After you gather your data through various means, such as reviews and meetings, you need to analyze it. You want to look at various aspects of your data, including the following:

✔ Action steps and responsibilities you identified in a prior meeting

✔ Key performance indicators for the organization's objectives

✔ Current problems and potential problems

Evaluate the problems by using a red/yellow/green light report. In this kind of report, you categorize elements of the program into three possible areas of discussion:

- **Red:** A problem is identified, and it materially affects the program and key performance indicators.

- **Yellow:** Data and reports show a possible problem that should be investigated and researched to determine whether it's an anomaly or something to address via a program change.

- **Green:** The reports and data indicate that all program elements are working according to program specifications.

✔ New information discovered via research, reading, conferences, and so on that could impact the way in which a program is operated

This information could include new technologies, new metrics, new areas to impact with respect to audience influence and/or areas to remove because evidence is showing some negative impact to client objectives (that is, too many recognition events can reduce recognition impact.)

✔ Product selections, website usage details, contact center reports, marketing and communication program elements, and other account management developments

Program modification

After you review and analyze your program, you need to make modifications. One of the best ways to revitalize a recognition program is through program tweaks. Here are just a few of the possibilities:

- ✔ **Add variety:** Brainstorm the ways in which variety can be added, without necessarily changing any of the core aspects of the program. You might recognize all employees who praise or nominate another employee for an award during a one-month period, for example. Sometimes simply adding a new celebratory activity can do wonders to revitalize recognition.

- ✔ **Provide new recognition opportunities:** Establish new opportunities for recognition and celebration. Even within a well-defined area of recognition, you should be able to identify many new recognition opportunities. For instance, if you have individual safety awards, establish a new category for team safety awards.

- ✔ **Add new recognition levels:** Choose new triggers for recognition. To make sure employees do not feel you are constantly changing the rules for recognition in your organization, be consistent in what you recognize, but add new levels for greater forms of employee achievement.

- ✔ **Offer "flash incentives" that reward a specific behavior for a short time:** You can think of this as a "Do This, Get That" model. For example, employees get points on initial login or the first five recognitions they send. Other simple fixes can involve feedback to upper management, where specific changes can be made to fix recognition problems that are identified.

Chapter 9

Engaging and Recognizing Individuals

In This Chapter

▶ Taking stock of individual recognition preferences

▶ Making recognition part of your job

▶ Recognizing managers too

I feel one-on-one interactions is where the rubber meets the road when it comes to employee motivation, recognition, and engagement. In this chapter, I explain how best to recognize individuals, and I give you tips, techniques, and plenty of examples for moving forward.

Starting with the Basics

One of the challenges of employee motivation is that, because the concepts are so simple, they seem like common sense and thus no effort is needed to implement them. The concepts are simple, but they will not happen by magic. You need to look at the fundamentals and master those until they become a habit in how you deal with others on an ongoing basis. Here are a few fundamental concepts and principles that you can use to create a strong behavioral foundation before you act.

Start in your immediate sphere of influence

Good recognition is very personal. To be successful with it, you need to operate on a one-on-one level, so starting with the people you work or deal with on a daily basis makes the most sense. This would include your direct reports, your manager, and your colleagues. Because you already know these individuals fairly well and likely have a good rapport with them, it's the best place to improve your relationships. You are probably also more aware of what they've done or are doing that most deserves recognition. When you recognize people you know well, your recognition is more likely to be natural rather than a little awkward, which it might be with employees you aren't as close to.

Do just one thing differently

The best goals are ones that are simple and attainable, so start small: Focus on doing just one thing differently. For example, make a point of telling others what you like about working with them. This is a simple thing to do, but one that is a great relationship builder. After you achieve some success and momentum, you can always build on this one practice. Remember, it's far better to focus on one thing, do it well, and do it consistently than to try to do a dozen things that never go beyond your initial intention.

 Here are some easy ways to begin: At the end of the day, take a moment to reflect and jot a note to anyone who achieved some success that day. Or start each staff meeting with good news and praise for individuals who deserve it, perhaps reading thank-you letters from satisfied customers or employees from other parts of the organization. It's estimated that over 90 percent of our daily behavior is routine, so don't underestimate the power of selective daily focus.

Ask employees what motivates them

Whether you have them jot down ways they like to be thanked or complete a simple recognition survey of items they find motivating, ask employees their preferences for recognition. Motivational preferences differ from person to person, and for the same person over time. Find out what's important to your employees and then get creative so that you can make those things happen when your employees perform well.

Spend time with employees, finding out what types of work activities most interest them, the kinds of skills they'd like to learn or develop in their jobs, where they want to go with their career, their personal hobbies, and their family situation. All this information is fodder for motivation, and the more you know about your employees, the better able you will be to motivate them. This information is especially useful if you have employees who are a little more reserved or are coming up short when you ask them directly about what kind of recognition they'd like.

Here's some sample questions I recommend asking new employees to get to know them better and learn what motivates them:

- ✔ How do you like to be recognized when you do a good job?
- ✔ Are you more introverted or extroverted?
- ✔ What type of work do you most enjoy?
- ✔ Do you more enjoy working alone on assignments or as part of a team?
- ✔ If a special task force is created, would you want to be a part of that?
- ✔ What do you most want to learn on this job?
- ✔ Do you have any development goals for yourself?
- ✔ What would your ideal job entail?
- ✔ Where do you want to be five years from now?
- ✔ When you're not at work, what are your favorite hobbies or activities?
- ✔ Are you married? If so, do you have any children? What are their names and ages?
- ✔ Do you have any siblings? Are they older or younger? What do they do?
- ✔ Are your parents still alive? Where do they live?
- ✔ Do you have any good friends that work in the organization?
- ✔ Where did you grow up? Where did you go to school?
- ✔ Do you like to travel? Where are your favorite places to visit?
- ✔ Do you have any pets? What types?
- ✔ What are your favorite foods? Your favorite music? Your favorite flower?
- ✔ What activities do you find most relaxing?
- ✔ If you had a free night with a friend how would you want to spend it?
- ✔ If you could get something for your work or office, what would it be?

You can include these questions in a simple survey, or ask them in individual discussions or even in a group setting to get to know people better.

Focus on what you can do, not what you can't do

No matter what your situation, there are always a lot of things you can do to thank and recognize others and call out those things that are going well. Yet from my experience, most people tend to focus on what they *can't* do — that is, they focus on the limitations and constraints they have in their position or company.

The best forms of recognition tend to be simple acts with little or no cost, so start there. Then look to what tools and resources your organization provides for employee recognition. If your organization has recognition tools you can use, take advantage of using those. If it has recognition programs you can nominate people for, do that as well. And if you're provided a budget to make recognition happen, all the better.

At the same time, almost every work environment has constraints, such as time, budget, and creativity, that can keep you from implementing recognition and recognition-related activities. Instead of dwelling on what you can't do, focus on the hundreds of things you *can* do. Anyone can write a simple thank-you note expressing heartfelt appreciation for a job well done, for example. It only takes a moment and doesn't cost a dime.

Don't expect perfection

Far too many managers abandon their initial efforts when those efforts don't live up to their expectations. Maybe things initially felt awkward or even silly. Maybe they didn't get the employee response they hoped for. Remember that there is no perfect way to recognize employees, and any new behavior or change will be awkward at first.

Before you give up, try out some small things, learn from what works, and then seek to improve. Ask others in your work group to provide feedback and ideas as you try new recognition behaviors and activities. Also keep a list of different, easy ideas that you can try if your first attempts don't quite work the way you envision. Always give yourself options and be patient with yourself and your colleagues. Recognition is supposed to be a positive experience, so focus on having fun in the process, and you will seldom go wrong!

Embrace simple gestures — they count the most

Recognition does not have to be anything fancy. In fact, the simpler and more direct, the better. The more I work with recognition and rewards, the more I marvel at the simple and sincere ways that employees find to appreciate each other, ways that take little cost, minimal time, and little to no administrative work.

Following are some ideas used successfully by other companies:

- ✓ **Put notes on business cards.** John Plunkett, senior vice president of human resources for Cobb Electric Membership Corporation in Marietta, Georgia, says, "People love to collect others' business cards. Simply carry a supply of your cards with you and as you 'catch people doing something right,' immediately write 'Thanks,' 'Good job,' 'Keep it up,' and what they specifically did in two or three words. Put the person's name on the card, sign it, and give it to the employee." In fact, one hospital in Chicago even uses praising cards such as these as a recruiting device. When one of their employees has received exceptional service in a restaurant or department store, for example, they hand the person a thank-you card and say, "Thanks so much for your service today. If you ever consider leaving your job here, we'd be glad to consider hiring you for our firm. Please give me a call." The technique has been very successful in hiring new talent!

- ✓ **Appreciation days.** ARMARK, headquartered in Philadelphia, Pennsylvania, organizes a day of appreciation for worthy employees. They send out a proclamation announcing Bob Jones Day, for example, and explaining the reason for the honor. The honoree enjoys all sorts of frills, such as computer banners and a free lunch.

- ✓ **Thanks a Bunch.** Maritz, Inc., a performance improvement company in Fenton, Missouri, has a Thanks a Bunch program in which a bouquet of flowers is given to an employee in appreciation for special favors or a job well done. That employee then passes the flowers on to someone else who has been helpful. The intent is to see how many people can be given the bouquet throughout the day. With the flowers is a written thank-you note card that each recipient gets. At certain intervals, the cards are entered into a drawing for awards such as binoculars or logoed jackets. The program is used during especially heavy workloads or stressful times.

- ✓ **The Wingspread Award.** The Office of Personnel Management in Washington, DC, uses a pass-around award that travels from one person to another. The first such award was given to a special performer in a division, who later passed the award to another person who the original recipient believed truly deserved it. Over time, the award took on great value and prestige because it came from one's peers. A recipient can keep the award as long as he or she wants or until another special performer is discovered. When the award is to be passed on, a luncheon ceremony is scheduled.

Planning Individual Recognition

The best way to successfully embark on a new effort of any kind is to plan, and individual recognition is no exception. Planning doesn't need to be elaborate or even formal. A plan can be as simple as consciously deciding to tell someone who's done a good job that you appreciate it.

An essential element in every effective plan — no matter what its purpose — is the action itself (not just the commitment to do it)! How often have you had the best intentions to do something but just never got around to it, thinking, "I'll do it as soon as I have the time"? Good intentions alone have never accomplished anything, but a plan backed by a commitment to act provides a powerful springboard for results. And to be most successful with your individual recognition efforts, your plan should take into account the stages before and after the recognition.

Effective planning can go a long way in helping you master the art of individual recognition and practice it consistently.

The prep work: What to do before you recognize an employee's efforts

When planning individual recognition, you should use the "what, who, when, where, and how" format:

- ✔ **What do I want to recognize?** As I mention in Chapter 5, the best recognition is contingent; that is, it is given in response to a specific behavior or performance. Therefore, you should clearly identify the behavior, performance, or results that merit recognition. Make sure the behavior or performance is important to you, the work group, or your organization's success.

- ✔ **Who do I want to recognize?** Identify the person or people whose behavior or performance you want to recognize. You may already have some names in your head, or you can jot down notes to yourself as you observe your employees throughout the workday. You can even ask around a little to see whether others know of someone who deserves recognition.

- ✔ **When do I want to recognize?** The most effective recognition takes place soon after the desired behavior or performance. Sometimes, however, you may not be able to provide recognition immediately, so in your planning stage, think about other times you could offer recognition if your initial attempts don't work out.

- ✔ **Where do I want to do the recognition?** The best recognition is personal — that is, delivered in person directly to the individual being acknowledged. It seems easy enough, but sometimes, the immediate location isn't always the best (it might be too loud, too busy, or otherwise not ideal), so always have a few options in the back of your head. For example, you may decide to look for an opportunity to provide the recognition in front of others.

✔ *How* **should I offer the recognition?** The best recognition is given in a way that enhances its motivational value to the recipient. So go back through your mental inventory of the individual you want to recognize. Why is this person's success significant? What is the context that made it especially notable? Who would that person prefer to provide the recognition? Would he or she prefer to receive it in public or private? Do you need any additional information, materials, or supplies to recognize the person? Asking yourself these questions and thinking through the situation will help make sure that the recognition activity has the greatest impact.

You don't need to write answers down to these questions; just systematically thinking through these questions will help you do a better job with recognition — especially when you are just getting started with your recognition efforts.

Implementing individual recognition

After you have all your plans laid out, it's time to take action. Sometimes, you may decide to implement your recognition efforts gradually. In other cases, you may decide that starting several different initiatives at the same time is more appropriate. To figure out what would work best for you, consider things like

✔ Your personal bandwidth

✔ The support you have from other people in your company

✔ The access you have to supplies, budget, and opportunities

Consider these examples of unique ways to implement individual recognition:

✔ William Pickens, owner of Pool Covers, Inc., in Richmond, California, found a way to use his limited time for recognition in a unique way. He often hangs a number on the wall and rewards employees who know how that number relates to the business. For example, 22.5 is the average miles per gallon of the delivery truck fleet, and those who knew that received a $10 prize, which he personally presents to them. Pickens says this game gets employees to think about the business and also creates camaraderie.

✔ Knowing that it had employees that would support the recognition effort, a mobile camera business in Houston, Texas, got sales staff to recognize individuals who had helped the company. In this initiative, a response to a complaint that customer service reps were underappreciated compared to salespeople, salespeople were given blue poker chips to award to a customer service clerk they felt was instrumental in helping them either close a sale or satisfy a customer. The customer service clerks then got to a pull a prize out of a hat.

Evaluating the results after your efforts

After you give recognition, take time to evaluate and learn from the experience. Learning from your actions is a critical part of developing effective recognition practices. Here are a few questions to ask yourself after you recognize someone:

- ✔ How did I do?
- ✔ Did I get the response I expected? Why or why not?
- ✔ What did I learn from the experience?
- ✔ What would I do differently as a result next time?

Then, if possible, get feedback from others — especially those employees you have recognized — so that you can answer these questions for yourself:

- ✔ How did I come across to others?
- ✔ What did the other person feel worked well?
- ✔ What did others think I could have done to be more effective?

Like any skill, this feedback loop can help you master the behavior so that you are improving every time you recognize an employee.

Making the Commitment to Employee Recognition

Probably the biggest obstacle to doing more recognition in the workplace is *time*. Managers often feel they are too busy focusing on what's urgent to focus on what's *important* — namely, the people they manage.

The situation is made worse by managers' false perception that they are already providing employees with plenty of praise and recognition. According to Aubrey Daniels, founder and chairman of the board of Aubrey Daniels International of Atlanta, Georgia, and a leading authority on the topic of performance management, "Those managers who feel they do positive reinforcement the most, in my experience, actually do it the least."

Managers may know that they need to positively reinforce their employees, and they feel they are doing so, but on a day-to-day basis, they generally do very little to catch their employees doing something right. Worse yet, the positive reinforcement they often provide is incorrect: The feedback is non-specific or insincere; the praise is random and overlooks employees who have contributed equally to a given success; or the facts about one specific acknowledged behavior or performance are wrong.

So how can you help managers act on their best intentions to recognize employees on a more frequent basis and to do so more effectively? One way is to raise their awareness about the importance of recognizing employees. You can also have them practice interpersonal skills so that they grow comfortable recognizing others. Still, the key is that they keep up the desired behavior going forward. I'm convinced that the percentage of success increases when you help people find ways to keep their commitment to their commitment, which generally means developing an individualized strategy and support plan that increases the likelihood that they will continue with their recognition efforts. Following are some tactics that I've seen work in a variety of different organizations. Try them, adapt them, combine them as you see fit for your circumstances.

Make recognition part of your job

To really own the topic of recognition, you need to make it part of what I like to call your *behavioral repertoire* — that is, it must become a natural practice and habit that you doing throughout the day, every day. Here are some suggestions about how you can make that happen:

- ✔ **Have a reminder system.** Hyler Bracey, former CEO and chairman of the Atlanta Consulting Group, kept five marbles in his pocket, transferring one to his other pocket each time he praised someone. His goal was to transfer all five marbles from one pocket to the other each day. The technique helped Bracey make praise a habit and a routine part of his workday.

- ✔ **Write notes at the end of the day.** If your days fly by without ever getting a chance to recognize others, take a few minutes before you go home to jot some personal notes to individuals who made a difference that day. Get some personalized note cards made up and keep a stack of them next to your telephone on your desk as a constant reminder of this powerful tool.

When Steve Wittert was president of Paragon Steakhouse Restaurants, based in San Diego, California, he told me that although the restaurant business kept him constantly busy, he could always take a few moments at the end of the day to jot a few notes to the individuals who made a difference that day. It was a simple practice that made their day!

- ✔ **Be accessible.** If you have an open-door policy, make sure you are actually around for employees to use it. Be accessible when your employees need you to be, not just when it is convenient for you. As Roy Moody of Roy Moody & Associates in Albuquerque, New Mexico, says, "The greatest motivational act one person can do for another is to listen."

> ✔ **Make people a part of your to-do list.** Add the names of those individuals who report to you to your weekly to-do list and check them off when you "catch them doing something right" during the week.

As simple and as relatively easy as these activities and techniques may seem, they can have a significant impact on the morale, productivity, and performance of your employees. Try one or more of these techniques and stick with those that work for you.

Create a habit of recognition

How can managers start recognizing their employees more? Like any behavioral change, you have to find a way to make it habit, a natural part of your daily routine. Start off the work day with a quick walk around the office or enter your building from different entrances so that you're more likely to bump into different people each day. Carry tokens, note cards or gift cards so that you can "spot awards" during the day. End the day by reflecting on who stood out — finishing a project, helping a client or team member, or solving a critical problem the department was facing — and then sending those people a quick e-mail, voicemail, or note. All these — and many other tactics you can come up with yourself — can help you make recognition a habit.

As illustrated by the story of Hyler Bracey, who transferred marbles from one pocket to another each time he praised an employee, the use of a simple reminder can help you turn recognition into a habit. Says Bracey, "Praising employees truly works. There is so much more energy and enthusiasm in a workplace where praise has become ingrained in the manager."

Managers who really *are* too busy or are unable for some other reason to praise employees personally need to find out what recognition activities they *are* willing and able to do. For example, a manager can sanction a department celebration, even if he or she doesn't personally attend the party, or can ensure that someone else on staff consistently does things to recognize others.

Link the activity to your day planner

For many people, the key to changing their routine is to make the new behavior part of their current planning and organizing system. I've seen success getting analytical, task-oriented managers to praise employees more by getting them to think of their people as things to do. I have these managers list the names of each person who reports to them on their weekly to-do list

The power of I's: No-cost, on-the-job recognition that works

Praise and simple gestures of sincere thanks are important to employees today, but there are many other things you can do within the job itself to acknowledge individuals and make them feel special. I'm convinced that the most important things managers can do to develop and maintain motivated employees are the daily work-related interactions that they have with employees. You can remember some of the best motivators from the first letter of each category of motivator, which I call "The Power of I's":

✔ **Interesting and important work:** At least part of every job must be of high interest to an employee. As the management theorist Frederick Herzberg once said, "If you want someone to do a good job, give them a good job to do." Yes, some jobs may be inherently boring, but you can give anyone in any job some variety or at least one task or project that's stimulating: Send the employee to meetings in your place, for example, or assign an employee to a suggestion committee or some other special group that meets once a week. The time away from the regular job is likely to be more than made up with increased productivity.

✔ **Information/communication/feedback:** Now that employment for life is largely a thing of the past, employees want more than ever to know 1) how they are doing in their jobs and 2) how the company is doing in its business. Tell them how the company makes money and how it spends money. Make sure ample channels of communication are available to encourage employees to be informed, ask questions, and share information, and make sure that at least some of these channels directly involve management in nonintimidating environments. Soon you'll have employees taking initiative to suggest ideas that can improve processes and save the organization money and time.

✔ **Involvement/ownership in decisions:** People who are closest to the problem or customer typically have the best insight into how a situation can be improved. They know what works and what doesn't, but they are rarely asked for their opinion. That's why involving employees — especially in decisions that affect them — is both respectful and practical. As you involve others, you increase their commitment and the make it easier to implement new ideas or change.

✔ **Independence/autonomy/flexibility:** All employees appreciate having flexibility in their jobs. Most employees, especially experienced, top-performing employees, value being given room to do their job as they best see fit. When you base your decision to provide flexibility and autonomy to employees on performance, you increase the likelihood that they will perform as desired — and bring additional initiative, ideas, and energy to the job as well.

✔ **Increased visibility/opportunity/responsibility:** Everyone appreciates a manager who gives credit where credit is due. The chances to share the successes of employees with others throughout the organization are almost limitless. In addition, most employee development happens on-the-job: Give employees new opportunities to perform, learn, and grow as a form of recognition and thanks.

Beneath all these techniques is a basic premise that you trust, respect, and have the best interests of your employees at heart. If you do, you can inspire extraordinary results from ordinary people.

and then cross off the person's name after the manager gives the employee a praising based on that person's performance. For some managers, such a specific technique helps take the activity from being a general, intangible activity to a specific, finite action item — an item that is therefore much easier to complete.

Managers can also write reminders in their calendars of employees' birthdays or anniversaries of their dates of hire. You can also provide processes or systems that encourage praise, such as scheduling a celebration or "bragging session" with upper management to update them on completed projects.

Elicit the help of others

Many people who are inspired to initiate a new behavior think of it as a personal quest they must do on their own. Not true! In fact, you're likely to have significantly better results if you discuss what you are trying to do and involve the people you work with. For example, you can partner with someone else — a colleague you met in a training session or a person who works in a different department who you want to have a reason to keep in touch with. The two of you can exchange action plans and set specific times for follow-up and to discuss the progress you've made. This partner in recognition acts as a designated monitor, counselor, and enforcer all in one — and as such can help you follow through on the new behaviors.

Alternatively, at the next staff meeting, you can say, "I'm going to be trying some new behavior and would appreciate getting feedback from people about it. Specifically, I'm going to be acknowledging people when I see them doing a good job. I'm trying to do this in a timely, specific way. Let me know when I do it right — and if you value my doing it."

Promoting Peer-to-Peer and Employee-to Manager Recognition

Increasingly, recognition can come from anyone at work, not just from a manager. For this reason, you should encourage *all* employees to recognize others, and provide to everyone the opportunities and recognition tools for doing so.

Increasingly, as organizations move to more team-based work environments, the recognition from peers, team members, and coworkers can be just as important as, or even more important than, manager-initiated recognition is to employees. The best organizations look for ways to encourage and legitimize praise and thanks between employees at all levels and among management as well. As organizations continue to flatten their hierarchies and to empower frontline workers with more responsibility and authority, the use of teams will flourish. With that growth, new approaches for team recognition need to be developed, since learning how best to recognize teams will increasingly become essential for their continued success in organizations — both today and far into the future. You can read more about giving recognition to teams in Chapter 10.

Recognition from your peers

All employees like to be recognized for a job well done, but recognition from one's peers has special significance. Perhaps this significance is because people seldom expect such recognition from their colleagues. Perhaps it's because everyone knows managerial favoritism played no part in the selection. Whatever the reason, when employees select someone from their ranks to single out for recognition and praise, the recognition tends to be both well-earned and heartfelt.

Here are some examples of peer-to-peer recognition, which should make up the basic foundation of interpersonal interaction in any strong recognition culture:

- Employees of Royal Victoria Hospital in Barrie, Ontario, use a "fish line" for peer-to-peer recognition. Says Nikki Sturgeon, employee services coordinator in Human Resources, "The fish line is a voice mailbox used to leave anonymous appreciative messages for anyone who has been caught doing something right. The messages are recorded on notes, attached to a special "fish" ribbon and sent to their managers who then get to recognize the individual personally. Because of the ease and simplicity of leaving a message, it's widely used by employees at all levels in the organization.

- Julie Blind, administrative director of Business Services for Sierra View District Hospital in Porterville, California, designates a "Pal of the Week," in which she asks everyone in the department to do or say something nice to the person during the course of the week. The designation rolls over to another member of the department the following week, and the previous designee is responsible for reminding everyone to do something nice for the new Pal. The honor continues until everyone has served as a Pal and then the process repeats. Members of Julie's department also use "kindness coins" — simple medallions — to thank others for their help and actions. The coins represent an emotional currency of personal appreciation that has a real payoff to those that receive them.

- At KFC restaurants in Australia, workers reward colleagues with "champs" cards, for cleanliness, hospitality, and accuracy. Recipients are entered in drawings for prizes, such as movie tickets, car washes, or babysitting. Yum Brands, Inc., the Louisville, Kentucky, parent of restaurant chains KFC, Taco Bell, and Pizza Hut, believes peer recognition helped lower turnover, which used to measure 181 percent for its hourly restaurant workers.

✔ Anyone at Spectrum Chemicals & Laboratory Products in Gardena, California, can give anyone else a written note of thanks that includes a $25 gift certificate for Trader Joe's or a restaurant of the recipient's choice. Most often, the person offering the thanks personally presents the note and certificate to the honoree in front of the sales department. Individuals are also allowed to give themselves a Thumbs Up award for those times when they are the only person who knows the specifics of their achievement.

✔ Human resources employees at software maker Symantec Corporation, based in Cupertino, California, give each other Serendipity awards, when someone does something worthy of recognition. At the end of the quarter, the vice president of HR randomly selects names among the recipients for prizes worth $40 to $50.

✔ Wellstar Hospital in Atlanta, Georgia, created a simple peer-to-peer award exclusively used by managers. The hospital printed notepads of the organization's core values and distributed them to all managers to be used for other managers. When a manager spotted a fellow manager demonstrating a core value, the person wrote the manager's name on the note pad with the corresponding value checked and gave the paper to the manager. During quarterly management meetings, managers who had been spotted demonstrating the hospital's core values were asked to stand, and those recognized for multiple core values were asked to the front of the room to receive a standing ovation. On the way out, each manager got to choose from a number of books on leader development. This is one of my favorite examples because it shows individual recognition from one's peers, public praise, and personal development all in a simple single program!

Managers need recognition, too!

Creating opportunities for managers to be recognized is an effective strategy for increasing the overall level of recognition in your organization. When managers feel the power of recognition on a personal level, they are more likely to both use recognition themselves as well as support other recognition efforts as they arise in the organization. So consider creating a management award that allows employees to honor their managers for certain performance criteria, or create recognition activities in which managers help and learn from each other on the topic of recognition.

Following are some ways that you can create an environment in which managers can help and learn from each other about recognition:

✔ A store manager at one Long's Drug telling me he brings in a silver dollar every Monday morning, hands it to one of his supervisors, and asks that supervisor to pass it on to another supervisor after the first supervisor recognizes an employee. During the week, supervisors encourage and remind each other to recognize employees in order to pass on the coin. If the silver dollar has passed through the hands of all supervisors in any given week, the store manager hosts a celebration for the team.

✔ A general manager at Xerox told me how he saves time at the end of each of his manager meetings to go around the room and have each manager share at least one thing he or she did to recognize a staff member since the group had last been together. He said you can feel the energy in the room rise as the managers share what they did. In addition, he noted, other managers took notes on the other's ideas, an example of how they were able to learn effective recognition techniques from one another.

Five tips for using technology to recognize others

✔ **Use it, don't abuse it.** Use technology sparingly and make it meaningful. Overusing technology constantly to deliver praise and recognition will undermine the value of your messages and simply make it part of a person's daily noise.

✔ **Get personal.** When leaving praise messages, be as specific and sincere as you can. Avoid the simple too-general "Good job." Embellish the praise with specifics.

✔ **Just do it now!** The beauty of technology is that it allows you to act immediately. Recognition is most effective just after desired behavior or performance. Seize the moment and follow through.

✔ **Say it right the first time.** We all love to dash off e-mails, but take a second look and make sure your message says what you want it to say. I know of one employee who was more than a little perplexed when she received an e-mail that said, "Great job on that affair."

✔ **Follow up face-to-face.** To anchor recognition in memory, follow up any technical communication with face-to-face interaction. Face time is still the best way to convey heartfelt appreciation and sincerity.

You can find many more tips and strategies about effectively using technology to recognize others in Chapter 12.

Chapter 10

Engaging and Recognizing Teams

. . . .

. . . .

*E*ffective managers don't only have to be good at engaging and recognizing individuals, but they should also be adept at engaging and recognizing groups of people, like departments and teams, whether they're quality teams (focused on improving the quality of products and efficiency of operations), cross-functional teams, self-directed teams, or even remote, virtual teams. As a manager, you need to know how to put together teams that can function at their highest potential and then recognize the successes of the team members, much like you recognize any individual. In fact, some of the best forms of team engagement and recognition are personal, such as publicly acknowledging group members for their involvement, suggestions, and initiative, or sending an e-mail or letter to all team members thanking them for their contributions.

In this chapter, I go over how to work with a team as a unit to maximize strengths, improve weaknesses, and keep the group operating well. I also outline how to make and implement a plan to recognize multiple people at once for collaborative achievements, and I give you plenty of real-world examples from my work with companies all over the country. Although engaging teams and implementing group recognition can be a bit more complex and challenging than implementing individual recognition, the payoff can be great. Read on to understand how to successfully motivate and reward the groups in your organization who deserve it.

Creating and Engaging High-Performing Teams

Before they can be recognized, teams have to do something worthy of recognition, because recognition is all about driving performance and reinforcing the desired behaviors that are most beneficial to the organization's success. In this section, I outline how to work with your team leaders to create and engage high-performing teams.

PERFORM: Setting the stage for success

The objective of every team leader should be to create a team that's a cohesive, interactive group that can work together to achieve a common goal. The Ken Blanchard Companies in San Diego, California, have outlined seven characteristics, represented by the acronym PERFORM, that summarize the behaviors necessary for a group to become a high-performing team: **p**urpose, **e**mpowerment, **r**elationships and communication, **f**lexibility, **o**ptimal productivity, **r**ecognition and appreciation, and **m**orale. When team members and leaders adopt these characteristics, they can better visualize and achieve a positive working environment that can more easily produce better results.

Purpose

Members of high-performing teams share a sense of common purpose. They discuss their objectives so that all have a clear understanding of the mission and its importance, and know precisely what they intend to achieve. Their discussions about purpose set specific objectives that clearly relate to the team's vision. Strategies for achieving goals need to be clear, and each member needs to understand his or her role in realizing the team's vision. Getting to this point requires having numerous group discussions until the team reaches a consensus of agreement around the group's purpose. These discussions often include brainstorming, prioritizing, and setting specific achievable actions.

If your team leader cannot facilitate the discussion well enough to yield a clear purpose, objectives, and expectations, you may have to coach him or model those behaviors yourself with the group.

Empowerment

Team members need to be confident about the team's ability to overcome obstacles, and they need to know that you and the organization support their efforts. This sense of mutual respect enables members to share responsibilities, support each other, and take initiative to meet challenges that arise. The established policies, ground rules, and team processes enable members to achieve their objectives. To empower members to be respectful and to focus on listening, for example, the group might establish the ground rule that only one person speaks at a time and others are not allowed to interrupt. Or the team may decide that members will summarize group discussions and outline any needed actions prior to addressing the next agenda item. Along the way, team members will have opportunities to grow and learn new skills, to be empowered, and to capitalize on their new skills. As personal empowerment becomes collective empowerment, the team's efforts will lead to the betterment of the team members, the team, and the company.

Relationships and communication

A properly engaged team is committed to open communication, where group members can state their opinions, thoughts, and feelings without fear. A high-functioning team considers listening as important as speaking and values differences of opinion and perspective. Additionally, all members understand the methods for managing conflict. Through honest and constructive feedback, members become aware of their strengths and weaknesses.

This atmosphere of trust, acceptance, and community creates a cohesive group. One of the checkpoints for achieving this level of trust within the group is a commitment to the free expression of concerns that team members may have about how the group is functioning. This kind of open communication helps to ensure that individuals remain committed to the group's success as opposed to "tuning out" when disagreements arise over how the group is functioning.

Flexibility

Group members need to be flexible — that is, able to perform different tasks and functions as needed to keep the team on track. All members need to share the responsibility for team development and leadership; that is, they should speak up when they think the group is off track and offer help to get it back on the right path. They should identify and play to the strengths of each member and coordinate individual efforts as needed. The team is fluid and open to both opinions and feelings, hard work and fun. Members recognize the inevitability and desirability of change and adapt to changing conditions.

Optimal productivity

High-performing teams produce significant results because everyone is committed to high standards and quality performance. Team members get the job done by meeting deadlines and achieving goals. The team establishes effective decision-making and problem-solving methods that result in achieving optimum results and that encourage participation and creativity. Members develop strong skills in group processes as well as task accomplishment.

Recognition and appreciation

Both team leader and members alike frequently recognize individual and team accomplishments by celebrating milestones, accomplishments, and events. Team accomplishments are valued by the entire organization. Members feel important within the team and experience a sense of personal accomplishments in relation to their team and task contributions.

Morale

Members are proud to be a part of the team and are enthusiastic about its mission. Confident and committed, members are optimistic about the future. There's a sense of excitement about individual and team achievements, as well as the way team members work together. Team spirit is high.

Putting PERFORM into action

Of the seven PERFORM characteristics, two are most important: optimal productivity and morale. To be a successful team, a group must be able to produce results, and team members must feel a high degree of satisfaction from working together. Recognition is the bridge that connects these two elements. As you and others recognize the group's performance, the group feels better about working together and can better achieve additional success and productivity.

What you as a manager can do

Any member's behaviors can shape the group's overall level of productivity and morale, but it is especially important that managers provide direction to increase productivity and support to increase morale. You can provide direction in three ways: structure, control, and supervision:

- **Structure:** Groups need structure, or a game plan, to make progress. The structure can come from your own agenda or from asking questions of the team that help clarify the goals of the group and group members' roles.

- **Control:** After the group establishes a plan, you need to help them manage their activities so that the group can stick to the plan. For example, you may set discussion time limits for each item on the agenda, and then stick to that schedule or modify or postpone the agenda as needed to keep to the schedule.

- **Supervision**: You need to provide supervision — the systematic observation, reinforcement, or redirection of behaviors — that is important in shaping any behavior. For groups, this means monitoring and evaluating how the group is doing, pinpointing what it needs to do to reach its goals, and helping in appropriate ways. As a manager, you can be helpful to the team by providing additional information, making suggestions, or summarizing and recasting what still needs to be done.

What team members can do

To develop a team that functions well, team members also need to support each other in three main ways: praising, listening, and facilitating:

✔ **Praising:** Giving specific praise on a timely basis is one of the most effective means of reinforcing desired behaviors. In a group context, team leaders can give praise for productive contributions, such as new ideas, suggestions, or factual data. Praising encourages others to continue to be involved with the group in a positive way.

✔ **Listening**: Few behaviors underscore the value one places on another person as much as listening. Team members can demonstrate they've heard each other and been understood by using both verbal cues (such as paraphrasing) and nonverbal cues (such as nodding their heads in agreement).

✔ **Facilitating:** An effective leader serves as a facilitator to help move the group toward its goal in a way in which both participation and commitment to the group process remain high. Assisting with the interactions of team members can take many forms, such as leading the discussion, helping the group stay on track, or encouraging quiet members to contribute to the group discussion.

Ideally, all members should share the responsibility of initiating behaviors that give direction and support to the group, but it's ultimately up to the team leader to develop and implement effective ways to recognize the accomplishments of the team as well as the achievements of individual team members. When this recognition occurs, the group can more easily assume the other team-building characteristics needed to perform and will be well on its way to becoming a high-performing team. Only if the team is performing as a team should it be recognized as a unit for its successes; in other words, avoid recognizing dysfunctional teams whenever possible.

A Quick Look at Team Recognition

Team recognition relates to work employees do and the achievements they enjoy when they work together as part of a group. Even though you may end up recognizing someone individually for his or her contributions to a team, your praise is still considered team recognition.

Just because a team recognition program or activity involves some individual recognition, that doesn't make it an individual recognition program. The distinction is a subtle one, but it's a distinction that is important to remember, because the approach you take when recognizing group-oriented work is different from the approach you take when you're recognizing individual-oriented work. Think of individual recognition as something that is between and relevant to just two people: you and the employee you're recognizing. Team recognition, on the other hand, involves more people and a larger context. Likewise, organizational recognition, which I discuss in Chapter 11, occurs within a larger context yet, the context of the organization, but it can and does involve both group and individual recognition.

Recognition can often take the form of simply empowering employees: Involve the team in the goal-setting, brainstorming, or problem-solving process; place a priority on open communication by encouraging and making time for questions; and grant the group sufficient authority to achieve their objectives. For example:

- ✔ What drives team members to take on responsibility at GDX Automotive (now Henniges Automotive)' plant in Shelbyville, Indiana, is the autonomy granted them by management to determine for themselves exactly how they do their jobs. According to Gary J. Goberville, former vice president of Human Resources, teams have the authority to pick one of their own coworkers as their team leader: "If you want a motivated workforce taking on the responsibility for good-quality products delivered on time, you have to give them the fullest authority to work out the best way to do it."

- ✔ All 80 employees at Techmetals, a small, Dayton, Ohio, metal-plating company, are involved in plant layout, scheduling, and delivery.

- ✔ Self-directed teams at Motorola's Arlington Heights, Illinois, cellular equipment manufacturing plant not only decide on their own training programs and schedule their own work, but they are also involved in the hiring and firing of coworkers.

Applying individual recognition principles to teams

Recognition works best with individuals when it's immediate, sincere, specific, based on performance — and when it comes from an employee's immediate manager or from others in the workplace whom the employee holds in high regard. These same principles hold true for teams. Some of the best forms of team recognition are personal — a manager taking time to thank group members in person for their involvement on a project, for example, or sending a letter to all team members thanking them for their contributions.

As a manager, you can demonstrate an immediate and sincere personal interest in a special project team's work by attending the team's initial meetings (and subsequent meetings) to help emphasize the importance of the group's purpose. You can conduct informal retreats for team members to set goals, stimulate communication, or focus on certain problems. During such retreats, you can hold team-building activities as well as order in special food as a way to celebrate a team's progress toward its specific goals, while verbally expressing appreciation and encouraging team members' continued success. At the end of the project, you can discuss with the team how they'd best like to recognize and reward their success.

Gestures of recognition do not have to be elaborate. To ensure that you carry recognition out personally and in a timely fashion, think small. Simple ideas are easier to implement, they are no less appreciated than complex ideas, and they can go a long way toward developing team spirit and positive group morale. Creating symbols of a team's work or effort (T-shirts or coffee cups with a special motto or project logo) or including photos of work teams in different company publications — as is commonly done at Advanced Micro Devices in Sunnyvale, California — can help you reinforce effective behavior. Ideas such as these are limited only by the creativity of the people in the organization.

Of course, you can always do something more elaborate when the occasion — such as a significant achievement — calls for it:

- ✔ **Provide a special award.** Executives at JASCO Tools of Rochester, New York, made a formal presentation to employees who produced the components that won a quality award. They put the award on permanent display on the shop floor.

- ✔ **Do an activity.** A manager at San Francisco, California-based Gap Inc. wanted to thank everyone for working madly to meet a big deadline. She handed out gift certificates from a spa for a facial or massage. Says Carol Whittaker, another Gap manager, "It was a much appreciated treat to help employees calm down and relax after a tough time."

- ✔ **Do both!** At First Chicago (now part of JPMorgan Chase & Co.), management recognized team achievements by inviting the team being honored on an outing — dinner, theater, or a sports event — and presenting the team with a plaque commemorating its achievement.

Tackling the challenges of team recognition

Recognizing individuals is one thing, but recognizing teams is a bit trickier. While managers report that they spend 60 percent to 90 percent of their time participating in group activities, they also indicate that group meetings are often inefficient and waste a significant amount of time. To exacerbate the problem, managers believe they receive little or no training in the skills needed to get their group to function like a team. Recognition is one of those skills.

The task of recognizing teams differs from the task of recognizing individuals and presents a dilemma: How does a manager affirm a team's collective effort on the one hand and the contribution of different individual on the other — especially when each individual's effort isn't the same? Members of a team seldom contribute equally to the group's work. Each member brings a different degree of skill, knowledge, experience, and enthusiasm to the table. As a manager, you want to acknowledge the group performance in a way that neither undermines those who contributed the most to the team's work nor reinforces the behavior of team members who added little or nothing to the team. "Jelly bean motivation" — giving equal recognition for unequal performance — is detrimental to the group's sustained productivity (more on this topic in Chapter 14).

One way to resolve this conflict is to enable and encourage the recognition among team members within the group. Initially make sure the team leader knows how to recognize individual members of the group when their performance warrants it, and that he or she follows through. As the team spends more time working together and observing the team leader giving recognition, each member can then assume this leadership role of recognizing others as warranted. By the time the group becomes a high-performing team, all team members should be recognizing and praising one another, and the job of the leader will be that much easier.

Another solution is to find ways to recognize both individual and team contributions simultaneously. For example, when a team's project is finished, you can publicly praise the team as a group for its work and give additional individual praise to top performers within that team.

In terms of rewarding teams as a whole, managers must also learn to pair individual performance with group output, according to Deborah Crown, Dean of the College of Business Administration at Hawaii Pacific University. Her research shows that a combination of group-centric individual goals (that is, individual goals that related to group objectives) coupled with overall group goals results in team performance that is 36 percent greater than what would happen otherwise. "It might be as simple as changing to rewarding people for the percentage of goals to which they contribute," says Crown. "You're more likely to have success if you give people a goal and direct their action where you want it directed, rather than hoping over time they'll try to do the right thing because they identify with the group."

An easy way to pair individual and team performance with the group output is to discuss recognition and rewards during the planning or launch of the team. After the mission, purpose, and objectives of the team are established, ask the group, "If we are successful in achieving these objectives, how would you all like to celebrate our success?" The end recognition and rewards can be useful in helping to motivate the team along the way — especially when it gets bogged down.

Planning Team Recognition

When your groups are functioning like they should, it's time to plan out how you can best recognize them! Because more factors are involved with team recognition, planning can be a little more involved than planning individual recognition.

Who, what, where, when, and how?

The key, however, is simply to get started and to not make it more complicated than it needs to be. Just as with individual recognition, you can use the "who, what, where, when and how" format by addressing the following questions:

- **Who should I recognize?** Discuss the topic of recognition with the team and ask the question, "Does anyone think we need to do more recognition in our group?" Incidentally, I've never heard of an employee anywhere saying, "I get too much recognition where I work," so it's safe to assume you will get a "yes" response. When you do, focus the discussion on recognition efforts that can be ongoing, not just a one-time celebration or activity. Then take the initial interest you receive in having more recognition and ask, "Who would be willing to help get a recognition program or activities going?" Volunteers who see a need and have an interest in the topic drive some of the best recognition programs and activities.

- **What should I recognize?** As with individual recognition, the best team recognition reinforces desired behavior — either by the whole group or by selected outstanding individuals within it. Activities can range from thanking individuals who completed team assignments to celebrating an important group milestone or achievement.

- **Where should I do the recognition?** You can recognize a team wherever the team congregates, or you can plan an off-site celebration. You can also recognize teams for their achievements during larger gatherings, such as at an organization-wide awards banquet or at an annual "all-hands" employee meeting.

- **When should I do the recognition?** As with individual recognition, your team recognition should follow as closely as possible the desired behavior or performance that was exhibited. You can do recognition instantly, as in the case of acknowledging a helpful suggestion made within a team meeting, or you can plan the recognition to coincide with the completion of a significant contribution by the entire team.

- **How should I recognize the team?** Ideally, team recognition should match group values. Ask team members to give you their preferences and feedback on the effectiveness of your own personal style of praising. Your openness in seeking their feedback will enable them to try new behaviors more easily as well.

You don't have to limit team recognition to something verbal. You can be visually creative, too. Create a team logo on coffee mugs, for example; create a "Successful Projects" scrapbook for photos of different teams and their accomplishments; or designate a "Team Spirit" wall where you display photos of past and present teams and each team's achievements. These are just a few of the ideas you can implement.

Developing a low-cost group recognition program

The best forms of team recognition cost little or no money. For example, The Ken Blanchard Companies in San Diego, California, created an Eagle Award to recognize team members who are "caught delivering exceptional customer service." Any employee can nominate another employee for the award. Typical examples include staying late to ship materials, helping a customer locate a lost order, resolving a billing problem, or rearranging schedules to deliver a last-minute customer request.

The nominator submits the employee's name with a brief description of the activity that is worthy of recognition. A committee reviews the recommendations, primarily to screen out actions they consider to be a normal part of someone's job. The Eagle Committee then surprises the winners with a visit and takes a picture of the person holding an Eagle Award — one of several eagle trophies that rotate around the company. They then display the photo on a lobby bulletin board along with a brief description of the recipient's special efforts. The winner gets to keep the trophy on his or her desk until it's needed for a new recipient — typically a week or so. At the end of the year, an Eagle of the Year winner is selected from the multiple award winners, and that person gets an engraved clock at the company's annual celebration event.

Using the Eagle Award as a running example, I look at other guidelines for creating an effective low-cost group recognition program.

Focus on areas that have the most impact

You make the most progress with your recognition efforts if you focus on only a few goals at a time. Select one or two objectives that, if implemented, will make the biggest difference to your group's success. For example, the Eagle Award focused on improving customer service at Blanchard and was thought to have a significant positive impact on sales and repeat business for the company.

Involve your target employee group

After helping the team establish goals, have the team develop the criteria and mechanics for the recognition program. By involving the group in this discussion, group members will feel a sense of ownership in the program and be vested in its success. Remember, the best management is what you do *with* people, not what you do *to* them. Make employees partners in their own success. At Blanchard, a group of employees pulled together to create a program that could impact customer service and came up with the specific criteria of the Eagle Award, which focused on recognizing desired customer service behaviors at nominal cost.

Announce the program with fanfare

A recognition program should be fun and exciting — starting with how the program is announced. So even if your program is low cost, take time to launch it with some fanfare. In the case of the Eagle Award, the program was announced and explained at an all-staff meeting, and nomination forms (and refreshments) were distributed to all who attended.

Publicly track progress

Even a low-cost recognition program needs to have objectives that are monitored. If you don't measure it, you can't manage it! If you do measure it — and do so publicly — you increase the chances that members of your team will pay attention to the behavior you want. In addition to the bulletin board of Eagle Award recipients that was very visible to all employees in the organization, all Eagle Award recipients were listed in the company newsletter along with a description of what they had done to demonstrate exceptional customer service.

Have lots of winners

Because some of the best forms of recognition — personal, written, or public praise — are free, why not do as much of it as possible? The Eagle Award had no top limit: Any number of people could be honored and, subsequently, additional "traveling trophies" were added to the mix so that recipients could keep the awards on their desks for longer periods of time.

Allow flexibility of rewards

What motivates one person may not motivate another, so allow individuals some flexibility in their choice of rewards whenever possible. This can be a choice of recognition activities, a choice of assignments, or a choice of merchandise. All Eagle Award recipients, for example, were given a choice of a car wash coupon, a restaurant discount coupon, or a zoo pass — all items that had been donated to the program or purchased in bulk.

Renew the program as needed

Even the best recognition program eventually runs its course, often within just a few months. So you must strive to keep the program fresh and exciting. Build on the success of the program, learn from your mistakes, and try something new to keep things fresh. Although it was implemented inexpensively, the Eagle Award was highly successful, and customer service became a leading attribute of the organization. After some 60 percent of employees received the award, the criteria of the program were modified to include measures of *internal* service so that an even greater number of employees could participate.

Link informal and formal rewards

Get the best of both informal and formal rewards by combining their use. For example, recipients of an informal recognition program that encourages employees to use "praising forms" can be tracked and given a formal award that more permanently signifies the event. An employee team merged informal and formal award programs when it revised the Eagle Award program, issuing recipients eagle stickers each time they received the Eagle Award. Employees placed the stickers on a card that, when completely filled, could be redeemed for a wall plaque (a formal award), presented at a company meeting with much fanfare. At the end of the year, all recipients of a wall plaque were invited with their spouses or significant others to have dinner with the president and founder of the company.

Find ways to perpetuate new behaviors

Driving specific desired behaviors with recognition is effective, but to truly sustain the new behavior, the recognition needs to be tied to organization systems such as hiring, orienting, communication, training, career development, merit pay, and promotion practices. The Eagle Award became a starting point for making customer service a core value for the entire organization — far beyond its humble beginnings in the sales department — and an established part of the company's culture and competitive advantage.

Ways to Recognize Your Team

There are all sorts of ways to praise and recognize teams — the sky's the limit! Whether simple or complex, wild or a little conservative, feel free to get creative. This section offers some suggestions to inspire you.

For team recognition to be effective, you must acknowledge success. If you don't focus on positive results along the way, you won't get more of the same.

Eight quick ways to praise and recognize teams

If you're finding yourself a little short on ideas, here's a list of quick ways to recognize teams:

✔ Open the floor for team members to praise anyone at the beginning or end of a department meeting.

✔ When a group member presents an idea or suggestion, encourage other team members to thank the person for his or her contribution.

✔ Hold a "praise barrage," an exercise in which team members write down and then read aloud things that they like about another member of the team.

✔ Assign one member of the team the job of creating and presenting an award for another member of the team.

✔ Alternate the responsibility for group recognition among different team members each week or each meeting.

✔ Host refreshments, a potluck, or a special breakfast or lunch to celebrate interim or final results.

✔ Ask an upper manager to attend a "bragging session" with the group, during which the group shares its achievements and group members are thanked for their specific contributions.

✔ Write letters to every team member at the conclusion of a project, thanking each for his or her contribution.

Planning group celebrations

Celebrations, parties, and special events are more organized forms of public recognition that are especially appropriate for groups. Although it's often traditional for companies to host holiday or year-end celebrations, group celebrations are more effective when you link them to the performance of your team. With a little forethought and planning, you can make any team event a meaningful form of recognition.

You can create a team challenge or contest in which a team competes against its own goals or against another team. When the team is successful, let its members decide how to celebrate. Possibilities might include going bowling, playing laser tag, visiting a state fair, or having a "popcorn lunch" — that is, going to a lunch-time movie. Other meaningful team celebrations might be a pizza party, a potluck dinner, or a catered lunch.

Here are some other ideas:

✔ Hewlett-Packard uses informal beer busts in the afternoons to mark special events.

✔ At Dow Corning, in Midland, Michigan, management hosted an ice-cream social in which managers made and served ice cream sundaes to employees to thank them for an accomplishment.

✔ The morning after a product passes a crucial test at Odetics (now Iteris Holdings, Inc.), a company that makes robots and spaceborne tape recorders in Anaheim, California, a mariachi band paraded through the plant, followed by some employees from the local Baskin-Robbins franchise offering free ice cream.

Using money as a facet of team recognition

While money is certainly not the only motivator by itself, you can use it effectively as a facet of team recognition. Consider these examples:

✔ In the team program at Cal Snap & Tab, located in the City of Industry, California, everyone can win, but one team wins big. "We're using a combination spoilage/attendance program," says marketing manager Richard S. Calhoun. "We put $40,000 into a special fund and, every time a mistake was made, we deducted its costs from the $40,000. We ended up giving out about $7,000." The next year the employees were divided into four teams, with a prize kitty of 1.25 percent of shipments. One-fourth of a percent was credited to each team, and spoilage by any team member was deducted from it. At the end of the program, each team got to keep its kitty, and the team with the lowest spoilage also got the leftover 0.25 percent.

✔ At Boston's Beth Israel Deaconess Medical Center, the PREPARE/21 program has increased employee involvement, teamwork, and creativity. Under PREPARE/21— which stands for Participation, Responsibility, Education, Productivity, Accountability, Recognition, and Excellence for the 21st Century — employees are encouraged to organize teams to study ways to cut costs and improve the organization. The program allows employees to share in the monetary savings that accrue as a result of team suggestions. In the first year of the program, participating employees split $1 million — half of the $2 million that Beth Israel Deaconess saved as a result of employee suggestions.

Recognizing virtual groups

You should always reward the behavior you desire with recognition that is valued by and meaningful to your employees. This is especially important when you design virtual rewards and recognition because employees who are out of visual contact with their managers or coworkers are more likely to feel left out of the group.

When creating a virtual recognition program, start by identifying the baseline motivational needs of your employees. A corner office or a prime parking space does not have much significance in a virtual environment, but what about a faster or better computer, or a state-of-the-art cellphone or text pager? "Technology — actually the access to technology — can be a very effective reward in itself," says Roz Cleveland, of Continental Mills, in Seattle, Washington. "I've found that giving employees new computers is a very motivational act. Getting employees involved in the selection process and seeking their input is also an important motivator, as well as allowing them to actually purchase the items."

Alternatively, virtual employees might value learning and development opportunities, a bright plant to liven up a home office, or a reward that is linked to a hobby or personal interest, such as a gift certificate to a local restaurant or movie passes at a local theater.

When employees are not in the same place, organizations must still create and sustain a strong sense of camaraderie, commitment, and collaboration. Following are some important considerations for virtual team recognition:

- ✔ **Use team identification items.** These items (such as logoed coffee mugs, T-shirts, jackets, and so forth) are more important for the virtual team member because they remind them of their place on the team. Make a point of employing a variety of team recognition items when rewarding members of virtual teams.

- ✔ **Keep a recognition log of remote team members.** Doing so can ensure that they don't fall through the cracks — a particularly important consideration for "mixed" teams (ones with both traditional and virtual team members).

- ✔ **If your employees are in the office infrequently, make it a priority to meet with them when they are around.** Establish a set time each week or during core business hours, when everyone is present, to meet with virtual employees. Alternatively, coordinate schedules so that you are at work at the same time as your employees. One executive I know schedules office hours at his company's plants so that anyone can sign up for a meeting. Employees sign up to meet and are given a number, and using a Baskin-Robbins-style "now serving #47" electronic billboard on the plant floor, they know when to make their way to the plant office for their meeting.

- ✔ **Spend time with your virtual employees.** Talk about real issues of importance to employees. Ben Edwards, CEO of the stock brokerage A.G. Edwards and Sons (now Wells Fargo Advisors) conducts a nationwide audio conference call with all employees on the last Friday of each month. The meetings begin with a brief state-of-the-company talk; then the phone lines open for a real-time, question-and-answer period.

- ✔ **Set regular times to communicate.** Managers can take a proactive role in fostering a sense of teamwork by establishing regular times for telephone calls, e-mail messages, teleconferences, videoconferences, and computer chats. Electronic message boards can be used for ongoing communication about progress on critical aspects of the team's work. Communicating in these ways gives virtual employees the opportunity to exchange ideas with team members, talk about the problems they may be having, discuss ways to improve, evaluate the team's progress, share ideas, get feedback, brainstorm new ideas, and discuss strategies. Everyone needs a forum in which to share problems and acknowledge successes.

To find out what virtual employees want, ask them. Conduct a survey asking virtual employees what kinds of recognition would be meaningful to them, have a discussion with your work group about the topic, or ask your virtual employees to select recognition and celebration activities for the end of the project. Not only does this tactic involve your employees in the process of planning their own recognition, but it also stimulates their desire to perform and gives them something concrete to look forward to when the project is successfully completed.

Putting It All Together with Perkins Coie

Perkins Coie LLP is a law firm of 450 lawyers serving a veritable Who's Who of successful companies, from Boeing to Bristol-Myers Squibb. While Perkins Coie has seen tremendous success over the years, the company's management is far-sighted enough to know that there is always room for improvement. In fact, "Continuous Improvement" is the second of seven of the firm's formal guiding principles (the fourth is "Rewarding Work Environment"). To gauge employee job satisfaction, the firm conducted a firm-wide employee survey. In the case of its 40-person-strong Finance Department, the score was only average — lower than expected. In this section, I outline exactly how Perkins Coie improved and implemented a specific team recognition effort to address this.

In response, Perkins Coie's then-director of finance and CFO Wayne Robinson created a "book club" with a focus on leadership. The group read books, discussed a selected chapter each month, and tried to apply the author's concepts in a real-world setting. Included in this group of books was my book *1001 Ways to Reward Employees.* According to Carla Stroud, a project manager at Perkins Coie at the time, reading the book started a chain of events that has not only improved employee morale within the Finance Department, but also improved employee productivity.

Said Stroud, "We decided that we didn't do enough to thank employees and that we needed to focus on that. During one of the first meetings we had regarding the issues, we came up with the idea of forming a Happiness Committee — I think the book called it a Morale Committee. Another supervisor from payroll and I just went around and asked people privately to participate. You see, it's a secret committee. At first, we just gave people a basic outline of what we were doing and asked whether they'd like to join. And some really enthusiastic people jumped on board, but no one knew all five of the members. In fact, no one knows even now."

Employees never know what to expect from the Happiness Committee, or when to expect it. The group's first formal act was to fill little Easter eggs with candy and wrap each one in a Dilbert cartoon in which the artist Scott Adams made reference to a "happiness committee." Other creative Happiness Committee activities and have included the following:

- ✔ **An end-of-summer barbecue.** It took place in the pouring rain on the outside 48th-floor deck of the building (which just happened to be under construction at the time)

- ✔ **An Earth Day competition.** On Earth Day, department employees received plants, bags of dirt, and fertilizer with a prize to whoever could grow a plant the most successfully. (One unexpected benefit: Employees were asking one another about their plants. Said one employee, "I don't know if I'd ever have talked to some of these people before. These kinds of things really break down the barriers.")

- ✔ **A sack lunch picnic trip on a ferry across Puget Sound.** Employees were required to bring permission slips signed by a coworker allowing them to attend.

- ✔ **A Veteran's Day celebration.** The department's five veterans were honored by their 35 coworkers with a potluck lunch, complete with red, white, and blue balloons, and a sheet cake.

According to Carla Stroud, "One of my personal favorites was when we brought in a clown for some surprise lunch hour entertainment. And we served McDonald's Happy Meals — from the Happiness Committee, of course! One reason that event was so special was because we hadn't done much for a while.

Sustaining the efforts

For a rewards program to be effective, it's not just enough to come up with a creative idea once in a blue moon. Rewards and recognition programs have to be sustained, and employees have to know that the organization cares enough about their well-being to make them a priority. Said Carla Stroud about the clown-and-Happy-Meal lunch, "It's interesting — it's like a garden. You've really got to tend it. And if you don't do something for a while — it's not that people feel entitled, but they notice. At the end of last year, people were a little burned out, and people began asking me, 'What are you guys going to do?' And I decided to hire a clown. It was only about $75 an hour, and well worth it. It's great to see 40 adults making balloon animals. That was our kick-off."

Assessing the results

The Happiness Committee has been effective. Perkins Coie conducted a follow-up survey, asking employees the exact same questions they were asked two years prior. In the company's Finance Department, the results, outlined in Table 10-1, were dramatic.

Table 10-1 Finance Department Employee Survey Results	Percentage Who Agree	
	Baseline	*2 Years Later*
My supervisor encourages independent thought and action	56%	95%
My supervisor creates an atmosphere that inspires trust	60%	88%
My supervisor treats me fairly	60%	88%
Overall, I am satisfied with my job	48%	73%
I am accepted by my workgroup	80%	90%
Ours is a blame-free work environment within my workgroup	76%	73%
Our guidelines and procedures help me do my job	52%	76%
There is good communication among departments	40%	38%
We have good unity of purpose (firm wide)	20%	33%

Not only did employee morale improve, but so did productivity. For example, the workload of accounts payable bookkeepers increased 36 percent during a four-year period while staffing decreased from ten full-time equivalents to nine, indicating a productivity increase of 52 percent.

And the fun spreads

All this fun — and an improved work environment — did not go unnoticed by other employees in other departments. With the assistance of the Perkins Coie Finance Department Happiness Committee, the firm's Information Technology and Technical Support Departments started their own recognition programs. To kick things off, they put up happiness boards like the ones established in the Finance Department. Employees use them to post items about their families, their children, or whatever was going on in the firm. Said Carla Stroud, "I see them slowly starting to do some things and forming their own ideas. They have a supervisor who is thinking of great ideas and trying to implement them herself. It has taken a while, but people in some other departments have noticed what we've done. Someone on the operations department staff said to me, 'You people seem so happy down there.'"

Chapter 11

Implementing Organizational Recognition

. . . .

In This Chapter

▶ Comparing organizational to individual and team recognition

▶ Discovering the three purposes of organizational recognition

▶ Implementing organizational recognition strategically

▶ Identifying the four phases of organizational recognition

. . . .

*O*rganizational recognition refers to formal recognition programs and activities that you organize and execute on a facility-, business unit-, or company-wide basis. Organizational recognition can be very diverse, going from very simple (recognition of an outstanding employee in the company newsletter, for example) to very complex and sophisticated (like a multitiered nomination process culminating in an award presentation by the company's CEO at a glitzy annual ceremony). Regardless of the complexity, an effective organizational recognition program can help you create a culture of recognition that perpetuates itself and outlasts individual employees and managers who may come and go.

In this chapter, I take you through the differences between organizational and other types of workplace recognition, and guide you through the process of putting an organization-wide recognition program into place in your company.

Three Purposes of Organizational Recognition

Organizational recognition can be effective at improving performance (reinforcing specific behaviors and results that you want more of); modeling desired behavior (highlighting the personal characteristics that you value); and showing appreciation (demonstrating your gratitude for extra effort). As I explain in this section, these purposes are not mutually exclusive. Recognition can include a combination of any or all of these purposes. Here, I look briefly at each.

Improving performance

Recognition designed to improve performance can be in the form of contingent promises *(incentives)* and after-the-fact recognition *(positive reinforcers)* that result in desired behaviors or results. This type of recognition is a major motivator of both individual and group change.

Recognition is one of the greatest drivers of performance, and you can use it to help your organization achieve specific, desired outcomes. People do things largely for the positive consequences they anticipate receiving. As I say throughout this book, you get what you reward — a statement that is true on an individual level, a team level, and an organizational level.

Every organization has plenty of opportunities for potential improvement in, among other areas, sales, revenue enhancement, client referrals, quality control, productivity, safety, customer service, cost-saving suggestions, knowledge sharing, and employee retention.

My book *1501 Ways to Reward Employees* (Workman Publishing Company) showcases numerous examples of organizational recognition you can use to reward employees for meeting or exceeding performance expectations, but here are a few to inspire you now:

✔ In a praise-for-performance program, Weyerhauser, a paper company in Federal Way, Washington, increased the productivity of logging trucks from 60 percent to more than 90 percent.

✔ At Worzalla, a book-manufacturing company in Stevens Point, Wisconsin, the Quality Services department exceeded its goal of 99.85 percent accuracy in customer specifications for five years in a row. Bill Downs, the quality supervisor and continuous improvement manager, wanted to celebrate, and with a budget of only $20 per person, took the department to lunch and gave each member of the team a certificate of appreciation and a gift card for a movie rental and pizza. The group enjoyed the lunch and gift cards but seemed to take even more pride in displaying the certificates in their offices and explaining their achievement to anyone who would listen.

✔ In an effort to reduce both turnover and expenses, the Daniel Company of Springfield, a trucking firm in Missouri, challenged its drivers to cut their fuel costs by improving mileage — and then let them keep the difference. Since then, turnover has been cut by 25 percent, and trucks are logging fewer miles, thus, cutting overall costs.

✔ Kathy Atkinson, a program manager for a nuclear clean-up facility located in Buffalo, New York, created the Bright Ideas Program to meet improvement goals. The program had two parts: (1) generation of new, bona fide original ideas and (2) implementation of those ideas. Employees submitted narratives explaining their ideas and including estimated costs, benefits, and savings. As a reward for their new ideas, employees received scratch-off coupons for redeemable points for merchandise in a catalog. Those who implemented their ideas also received coupons. All recipients were eligible for a quarterly grand-prize drawing for a cruise. For a cost of $25,000 per year — less than half of what was budgeted — the program saved a documented $2.2 million in cost avoidance over the first 18 months. The program was written up as an innovative best practice by the U.S. Department of Energy.

Although recognition is frequently an important component in organizational performance improvement programs, it should be an integral component of *every* organizational improvement effort.

Modeling behaviors others can emulate

Another purpose of organizational recognition is *modeling* — that is, creating role models in the organization whose behaviors others can emulate. Every time you recognize someone publicly, you're sending a message to all other employees that the recognized behavior is what you want to see everyone doing more of.

When Lou Gerstner, former CEO of IBM Corporation, was at American Express, he instituted a highly visible Great Performers program in which posters of outstanding employees were displayed alongside posters of more famous American heroes. Gerstner also successfully used modeling to promote IBM's services organization, IBM Global Services. IBM bought newspaper and magazine ads that featured its high-achieving employees, along with the employees' accomplishments. Although IBM primarily targeted its customers with this effort, the advertising campaign served the additional purpose of establishing role models for the rest of IBM's workforce. Here are some other examples:

✔ Every month, Nordstrom department stores select a Customer Service All-Star who has demonstrated the greatest commitment to customer service. From those selected for recognition, it's very clear to employees exactly what types of behaviors Nordstrom's management considers most important.

✔ Stew Leonard, of Stew Leonard's Dairy (now Stew Leonard's Farm Fresh Foods) in Norwalk, Connecticut, was well-known for his frontline leadership in his grocery store. He provided very visible employee-of-the-month recognition for those who modeled his customer-first philosophy.

- Jack Stack, chairman of Springfield Remanufacturing Corporation in Missouri, has put so much emphasis on recognizing cost-consciousness among employees that they are reputed to even know how much the toilet paper costs!

- General Electric's former chairman and CEO Jack Welsh installed a special telephone in his office for the company's purchasing agents to call him directly to report price concessions they had won from vendors so that he could thank them immediately. No matter what he was doing, he would answer the special telephone, and then he would scribble a personal congratulatory note to the agent. This became part of the GE folklore and a powerful example for other executives to follow.

Showing appreciation

Organizational recognition isn't limited to rewarding people only for quantifiable results. Recognition that's based not on the achievement of predetermined goals but on more esoteric reasons, is *appreciation* — and it's important! Thank-you events energize employees to work hard and to improve their performance. They also become ingrained in the company's culture and part of the organizational folklore.

At Dow Corning Company, management hosts ice-cream socials at which managers make and serve sundaes to thank employees for special accomplishments. Another company sends flowers to the spouses of employees who have to travel extensively. And many organizations host surprise celebrations when employees make major efforts, such as satisfying a difficult customer or meeting a rush-order deadline. These signs of appreciation can range from one company's distribution of chocolate cookies to another's celebration of a new product by parading a mariachi band through its plant, followed by an ice cream party.

Organizational versus Individual and Team Recognition

You can distinguish organizational recognition from individual and team recognition by three characteristics: extensiveness, visibility, and formality:

- **Extensiveness:** Organizational recognition affects a large number of people, both directly or indirectly. Individual and team recognition impacts much smaller numbers. Therefore, organizational recognition requires a broader, more strategic, more systemic perspective than individual and team recognition. You have to be much more aware of the consequences of putting an organizational recognition program into place, and you have to keep a close eye on its impact on employees.

✔ **Visibility:** The message you send through organizational recognition is seen or heard by many employees at all levels throughout the organization. When an award becomes highly visible, employees tend to view it quite differently than they view private, individual recognition.

Visibility can be an advantage, with the award operating as a positive model for a wide range of the company's employees, or it can be a disadvantage, because any mistakes that management makes with the recognition are greatly magnified. A supervisor who individually recognizes an undeserving employee does minimal damage, but publicly recognizing a clearly undeserving employee as part of an organization-wide program can result in enormous and long-term damage to morale, credibility, and trust.

✔ **Formality:** A characteristic of organizational recognition is a more formal structure. Such structure can be good because it increases the consistency of recognition and the likelihood that recognition will occur. The downside of a more formal structure is that it's less flexible and more difficult to change. Design flaws are hard to fix; if you change or discontinue organizational recognition, even in an attempt to make it better, employees can become demotivated and cynical about the sincerity of management when a program employees have come to expect is being changed.

Read on to find out about a few other differences between organizational and individual/team recognition.

Challenges based on type of organization

On one hand, organizational recognition is — to some extent — an elaboration of the same recognition principles I advocate with individual and team recognition. On the other hand, it does have fundamental differences and special challenges you should neither minimize nor ignore. Many companies have relatively few formal recognition programs and tools in place, and the ones that do exist have often become stale. Large companies may seem impersonal and bureaucratic when they conduct recognition, while smaller companies or nonprofits may not have adequate resources to devote to effective organizational recognition. Public organizations must be careful with how they use public funds for recognition activities, while older companies may be slow to change from noneffective, paternalistic incentives. And then, many organizations are unionized, which can restrict some recognition practices.

Degree of impact

Although individual and team recognition might be a bit more nimble, flexible, and timely than organizational recognition, the effects of individual and team recognition are more limited than organizational recognition. Without an organizational-level focus on the topic, recognition tends to be fragmented, short-lived, and inconsistent, with redundancies and cost inefficiencies throughout the organization.

With individual recognition, feedback is usually fairly immediate — you know right away whether it is effective or not. With organizational recognition programs, because of their public nature, when you make a mistake, the negative consequences are amplified and more widespread. Consider these examples:

- At a company celebration where public recognition and awards were being given out, a number of deserving employees were overlooked. Those employees felt slighted and management looked out of touch. To avoid such a scenario, double-check recognition details in advance, including the correct pronunciation of recipients' names and whether the recipient will be at the event. Every effort should be made to follow up to apologize to the slighted individuals. You may also decide to select the next public opportunity to acknowledge the overlooked employees' achievements.

- A company implemented a nonmonetary employee recognition program at the same time that large executive bonuses were being announced. Employees were not happy with the financial disparity of the two programs, and understandably viewed the recognition program with cynicism and contempt. Unfortunately, because senior managers did not receive feedback for some time, they continued with the implementation, adding insult to injury in the eyes of most employees. This well-intentioned organizational recognition program became a major demotivator. Thinking though such actions in advance and making adjustments or delaying actions can help you avoid public ridicule and a toll to morale.

- An executive team decided to stop giving out added largess for long-term years-of-service employees (airline tickets, additional time off, and cash) because executives felt the program was getting too expensive. They ended the program with little advance notice and promised that something better was coming, but that "something better" had yet to be planned. Eliminating popular benefits without a plan for doing something else will always be viewed as a something that was taken away, resulting in a detrimental impact on morale.

Whereas people typically view an individual award as the isolated action of an individual supervisor or peer, and a team award as a team-focused activity, they see an organizational award as an organizational validation of their efforts.

The "permanence" of recognition

The individuals who take the initiative to recognize others typically don't receive much recognition or support themselves. If those high-use managers leave the organization or transfer to a different department, their recognition efforts leave with them.

As you expand and institutionalize your recognition efforts at the organizational level, you can increase the scope and impact of your efforts to encompass the whole company, and deeply and more permanently affect the culture of the organization in positive, productive, and meaningful ways.

Strategies for Implementing Organizational Recognition

Changing the recognition practices of your whole organization can seem daunting, but it is doable. To make organizational recognition a reality in your company, you can start in one of these three places:

- **At the top:** One or more senior executives decides that the organization needs a recognition program. If you're not at the top, you can approach someone at the top and ask whether that person is willing to support and sponsor the effort.

- **In the middle:** A manager, group, or unit within the organization designs a recognition program that expands to the rest of the organization.

- **At the bottom:** An individual or team recognition initiative is expanded throughout the organization, sometimes with such success that it changes the organizational practices and culture.

In this section, I look briefly at each of these starting points.

Starting at the top

A significant amount of organizational recognition begins with a CEO's or other top executive's inspiration. I've seen organizational recognition programs that involve an executive funding a budget line for recognition or asking a direct report to start a recognition initiative. That person can help lead a recognition task force to focus on the topic, set up annual or quarterly events to do organizational recognition, and establish an information feedback system to keep the CEO informed of various individual, departmental, and organizational successes as they occur.

Here are two examples of organizational recognition programs that started at the top:

✔ After reading about Japanese suggestion programs, Martin Edelston, CEO of Boardroom, Inc., in Greenwich, Connecticut, decided that his company needed one. His initial effort to recognize employee suggestions for improvement had such a positive impact on employee creativity and morale that it was expanded into I-Power, a formal program that uses a lot of social recognition and some very small monetary rewards to generate a large number of employee suggestions. As one employee said, "I never realized that making suggestions could be so much fun. Marty, as the CEO of the organization, saw the need and made it happen!" The program has evolved to now include quarterly profit gain-sharing for all employees who participate in the program. For more on the I-Power program, see Chapter 2.

✔ At WS Packaging Group in Green Bay, Wisconsin, launched a profit-sharing program with monthly bonus meetings called STP ("share the profit"), where the company shares information on every line item of its budget. The company shares profits that exceed company goals (if a loss occurs, bonuses are put on hold until the losses are recovered). In addition to launching this program, company leadership continues to provide monthly support to drive desired results.

Starting in the middle

In this scenario, an individual or group within the organization might sponsor a program to recognize the most productive, the most quality-conscious, or the safest employees. It's not unusual for the success of such a program to get the attention of other divisions and of senior management. After all, nothing succeeds like success! These successful functional programs are often expanded or are replicated in other locations or throughout the organization.

If you're having a difficult time getting support to launch a recognition program company-wide, start within your own department. Once you've proven the efficacy of your efforts in your own ranks, it's a lot easier to have it spread to other parts of the organization.

Here are some examples that all started with a manager trying something that caught on, was repeated, embellished, and expanded, and then came to be part of these organizations' lore and tradition:

✔ **Hewlett Packard** in Sunnyvale, California, uses the Golden Banana Award. It's a classic story of the HP software engineer who, having fixed a software bug, burst into his manager's office to announce his success. His manager, who recognized the importance of timely recognition, wanted to do something right away. He groped around his desk and handed the engineer a banana from his lunch with the words, "Great job! I knew you could do it!" The employee showed everyone around the office the banana the boss had given him and explained why. The story took hold, HP repeated the award, and added elements such as a lapel pin of a banana to commemorate the recipient. Soon the Golden Banana was the highest honor for technical achievement in the organization.

✔ **The Walt Disney World Dolphin & Swan Resort** in Orlando, Florida, uses Captain Wow. Initially the resort printed "Wow!" cards — tri-folded wallet cards made from different colored construction paper — with which employees and managers could provide a quick written thank you to others who wowed a customer or another employee. As that program unfolded, participants soon expanded the concept to include creation of their very own superhero, Captain Wow, who, wearing a motorcycle helmet and cape, drops by regularly to thank people for providing great service to others.

The evolution from a one-time award

And here's yet another example of the evolution of recognition from a one-time celebration to an ongoing tradition. "We used to reward just the salespeople (customer service reps) when they did something good, but the rest of the staff felt left out since they weren't 'selling,'" says vice president Patty Nuzzo of Restaurant Equipment World (REW), of Orlando, Florida, so the company started throwing celebration parties when there was good news to share.

Nuzzo comments, "The parties help us recognize the people behind the scenes who help the salespeople. For example, our web development staff keeps the websites up to date; our warehouse staff ships out the orders to the E-Com customers; the accounting staff keeps the bills paid on time so that our merchandise ships in a timely manner from manufacturers. We want our people to work as a team so that customers get the same level of service no matter how little or how much they spend. Our theory is that if we did quotas, commissions, and bonuses, the little orders would get ignored."

In recent years, celebrations have since ventured outside of the office to avoid workday interruptions as well as to give employees more of an opportunity to bond. Trips have included visits to a factory to make chocolate, group cooking lessons, pottery classes, bowling, laser tag, and an outing to an outdoor high-rope and zip-line park.

"It's a good return on investment," says Nuzzo, who takes photos of evening activities and displays them in the cafeteria the following day. "People immediately run to check them out. Anyone who attended has happy memories of the night before, and those who didn't go wish they had after seeing the pictures. They really seem to enjoy the evening outings, especially the warehouse staff. They attend everything we do; accounting, too. We get a mix of salespeople, depending on their schedules. It's nice to see them do things as a group where everyone is equal, regardless of their role in the company. We have been able to retain a lot of great people because of the friendships they make at work."

The company now throws million-dollar parties for everyone in the company when a department reaches $1 million in sales.

How do you put a price tag on teamwork?

Starting at the bottom

Although not as common as the previous two starting points, spontaneous awards occasionally do evolve into major organizational awards. There are literally hundreds of examples in which team or department recognition gains visibility and sponsorship and is expanded to other areas in the organization.

One of my favorites is the Spirit of Fred award I discuss in Chapter 5, which originated with an employee named Fred and spread to become a full-blown organizational recognition philosophy. Here's another: Janitors on a shift at the Worthington Renaissance Hotel in Ft. Worth, Texas, decided to acknowledge the particularly meritorious work of one colleague by presenting him with a broom in an on-the-job ceremony. This spontaneous recognition evolved into a highly successful ongoing program aptly named The Golden Broom Award.

The Importance of Strategic Recognition

While you might be able to get away with winging it when it comes to your individual or even team recognition, you can't really do that on the organizational level. With so much at stake, you really need to strategically plan and implement your recognition initiatives.

In my research, 89 percent of today's employees report recognition is very or extremely important to them. If, in the years ahead, you want to attract and retain top talent, your organization needs to be exceptional at recognizing employees in ways they value. If you want to maximize the performance of those individuals who work for your organization, recognition is a key driver for obtaining that performance, yet your organization might be wasting as much as 90 cents of every dollar it currently spends on reward and incentive programs. In fact, I guarantee this is the case if you fund your reward and incentive programs, year after year, based simply on what you budgeted the previous year.

This doesn't mean you need to scrap your recognition programs; it just means you need to 1) better align your recognition efforts to drive strategic objectives and 2) shift your focus from programs to desired behaviors and results. Doing so fosters a broader organizational culture of performance, recognition, and engagement.

Using recognition to drive strategic objectives

Research shows that the best forms of recognition are performance-based, yet many organizations spend the bulk of their recognition dollars on programs that reinforce presence over performance, such as years-of service awards, holiday parties, and birthdays.

Organizations have typically used incentive programs in a reactive way: Sales are flat? Install an incentive program to spark business and get the sales force cranking. Insurance costs on the rise? Institute a safety program to incentivize reduced accident claims. Quality is off? Install a quality program to reduce errors and defects.

This piecemeal approach to using incentives leads to uneven and redundant efforts and inconsistent results that can be counterproductive to the organization's overall goals. If your organization has taken the time and effort to clearly establish a core mission, values, and strategies, then your reward and recognition systems should clearly and systematically reward the behaviors and results that reinforce those elements.

The more recognition activities and programs drive significant organizational performance and strategic results, the easier it is to justify the effort and resources needed to support them. To do this, you must reverse the evaluation strategy and begin with the end in mind; that is, instead of engaging in some recognition activities and asking whether they were effective after the fact, specifically link the recognition and incentives to the desired results you are after in advance.

To obtain consistent recognition efforts, you must have effective measurement strategies in place. As my former professor, Peter Drucker, used to say, "If you can't measure it, you can't manage it." While many human resources processes are notoriously difficult to measure, recognition need not be one of them. You can measure recognition effectiveness by its ability to produce results and desired performance, such as progress towards specific goals.

So how do you best measure recognition? First, clearly understand what your employees want and value. Then define the results you desire. Starting with a clear idea of your audience, and the goals and performances you want from them, strengthens the link between recognition and organizational results, now and in the long term.

According to psychologist Donald Kirkpatrick, four levels of measurement are relevant to measuring desired outcomes.

Level 1: Reaction

The first level of measurement is often an emotive response to the question, "Do you feel recognized at work?" that uses a scale of 1 (didn't like it) to 5 (thought it was excellent). This measure often surfaces in employee attitude surveys. When morale is low, employees typically rank one or more of the following items very low:

- ✔ "My manager recognizes me when I do good work."
- ✔ "My manager makes time for me when I need to talk."
- ✔ "My manager has discussed my future career aspirations with me."
- ✔ "I feel appreciated for the work I do."
- ✔ "I feel I'm a valuable member of the team/department."

Level 2: Learning

The second level of evaluation deals with what employees learned from the behavior. Kirkpatrick defines learning as the "extent to which participants change attitudes, improve knowledge, and/or increase skill."

As it applies to recognition, you can measure how certain skill or awareness levels have changed based on recognition training or the rollout of one or more recognition programs. Executives can ask managers(before and after recognition training) how important it is to recognize employees, how often they should do so, in what types of situations recognition is appropriate, and in what ways. In a seminar, managers can learn guidelines for effective praising and be allowed to practice the skill, taking advantage of feedback from others. Other measurable recognition skills include knowing how to praise publicly, how to write a persuasive nomination for an employee award, and what forms of recognition work well for different types of performance.

Level 3: Behavior

The third level of measurement involves the impact of recognition back on the job. Employees often learn new skills in training programs and then never use those skills after they return to work. Simply involving their managers in discussing ways to use newly learned skills on the job can make a significant difference in the use of those skills. The evaluation is somewhat easier if the measurement is established as part of the program (for example, a tracking report) and not as a separate activity to be done later.

Level 4: Results

If the recognition isn't getting desired results, it doesn't matter how people feel about it or how good they are at using it. Even when the intent of a program is simply to increase employee morale, indirect measures exist (or can be built) to examine the results of the program's effectiveness beyond morale. Here are some examples of recognition questions you can ask about results:

- ✔ What is the impact of employee recognition on improving the business?
- ✔ How much is recognition helping to increase revenues? Lower costs?
- ✔ How much does recognition reduce absenteeism? Turnover?
- ✔ Is employee recognition improving customer satisfaction?
- ✔ Is team recognition enhancing inter- and intradepartmental cooperation?
- ✔ Are safety recognition programs increasing safe behavior and reducing accidents?
- ✔ Are quality award programs increasing product quality?

Usually results are defined as the bottom-line outcomes of the organization (such as profits, sales, and so on), but the tendency to reduce everything to financial terms is dangerous because it trivializes many nonfinancial organizational effectiveness measures. Kaplan and Norton's "balanced scorecard," which has revolutionized management thinking about organizational evaluation, is a response to this bean-counting, quantifying mentality.

Shifting from a focus on programs to a focus on behaviors

The second major challenge is shifting from a focus on finite recognition programs to an emphasis on recognizing desired behaviors and results.

Historically, recognition efforts in most organizations start with an event, such as a celebration for some organizational milestone (making a sales goal or recognizing employees who have been with the company for ten years, for example); then, over time, those efforts become institutionalized as programs.

Today, the primary focus of effective recognition efforts is to create a true culture of recognition — one that doesn't start and end with launching programs or hosting one-off events but that is ever-present throughout the organization. The trend in progressive organizations is to create a recognition philosophy and recognition platform that allows for a decentralized focus on customization and flexibility on the frontline manager level.

Embracing recognition as a competitive advantage

Formal and informal rewards and recognition provide effective ways of encouraging higher levels of performance from employees. Yet few organizations embrace recognition as a competitive advantage in achieving their organizational missions, strategies, and objectives. The challenges and opportunities for executives to have an impact in their organizations are significant in the area of rewards and recognition.

By moving rewards and recognition from being a "nice to have" organizational perk to a "have to have" strategy for obtaining and enhancing performance, any organization has the ability to tap into a wellspring of energy that its employees are ready to bring to bear in helping the organization reach its goals and objectives.

The Four Phases of Organizational Recognition

Now you're ready to put your money where your mouth is — or, rather, to put your program where your planning was. Putting organizational recognition programs into practice involves four key phases: the design phase, the planning phase, the implementation phase, and the management phase. I end this chapter by providing a quick overview of these phases. When properly executed, organizational recognition will have a profound and positive effect on your organization's employees and bottom line.

The design phase

Everyone can appreciate the importance of a blueprint for a house. No matter how outstanding the subsequent construction work might be, the house will be no more functional than the blueprint design permitted. Likewise, no matter how well-constructed a bridge or a road is, if there are serious design flaws, neither the bridge nor the road will be safe to travel. While individual or team recognition is much more dependent on the initiative and skill of the recognition givers, organizational recognition is more dependent on the design of the program.

The planning phase

After you design an organizational recognition program, you need to develop an implementation plan. Here's a six-step organizational recognition planning process that helps you use your program design to successfully implement a program that will get the kind of results your organization wants and needs:

1. **Make an action plan.**

   This is the heart of the planning phase. Consider and write down all the steps needed to make your program design operational.

2. **Set a schedule.**

   Lay out the proposed timeframe for implementing your plan of action. Consider starting with the date you want to launch the program and work backward to set other deadlines.

3. **Detail your resource requirements.**

   List all the resources — human and otherwise — that your program requires for successful implementation.

4. **Set a budget.**

   Take into consideration all factors, all resources, and all contingencies, and write out the estimated cost of the program.

5. **Think through potential obstacles and factors that could result in your program failing and identify preventive actions you can take.**

   Make sure to take time to think about and list the factors that, if not addressed, could cause the program to fail or fall short of expectations. Also include the preventive actions that you should take to avoid or mitigate the possible impact of these obstacles.

6. **Write out a measurement strategy.**

   Decide and record what approach you want to take to determine how well the program implementation is going.

The implementation phase

After you design your organizational recognition program and develop the program plan, you can begin implementation. As the saying goes, "Once you plan your work, you need to work your plan." During the implementation phase, you work your plan. How well you implement the program is as important as how well the program is designed. As leading organizational systems expert John Keller explains, "The implementation of a motivational system, like the implementation of any other innovation, requires the use of strategies for change management, to gain approval, support, and participation." Follow the steps that you outlined and stay focused.

The management phase

You must manage organizational recognition programs as well as you implement them. Implementation will get organizational recognition programs launched, but that initial launch is not enough to float the program for very long. Understanding and managing this life cycle is critical to the ultimate success of your organizational recognition programs. The one constant in organizations is change. Organizational recognition must be kept dynamic and actively managed to address all the shifting circumstances, conditions, and problems that might occur.

Organizational recognition the Chevron way

The Chevron Corporation, based in San Francisco, California, is an international company that produces energy and chemical products and employs about 65,000 employees worldwide. To maintain and reinforce desired employee performance behaviors, Chevron has developed a set of corporate recognition and award guidelines each division uses to design its own specific recognition program. In addition, Chevron has developed a company-wide recognition program called the Chairman's Award, which rewards individuals or teams who've achieved extraordinary accomplishments, such as developing new technology, making work progress improvements, or designing innovative solutions to complex problems.

Although Chevron's programs seem robust now, that wasn't always that way. Chevron got exposed to the best practices of another company, Eastman Chemical, who had been incorporating recognition programs into its organization and was seeing great business success. Chevron's executives realized that, if they wanted their employees to do more — if they wanted them to push the envelope — then the organization would need to encourage and reinforce its employees' potential by rewarding the behaviors that company executives wanted to see again.

Natural reinforcers

The most effective reinforcement comes from what Chevron calls the "natural" reinforcers. For example, if you turn the key in your car, the car starting is a natural reinforcement that you'll do again and again to get the result you want (the car to start). The problem is that these natural reinforcers are not always present for the behaviors that organizations need to be successful. Even incentive programs can be limiting because, after the goal is attained and the reward received, there is no incentive to continue to do more. An employee who is paid to talk to a certain number of customers per day, for example, will work only to the set goal.

Therefore, Chevron tries not to set limits. The real goal is to use recognition as a business tool — to reinforce and encourage behaviors that are good for the business.

Chevron is training all managers on "reinforcement-based leadership." In this training initiative program, managers learn about positive and negative reinforcers — when to use consequences to continue and extinguish behaviors.

The Chairman's Award

Chevron has a corporate-wide formal recognition program called the Chairman's Award that is given out for exceptional performance. The company wanted something that was exclusive and meaningful yet that everyone could strive to attain. All employees are eligible. For example, one division saved the company millions of dollars; consequently, Chevron gave everyone in that division the Chairman's Award because it was a team effort. Everyone contributed, and all were awarded equally.

Customized recognition programs in each division

In addition to the Chairman's Award, each division develops its own customized recognition programs as well. If a division needs help in setting up a recognition program, it can always ask the training group for help with designing and implementing their program. The trainers first help the division clarify its business goals. Next, they help the division determine what behaviors are needed to meet those goals. Finally, the trainers work through the nuts and bolts of the best ways to reward and recognize the desired behaviors in the division's employees. They encourage the divisions to have equitable programs with very clear criteria for recognition — specific criteria ("volunteering to support a project," for example) rather than vague criteria (such as "going above and beyond the call of duty").

As a consequence, all of Chevron's divisions have some type of recognition program, but they are all very different and are customized to reward the specific behaviors that make that particular division successful. In one group, for example, everyone has signature authority to purchase recognition and reward items without formal approval, empowering individuals in the organization to reward as they see fit. In another division, committees evaluate nominations for awards, using scoring charts. Some groups use only instant awards — coupons worth $20, for example, that anyone can give to anyone.

Proven success

Overall, employee recognition at Chevron has improved dramatically over the years. The company does not track informal recognition, but the percentage of employees who have been formally recognized has doubled in just over five years. The company also conducts worldwide employee surveys to measure people's perceptions of feeling appreciated and getting recognized for the right things, and the numbers from these surveys improve each year. Recognition is highly valued and explicitly encouraged at Chevron. Everyone is encouraged to integrate the principles and philosophies of the Chevron Way into their day-to-day lives.

Part VI
Creating and Sustaining a Culture of Recognition

Top Five Ways Technology Helps Sustain Recognition

- **Makes integrating with business operations easier.** Technology helps business leaders and managers identify specific opportunities and provides clear recommendations on where and how to close performance gaps; it outlines how recognition benefits the bottom line; and it integrates all this information with real-time employee intelligence data that enables managers to impact key business outcomes.

- **Enables companies to consolidate their recognition and reward programs across the organization into a single over-arching system.** An online recognition platform allows for greater effectiveness, coordination, administration, and tracking and leads to reduced redundancy, waste, and administration costs to the organization.

- **Provides flexibility.** Having a recognition program that can adjust to the changing needs and priorities of your organization is important in these dynamic times. Rather than years-of-service awards, birthdays, or holiday parties, recognition can focus on the current year's strategic initiatives, core company values, or cost-saving ideas, for example.

- **Taps into social media.** Research by the Cicero Group shows the benefits of recognition get amplified six times when integrated with social media tools.

- **Gives greater choice in accessing reward options and activities.** Having an online reward selection allows you to add the latest products as they are available — as well as nonmerchandise items like travel, experiences, and so on.

 web extras

Find out more about current management trends that are influencing managers' efforts to sustain recognition and engagement at www.dummies.com/ extras/recognizingandengagingemployees.

In this part . . .

✔ Automate, streamline, and be more effective with your recognition efforts by using the technological tools outlined in this part

✔ Link your recognition efforts to the different departments, protocols, and policies so that they become part of the institution

✔ Anticipate and overcome common challenges to keep your recognition moving in a positive way

Chapter 12

Recognition and Technology

In This Chapter

▶ Recognizing the benefits of rewards and recognition technology

▶ Overcoming challenges of using recognition technology

▶ Anticipating the future of technology and recognition

More and more companies are applying technology solutions to their recognition efforts. This move creates a tremendous opportunity, but it also poses a number of challenges. This chapter discusses the pros and pitfalls of using technology for employee recognition, the gamut of technology that is being used for this purpose, strategies for setting up an effective online recognition and rewards program, and a look to the future.

The Pros of Rewards and Recognition Technology

Constructive use of technology can go a long way toward creating more positive working relationships and a more supportive work environment that better drives employee performance, productivity, and morale. Using technology for rewards and recognition today offers numerous benefits. In this section, I outline a few of the major ones.

Facilitating integration with business operations

Recognition is becoming an increasingly more important aspect of business productivity, and its scope and application is rapidly evolving to include increased customization, personalization, and accessibility. As organizations apply technology across all aspects of their operations, they are including recognition in the effort.

In addition, executives no longer invest in employee recognition and engagement merely because it's the right thing to do; instead, they need to see the impact recognition has on the business. With technology, they can identify specific opportunities that offer clear recommendations on where and how to close performance gaps and that outline how recognition benefits the bottom line — all integrated with real-time data to impact key business outcomes.

Consolidating recognition efforts, budgets, and administration

Most companies strive to consolidate their recognition and reward programs across the organization (recognition done geographically or by department, ad hoc rewards, and all other incentives) into a single overarching system. An online recognition platform allows for greater effectiveness, coordination, administration, and tracking, and leads to reduced redundancy, waste, and administration costs to the organization.

Allowing flexibility in response to changing needs

In these dynamic times, you need a recognition program that can adjust to the changing needs and priorities of your organization. Most recognition programs I've seen in companies tend to be plopped on the organization and operate independently of the organization's strategic objectives and needs. As a result, management spends excessive time, effort, and financial resources on activities that have little, if any, impact on the success of the organization.

Take years-of-service awards, birthday celebrations, and holiday parties. How much better would it be to have recognition that focuses on the current year's strategic initiatives, core company values, cost-saving ideas, hiring of talent, or client referrals? Multichannel recognition like this is possible (and you can run it all simultaneously) with an effective online recognition program.

Tapping into favorite social media outlets

Research by the Cicero Group shows that the benefits of recognition get amplified six times when integrated with social media tools. Properly utilized, social media can successfully combine public recognition for positive performance with the latest social communication technologies that connect a significant percentage of employees. For example, just as HR directors increasingly use social media for recruiting and marketing, they can also use it for broadcasting employee achievements to others within the company or to the public in general.

Social recognition is easier to do when you use social networks that are especially popular with the younger generations (which, incidentally, currently represent 58 percent — and growing — of today's workforce), and it's more powerful as well.

Offering greater freedom of choice

Making your rewards accessible online (whether through the web, a software application, or company intranet) provides an expanded choice of rewards; not just traditional rewards, such as plaques or logoed items. Having an online, brand-name reward selection allows you to add the latest products as they become available, as well as nonmerchandise items like travel, experiences, charitable donations, or green options (rewards that support conservation or sustainability initiatives). You can even allow virtual redemptions, where you recognize employees with debit cards that they can use like cash with whatever vendors you select. An effective online rewards platform also allows employees to create wish lists of rewards they would like to receive, making the process even more meaningful for them.

Easier tracking and reporting of recognition program success

An online recognition and rewards platform allows you to track and report on recognition and correlate the use of recognition with performance. In so doing, you will be able to make better decisions and improvements to the program as you go. You can enter every recognition, reward, and inquiry, and then easily pull this information to see how the reward program is trending, identify top performers, and make connections to your business objectives. Tracking all recognition online makes it easy for managers and employees to access the data they need to monitor progress.

Overcoming Challenges of Recognition Technology

Although today's office technology can help you work more efficiently, it also has the potential to alienate employees by creating more distance in work relationships. Each year, employees spend more time interfacing with their computers than they spend in face-to-face interactions with their bosses or coworkers. Ironically, the more "connected" we become, the less "connection" we seem to have to one another at work. As John Naisbitt predicted in his classic book *Megatrends: Ten New Directions Transforming Our Lives* (Grand Central Publishing), the more high-tech we become, the more high-touch we need to be to assimilate the technology; that is, the more that technology dominates our lives, the greater the need to establish and promote personal bonds with others to have meaning in our work and lives.

Another not so great trend has emerged: A recent study by Pitney Bowes on messaging tools and practices reveals that U.S. workers now receive over 200 messages per day — more than ever before. Globally, that amounts to an estimated *20 billion daily e-mail messages*, 40 percent of which is spam.

What's the impact of this constant bombardment of messages and increased use of office technology? And what can be done to minimize the problems of increased technology use? A lot. This section offers some advice that can help you keep the human element a priority at work.

Get to know people before you communicate

All rapport comes from shared experiences, which help to promote trust and respect among employees. This is key to every successful working relationship, but rapport is difficult to establish if you use only one-way, electronic communication. Since an estimated 90 percent of all communication occurs at the nonverbal level, what you don't see in your interactions because you're communicating online may hurt your relationships. If you send an e-mail to a colleague while you are upset, your negative energy quickly disperses, but your colleague has no way of knowing you are no longer upset and is more hesitant in his or her future dealings with you. If at all possible, get to know the people personally before communicating with them via e-mail. Another good rule to follow is to be more diligent in being friendly and courteous when you use online communication with your colleagues.

Be aware of technology's limitations when you communicate

Don't allow electronic communication to replace a personal meeting just for efficiency's sake. Before shooting off a message, take time to consider whether voicemail or e-mail is truly sufficient, or whether a personal meeting would be better. Avoid the use of electronic communication for dealing with sensitive or complex issues, which are better dealt with in face-to-face interactions. Even if is just to thank or praise someone, doing so personally and face-to-face will have a much greater personal impact than an e-mail alone. If the recognition is truly warranted, invest some time to personally connect with the other personal to thank him or her, if possible.

Use electronic communication to enhance, not degrade, relationships

Resist the urge to include criticisms with your positive e-mails. No one likes to hear, "You did great, but next time . . . ." Just leave it at "You did great." "But" is essentially a verbal eraser that deletes the value of what you initially said.

Copy related supervisors and peers on the e-mail for extra validation. For example, I know a manager who copies his boss on all praising e-mails he sends to any of his employees. When it comes time for him to do performance reviews and salary actions for his direct reports, his boss always agrees with his recommendations because he's been kept in the loop the entire year.

Use the power of technology to amplify good news

It's easy to forward e-mails to your employees, describing problems and directing them to fix the problems immediately, but you also have to find ways to instantly pass on good news to your staff when it occurs. One way is simply to forward positive e-mail messages that you receive when you receive them.

At Hughes Network Systems in San Diego, California, employees use an Applause electronic pop-up bulletin board on their Intranet system. Any employee can post public thanks and recognition to any other employee using the Applause bulletin board, and all employees get to see the most recent thanks each time they log on to their computers. In these days of relentless pressure and change in most organizations, hearing what's going well becomes a salve that helps to relieve stress and frustrations.

Try to be creative in how you use technology

Don't just stop at "job well done" e-mails. Technology can help you include others in discussions and decision-making that might have been left out in the past because finding a way to involve them was too cumbersome.

Home Depot used to schedule a weekly satellite feed to every store. Called "Breakfast with Bernie and Arthur" (their chairman and CEO at that time), these "breakfasts" gave everyone a chance to hear at the same time what was new and how things were going. And A.G. Edwards, the financial services company, has a weekly audio conference that includes every employee. Another company audiotapes a monthly message to employees that they can listen to at their convenience in their car. Web chats, message boards, and dedicated phone lines that enable employee access to top management are other ways companies can use technology to help their employees be more connected.

Using Technology for Recognition

Despite the (real or perceived) risk of "dehumanizing" communication, I believe you can use technology to actually *reinforce* human connection at work and increase opportunities to provide meaningful recognition and appreciation to others. Doing so won't likely happen by accident, but with a little forethought and planning on your part, technology can help you do more than simply complete work more quickly; it can help you build trust and develop relationships.

Companies often get stuck in patterns of behavior, even as employee preferences evolve. Some firms continue, for example, continue to give out traditional employee rewards even though employees would prefer more social recognition, which has the advantage of increased timeliness. As I explain throughout this book, employees want their work to be purposeful and have meaning. Companies therefore must do a better job of connecting the dots between employee tasks, corporate mission, and their recognition efforts. They can do so by adding more inspiration and motivation via online recognition platforms and communications. Most companies have moved to using a Cloud-based online SaaS (service-as-a-software) technology platform to drive their online recognition and rewards program.

One way to increasingly integrate recognition with company experiences is to use social networks. Social networking is already used for recruiting and branding and in other areas as well. Such recognition technology can be used to welcome and orient new employees, and to empower employees to initiate giving, as well as getting, recognition. In this way, recognition can help reinforce corporate values and corporate culture and encourage employees to live those values and thereby enable companies to attract and retain the best employees.

In this section, I outline some fundamental ways you can use technology in your recognition efforts.

Mobile — anywhere you are

Just as work doesn't end when employees leave the office, great performance doesn't either. According to Cisco, 60 percent of office workers use a mobile device for work (and that percentage is only going to grow as employees across the board become more dependent on their mobile devices). Most employees now have smartphones, and they expect to be able to interact with work-related technology in the same way they do with social media and texting, which means your recognition and incentive programs need to follow suit if you want to remain relevant.

Among other features, make sure you can track attendance and approve awards nominations through mobile devices. Also ensure that employees can redeem awards at any time convenient for them and from any web-enabled device they choose. Other mobile functions that add value include leaderboards (for managers who provide the greatest number of recognitions), badges (for mastered work skills by employees), discussion forums, and an events calendar.

Mobile is increasingly the recognition platform of choice. With more than 162 million mobile phone Internet users and 140 million tablet users in the U.S., all organizations must ensure that recognition platforms are fully accessible on mobile devices. New apps such as Culture Amp, Glint, and Waggl that can instantly provide management with anonymous survey responses and feedback about questions and problems perceived by employees are constantly being created.

Voicemail — a quick way to say thanks

How did we ever survive before voicemail? As useful as this tool is for communicating, most of us have had times when we felt we were a slave to the message system. Instead of task-oriented messages, consider also leaving positive voicemails simply to thank others for something they've done well. When you do, don't offer any criticism or assign additional work; simply say thanks. A great voicemail (from a client or customer, for example) can even be transcribed and distributed.

E-mail — put it in writing

When you have an e-mail praising to send to someone, copy that person's manager or others in the recipient's department. When you get a positive e-mail about someone's performance, pass it on to others or print it out and save the message to share in person or in an upcoming staff meeting. If appropriate, the message could even be posted in the department or company, or slipped into the employee's personnel file.

Texting — another quick way to praise

Leaving a text message of quick thanks is really easy. Doing so can be especially important in work settings, such as restaurants, hospitality, retail, and so on, where employees may not readily have access to a computer.

Video — the next best thing to being there

It's estimated that the U.S. has 190 million digital video viewers, and video is becoming quite a popular tool in recognition. With phones and computers that record and even help you edit footage, managers can easily incorporate videos into their communications. Increasingly, employees are submitting videos as part of nomination processes for recognition. This use of video is beneficial since the format captures emotions and tone in a way that the written word can't. Conveying recognition by video will only grow in popularity, replacing recognition delivered through text-dominated media. Videos bring recognition into living color and are the next-best thing to recognizing someone in person!

Social media — underutilized but effective

Although this is the age of social media, social media is underutilized in recognition. According to recent survey data, 98 percent of HR respondents said they believe that social networking is an important tool for recruiting, retaining, and managing employees, yet 43 percent of companies still restrict access to social networking sites. Connecting with and recognizing employees through social media (Facebook, LinkedIn, Twitter, Instagram, and Tumblr, for example) is critical for recognition programs in the future.

Most incentive companies have developed social recognition solutions. Some have apps that automatically post to news feeds so the public can see and share in the celebration. And some have a "recognition wall" that allows people to add personalized congratulatory messages to employees' posted achievements.

Virtual applications — great for off-site employees

Companies are becoming increasingly more virtual (according to Global Workplace Analytics, the demand for telework has grown by 80 percent since 2005), and you can leverage technology to deliver consistent, efficient, and appropriate recognition to employees wherever they are. The Internet provides a wide range of recognition opportunities: You can send virtual flowers, virtual greeting cards, or virtual postcards. Or use an "Applause" bulletin board, another great example that was suggested in the earlier section "Use the power of technology to amplify good news."

Anyone can post a public praising for anyone else in the organization on the electronic bulletin board, and most employees take a moment or two to read the praisings prior to going about their work. The praisings scroll off the bulletin board after a few days.

Customized reward options — include online rewards, too

To be successful and to achieve maximum impact, the types of awards your recognition program offers need to be diverse, and your reward program needs to include significant flexibility because reward preferences vary so significantly. Awards may include merchandise, gift cards, e-codes, travel, charitable contributions, auctions, branded items, paid time off, premium contributions, career development, and more. Creating truly unique experiences may include any combination of online and offline program elements. Use order history, popularity trends, and comment rating and reviews to devise the elements that best suit your company and recognition program.

Consider letting your employees customize the award offerings. The more they can be involved, the greater chance they will use the features that are developed. Doing so is a key part of a dynamic, successful program experience.

Analytics and data integration — for recognition in real time

Technology can help you go beyond annual performance reviews and get a more holistic view of employees' contributions on a daily basis. After you input employees' goals into the recognition system, you can track and encourage employees by recognizing their achieving milestones along the way.

You can integrate sales incentive programs with Salesforce.com and other customer relationship management (CRM) systems so you don't have to log activity in two places. Integrating with a human resource information system (HRIS) to receive employee data and send payroll information is more commonplace today, but expect these types of services to continue to grow.

Once you're collecting data, real-time analytics helps you analyze it. Such analytics give you a better understanding of who gives recognition, who receives it, how frequently either occurs, the kinds of recognition given, and results of recognition. You can also access information about the recipients and their recognized behaviors. Such insights allow you to better connect and engage emotionally with your people and make better workplace decisions.

As time moves on, analytical reporting tools and predictive analytics will continue to expand, so plan accordingly. Your recognition technology will need to incorporate additional data streams if you want to continue to enhance and update the effectiveness of your recognition efforts.

Other ways to use technology for recognition

Creating an environment in which employees recognize one another and get rewarded for doing so helps generate stronger manager-to-employee relationships, which in turn helps to improve employee morale. Technology can help, with applications like print-on-demand services (for certificates), mobile interactions (like an app for submitting recognition nominations), and integration with client systems (like registers). You can use the data to offer tailored reward suggestions, experiences, or communications and thus increase program engagement.

There are also other ways to use technology:

- **Gamification:** Companies are increasingly using gaming techniques to increase participation and engagement levels in recognition programs, making tools, programs, and contests more fun for participants.

- **Debit cards:** Almost all the major incentive houses now offer debit cards on which employees receive points when they meet some performance-related criteria; they can then use those points to purchase merchandise they select.

- **Knowledge, guidance, and tips for recognizing others:** When someone enters a recognition, you can have the recognition system show tips or guidance — what to mention in the recognition message, for example, or the suggested award point range for the achievement.

- **Recognition outside of the platform:** Some integrated online recognition systems are configured to pull e-mail praisings from Outlook based on subject line content and automatically copy it over to the recognition platform.

Be on the lookout for the opportunities for even greater interactivity. For example, you can use QR codes on gift packaging or awards to create an ongoing interactive communication element, making recognition into an interactive two-way dialogue! (A QR code is a graphic that someone can scan with a smartphone app. When scanned, the code directs the user to a new screen or links to a website where that person can get more information or access content about the item that enhances the employee experience.)

Seven Keys to a Successful Online Recognition Program

The best online reward and recognition programs have the following characteristics, each of which can be built into your program:

- ✔ **They are results-driven.** The best online recognition programs focus on the performance you most want to drive in your organization. All performance starts with clear goals and expectations, so you need to first give consideration to what performance and results you most want to achieve so that you can be sure that your rewards and recognition program specifically addresses those objectives.

- ✔ **They engage all members of the organization.** Recognition is not just a top-down, manager-driven activity, but should encompass all levels and locations of the organization, including peer-to-peer, employee-to-manager, manager-to-manager, executive-to-employee, and so on. They should even involve the organization's customers and vendors, where possible. Recognition must be available and accessible to *everyone* in the organization if it is to provide important and reliable feedback and help you create an organizational culture that essentially has recognition "without borders." Technology is the most viable way to achieve this objective in today's organizations.

- ✔ **They are custom-branded.** The customized online platform is branded to your organization. Whatever online solution you select needs to be customized to fit your organization seamlessly. Some organizations want to include certain options and brands, and use specific information for their recognition websites. They also want the flexibility to add or modify recognition tools that can be integrated within the program. Whatever you choose, make sure the online solution you select enables you to run simultaneous recognition programs.

- ✔ **They offer enhanced communication for launching (and sustaining) recognition use.** Communication is an important aspect of any recognition program, not only in initially launching the program, but also in systematically sustaining the initiative over time. Online recognition provides a more timely and less costly answer to communicating about the recognition program launch, but it also provides a way to ensure ongoing communication about the program, highlighting its successes and providing education and reminders that will help sustain the program's success.

✔ **They are effectively launched and inspire employee buy-in and excitement.** Any effective recognition program needs a successful launch. A successful launch includes training for both the organization's recognition program administrator, as well as training for everyone expected to effectively use the program. In addition, managers should receive training on the importance of recognition and how they can best integrate recognition into their daily practices at work. This last point is essential, given that my research indicates that the main reason managers don't use recognition is because they are not sure how to do it well.

ConAgra aligns employees with objectives, using online recognition

ConAgra Foods, a leading food company, had a recognition program. However, when an annual employee engagement survey revealed that 75 percent of ConAgra's employees were not satisfied with it, the leadership team decided to relaunch it. They implemented a program that helped align employees to company goals and improve employee engagement scores. Their four main objectives were to create a culture of recognition, meet diverse needs of their people, customize a program that fit the ConAgra culture, and make the program easier to use and manage.

ConAgra Canada partnered with an incentive company to create an online, points-based employee recognition program for all ConAgra employees. In the program, called "You Made a Difference," employees are awarded points from their managers and peers for exhibiting behaviors that are aligned to ConAgra's core operating principles. The program addressed all four objectives outlined by management.

A year after the launch of the new You Made a Difference recognition program, the company experienced a 264 percent increase in employee satisfaction. Key results included

✔ Eighty-two percent of employees believe that the program is aligned to ConAgra's business goals

✔ The company's gross margins have increased

✔ Employee engagement scores have increased 88 percent

✔ Turnover has significantly decreased.

As Luciana Oliveira, a ConAgra human resources manager, said, "We have had more than 500 nominations in six months, which has driven engagement and enthusiasm toward the company. Recognition is now part of our everyday activities!"

> ✔ **They include meaningful rewards that best fit employees' preferences.** One of the benefits of an online recognition and rewards program is its expansive potential. With an online program, employees can access almost any type of reward imaginable. Select those categories that most appeal to your employees — today, these increasingly go beyond merchandise to include activities, charitable giving, green options, and learning and development opportunities.

> ✔ **They involve periodic assessments that enable companies to change and build on the program's success.** To keep your recognition initiative fresh and vibrant, you need to constantly improve upon it, adding new elements as needed and eliminating those elements that have run their course. This kind of assessment and modification will help make the program a dynamic, long-term, strategic initiative as opposed to one that feels like a "flavor of the month" program that most employees grow weary of.

Overcoming Pitfalls in Setting Up Your Online Recognition Program

As great as online recognition programs can be, they do present obstacles and challenges you need to watch out for. Be ready to overcome the potential pitfalls I list in this section as you implement and manage your web-based efforts.

Making it accessible to all employees

In many fields (like manufacturing, retail, and hospitality), not all employees have access to a computer (usually because computers are not required for their jobs). A common solution is purchase kiosks that are readily available to employees in their departments, allowing them time on the job to periodically access those kiosks (you can use savings from the online recognition program conversion to fund the purchase of the kiosks). Also, your employees may be able to access online recognition programs from home computers, although training will still be needed to show all employees how to use the online platform.

Being sure it's more than a way to simply redeem rewards

Some incentive providers use technology just to provide a rewards platform. Employees go online, select their rewards (using points or not), and then receive them. Don't stop there, though; look for ways to provide a wider range of rewards and give employees a choice in the selection and timing of rewards. Also offer technology for virtual redemptions (for example, online gift cards for immediate delivery as well as ways to donate points to a charity of your choice and automatically receive a tax receipt). These things make the recognition and rewards experience more personal and meaningful to employees. Also look for an online solution that offers a more robust recognition and communication platform, as well as the capacity and flexibility to integrate a variety of tools into the online solution.

Looking for ways to minimize upfront costs

Many incentive companies require a substantial upfront investment to cover the development of the desired software solution. Be leery of agreeing to such a requirement. Upfront fees should no longer be necessary because technology in this area has progressed such that recognition applications are already developed and readily available. Also select an incentive company that is invested in your program's success (that is, one that doesn't make money if the program is not used and successful).

Maximizing flexibility

Because motivators vary greatly from employee to employee, be sure your online recognition program provides maximum flexibility so that it meets everyone's motivational preferences. Some employees might prefer electronics, while others prefer e-cards that can be redeemed for coffee, or debit cards that can be used to purchase gas. Perhaps others would like to save up points to use for more expensive reward options, such as trips or major appliances. These divergent needs obviously can't all be met though a single recognition tool such as gift certificates, so make sure you think through your needs before you design or purchase your recognition platform.

Getting people to use it

One of the greatest recognition obstacles I've seen in organizations is getting managers to use recognition tools that are provided to them. Using the tools is more than a function of knowing what tools are available and how to use them. More fundamentally, it's about developing in your managers the beliefs and values that help them see that recognizing employees is a viable business strategy. Therefore, it is important to provide managers effective training that can help raise their awareness and abilities in providing recognition to their employees.

The Society for Human Resource Management (SHRM) reports that 81 percent of organizations currently do not provide such recognition training for their managers. As a result, even excellent recognition tools and programs are not apt to be effectively used by their managers.

Overcoming loss of the "personal touch" of face-to-face recognition

Sometimes, when going to an online recognition solution in which praise is delivered online via the Internet, employees feel the loss of personal thanks.

Online recognition should augment, not replace, face-to-face recognition. You can heighten the awareness of achievements by using online recognition that echoes real-life employee contact. You can also use online recognition to trigger nominations for more formal recognition programs in the organization, and in this way, help to amplify and leverage the grass-roots recognition that is occurring.

Rogers Communications drives call center sales with online rewards

Rogers Communications is a diversified communications and media company and Canada's largest provider of wireless voice and data communications services. Rogers wanted to incentivize its reps in the retail fulfillment call center to generate upsell and cross-sell opportunities for every modem or terminal box activation. After an unsuccessful attempt at implementing a commission structure, the company partnered with an incentive company to implement a noncash rewards program tailored to meet the company's needs and goals.

The program, named RCAC Rewards, instantly took off, gaining momentum with management and fulfillment reps. Every time a fulfillment rep sells an additional service to a customer while on a call, he or she submits it online and is instantly awarded points. These points can be redeemed for merchandise, experiences, gift certificates, or travel awards from an online catalog. Supervisors and program administrators can download reports showing program activity in real-time to measure and track the additional upselling and cross-selling services sold by the retail fulfillment call center team.

Within two months, RCAC Rewards reported a 93 percent increase in the number of submissions made by fulfillment reps for additional services sold since the program's launch, as well as a high level of program engagement (69 percent of agents actively participated in the program). In fact, RCAC's robust reporting capabilities sparked enthusiasm with Rogers' partners to sponsor their own incentive plans. Overall, it was a great success. "The reporting capabilities and the success of RCAC Rewards online platform has automated what used to be a time-consuming process for us and allowed us to set clear targets for our fulfillment reps," said Maria P. Bazkur, the manager of sales support.

The Future of Technology and Recognition

Current technology makes the daily task of recognition so much easier and more efficient and effective. What could possibly be in store for the future? Here are some on-the-horizon technology solutions that are already helping to support the next-generation workforce:

- ✔ **Geolocating capabilities.** Just as many apps already use location information to pitch products and services to customers, companies will be able to utilize this same technology to show management where recognition occurs. Real-time information about recognition that's displayed on a map can be a vital tool in getting management to buy into and support recognition, as well as respond to efforts immediately and make changes if needed.

- ✔ **Digital recognition and reward delivery.** Information and processes move faster than ever, which just feeds into the "expect it now" mentality (especially within the Millennial generation). To meet this need, devices like smart watches and Fitbits are increasing in popularity and quantity. Those who oversee recognition programs would benefit from including ways to incorporate wearables into their strategies.

- ✔ **Corporate digital wallet.** A digital wallet is an electronic device that allows people to buy things without using actual money. In the very near future, corporate digital wallets will be available. They'll feature corporate-branded tools that enable employees to store value earned at work in the Cloud or on their mobile device and redeem their "currency" or gift cards for rewards. Customizations can reinforce the organization's brand and values. Other perks of using gift cards in a digital wallet include the following:

  - The company has the ability to partner with brands that resonate with employees.

  - Employees can easily select awards to use in person or online.

  - Employees can combine rewards with other forms of payment when they use them in a storefront.

- ✔ **Advanced analytical reporting developments.** To be truly successful at recognition, organizations are realizing they must use and integrate data such as employee turnover, profitability, employee engagement survey results, quality metrics, and customer satisfaction scores. In the future, look for companies to collect more relevant employee and customer data and to better integrate that data to make informed decisions that most benefit the organization.

Chapter 13

Sustaining and Reenergizing Recognition Efforts

*I*t's natural for a recognition program to become tired after the initial excitement of the program launch wears off. When the freshness is gone, sometimes the only things that remain are the administrative and bureaucratic elements of award nominations and awards events, which can sometimes get so drab that the award-winners themselves are bored. While no rewards and recognition program lasts forever, you can enhance the energy of your program if you are diligent in sustaining and reenergizing it as needed.

Sustaining a recognition program over time means raising and re-raising awareness of the importance of recognizing employees, constantly renewing the motivation for managers and staff to recognize others, and periodically introducing new elements into the recognition program. In this chapter, I present some strategies and techniques that will help you keep your recognition efforts fresh and effective.

Sustaining Your Recognition Program

So you've got an effective recognition program in place. Congratulations! Employee morale is up. Customer service is up. Productivity is up. So are profits. Now what?

The next step is to build upon this momentum to keep the energy of the program up, as well as to systematically start to connect recognition to other organizational elements at various levels: communication, celebrations, hiring, and other key organizational processes. Build or rebuild momentum for recognition by amplifying and multiplying recognition practices throughout the organization until recognition becomes part of the organization's culture.

To sustain initial recognition efforts, you must link recognition to the organization's strategic objectives and values, renew sponsorship commitment, institute management follow up, and tie the recognition program to the organization's ongoing communication vehicles.

Linking to strategic objectives

The most effective recognition programs tie recognition specifically to the achievement of important objectives for the organization. Ideally, you should create the link between things that merit recognition and organization goals during the design phase of the recognition program (see Chapter 11), but it's never too late to make this link.

At the outset, find ways to measure the impact of recognition on the goals of the organization so that you can demonstrate the actual, quantifiable differences that recognition efforts make on employee perceptions, performance, and results. Then work the evidence of the connections between recognition and results into any organizational activity you can, whether at an all-staff meeting about the annual report or in casual conversations with colleagues about the latest office happenings.

Acquiring and renewing sponsorship commitment

Any recognition program without an active upper management sponsor is bound to lose steam, so if your program's been surviving all this time without a sponsor, it's now time to get one! Few forms of support are more important to recognition than having sponsorship from someone on the executive leadership team, ideally the CEO. A sponsor is a senior staff member who serves as an advocate for your recognition program and related activities.

Acquiring a sponsor can be as easy as simply asking an executive who participates in recognition if he or she will fulfill the role, perhaps someone that has already demonstrated an interest in the topic. If your sponsor needs to be reenergized, consider taking the sponsor to a conference on recognition or on a field trip to another organization that has a highly energized recognition program.

Having more than one sponsor can help spread the workload and also prevents the loss of your advocate if one of your sponsors changes roles or organizations, retires from the organization, or otherwise steps down from the role.

Creating a recognition committee

One of the best ways to keep recognition programs fresh is to create a recognition committee whose ongoing responsibility is to focus on recognition. Ideally, the group consists of volunteers that represent all areas and levels of the organization and meets periodically, perhaps for lunch once a month. Participants are charged to be an advisory group for the organization's recognition programs, making recommendations as needed to keep the programs fresh and effective.

If you happen to have an executive sponsor on the committee, that person doesn't have to be the one to lead the meetings. The committee chair can come from the group itself and is ideally selected by the team.

Providing specific management follow-up

Get managers to recognize employees (and employees to recognize one another) on a continuing basis by providing awareness, reminders, assistance, recognition tools, and a budget. To hold managers accountable, some organizations require all managers to develop a plan for implementing recognition on an individual and group basis, along with time frames. Plan elements can range from asking managers to have new hires (or all employees, for that matter) make a list of things they find rewarding, to hosting a group discussion among their staff about new ways to acknowledge work well done.

Other organizations designate specific employees — perhaps from the organization's recognition team — to follow up with managers to discuss the topic. You can specifically focus on those managers who are not using the recognition tools provided by the organization and then focus on finding a way to get them using those tools. Review progress on the managers' recognition plans, brainstorm new strategies and techniques they can use, and encourage them to continue or expand their efforts. If a manager is stuck or having doubts about his or her recognition efforts, that person might be teamed with another manager who has more experience and/or success with recognition.

You can also ask managers to conduct "one-on-one" meetings devoted to issues that are important to their direct reports at least once every two weeks. What might initially be an awkward meeting often turns into a welcome opportunity for employees to seek advice, role-play a work problem, or discuss development plans and even potential career paths.

I provide more guidance for getting managers to buy into using recognition in Chapter 7 and for getting buy-in of senior managers in Chapter 15.

Don't set a quota for recognition! One organization told its managers that they each had to recognize four employees each week, which predictably resulted in hundreds of superficial, insincere compliments that did little to motivate employees — and made the managers feel kind of silly as well. To be effective, recognition has to be sincere and can't easily be legislated.

Inserting recognition into communication

Every bit of communication in the organization — whether it's a voicemail, e-mail, a speech given at the end-of-the-year awards banquet, or a chance passing in a hallway — is an opportunity to recognize employees and sustain your program. An exchange of praise and recognition in a company newsletter, an "applause" bulletin board on the company's intranet, or simple acknowledgements in meetings of jobs well done are just a few possibilities for formalizing recognition.

Other suggestions to sustain enthusiasm for your recognition program

Other successful communication strategies to sustain and enhance recognition programs include the following:

- Promote, advertise, and market recognition throughout the organization.
- Capture and share success stories.
- Use recognition publicly (like starting meetings with recognition).
- Highlight successful projects and milestones with internal and external thank you's.
- Encourage peer-to-peer recognition.
- Track and report use of recognition tools and recognize managers who use them.

✔ Find ways to spark existing recognition programs.

✔ Create special recognition activities for part-timers, people with high potential, Millennials, and volunteers.

A general manager from Xerox told me that whenever he gets his 30 managers together, he always saves time at the end of the meeting to go around the room and ask each manager to share something he or she has done to recognize a staff member since the last meeting. This simple technique renews the excitement of recognition while providing a practical source of new recognition ideas for managers to learn from one another. At other companies, the question, "Does anybody have any praisings?" is asked — and responded to — at the end of department or company-wide meetings. And managers at the Swan & Dolphin Resort in Lake Buena Vista, Florida, meet monthly to brainstorm new and creative ways they can recognize their employees to consistently strive to keep the topic fresh and top of mind.

Letting employees call the recognition shots

The managers at Comprehensive Rehabilitation Consultants, Inc. (CRC), a health care consulting company with locations in Miami, Florida, and New York City, realized that interest was waning in their traditional employee-of-the-month program. They wanted to revitalize the program with employees, instead of managers, driving the change.

They decided that to reinvigorate their fellow staff and eliminate the perception of a popularity contest, they needed to develop a new program they dubbed the "Star Employee" program. They identified nine star qualities that were important to the company's success and philosophy. Every current (and future) staff member received a coffee mug listing these nine star qualities and a stack of nomination forms.

Staff members now nominate one another, and a committee of other employees reviews the nominations and awards "star" bucks for behaviors that fall under the nine qualities. Rewards vary from a couple of bucks up to $20 or more. Employees may then purchase services or privileges with their bucks on a dollar-for-dollar basis. Rewards include video rentals, car washes, time off, restaurant gift certificates, classes, massages, weekend getaways, gourmet coffee delivered to their desks, and any other item that the committee approves.

At the end of the year, the person who received the most nominations receives the Star Employee of the Year award, and those who have made the most successful nominations also receive awards (small trophies and star-shaped baskets of goodies). Each year, different employees volunteer to serve on the committee for the following year. Managers do not serve on the committee and are not eligible to receive bucks but can nominate other staff. Bucks are awarded at monthly staff meetings and nominations are read aloud so that both the nominator and nominated are acknowledged.

The program has been in place for four years and has been a wonderful source of team-building, improvement of morale, and an opportunity for everyone to become involved in recognition.

Tying Recognition to Human Resource Systems

Another effective method for making sure recognition efforts last is tying them into HR systems as much as possible — including hiring and recruiting, orientation and training, and evaluation and promotions.

Hiring and recruiting

Because it's easier to hire the right attitude than it is to change long-established attitudes, recognition skills should be among the criteria you list when hiring new managers, and you can even try to work it into job descriptions whenever possible. Also add a question or two about recognition to your interview process so that you can talk at length with candidates and get a better picture of their skills and philosophies in this area.

 If recognition skills is too fine of a point for you to include in hiring documents and processes, try exploring the broader category of people skills. Candidates who have strong people skills and consider themselves "people persons" have a high affinity for recognition and should easily be able to provide examples of things they have done in previous jobs to recognize those with whom they work. The Walt Disney Company, for example, aggressively recruits people-oriented individuals — regardless of the position; other hiring considerations pale in comparison to this fundamental value for the Disney organization. Likewise, Southwest Airlines' policy is to "hire for attitude and train for skills."

Orientation and training

Management training in many organizations tends to focus more on business planning and operations at the expense of the soft skills — people skills, like communication — related to managing others. Not surprisingly, few organizations have a new-manager orientation that emphasizes the importance of employee recognition, and according to the Society for Human Resources Management, 81 percent of organizations provide no recognition training to their managers. By providing specific training on recognition, organizations can overcome the objection by low-use managers that they don't know how to do it well (see Chapter 7 for more on low-use managers).

All employees at Disney are required to attend a Traditions 101 course that teaches staff members the organization's values — including the importance of how people are treated — and what those values look like in practice. Managers and supervisors at AlliedSignal (now a part of Honeywell, Inc.) are required to attend a four-hour recognition training, which includes real-job situations for discussion and role-playing. And at CalPERS, the State of California retirement fund, training in recognition skills is provided to all employees — not just managers — to encourage the use of recognition at all levels throughout the organization.

Evaluation and promotion

If recognition is important to the organization, it makes sense that managers be evaluated on their use of it and that people-skills be a criterion for any promotion. If your organization uses a form for employee evaluations, it helps to add a category or a few questions about managing employees, such as "Do you provide positive feedback to employees?" and "Do you periodically discuss developmental opportunities and potential career paths with your employees?"

In their performance reviews, managers at Disney are evaluated in part on their ability to manage, develop, and encourage their employees. Managers who aren't considered competent people developers receive additional training and cannot advance in the organization until they demonstrate their commitment to the people side of their job. At AAA of Southern California, one-third of a manager's annual bonus is based on the manager's immediate employees' quantitative rankings of the manager's soft skills, such as making him- or herself available to listen and help employees, being supportive, and creating development opportunities for employees.

Reenergizing Your Recognition Program

Recognition can easily become rote and meaningless. The best way to battle this is to remain in tune with how your recognition program is actually playing out. Don't be afraid to admit when things aren't as effective as they used to be or that you need some help improving the program. For example, someone asked me once, "We currently have a weekly recognition program where we encourage employees to recognize others who have helped them in any way during the week. We track it, and if the number of recognitions reaches the target, everyone in the company receives a small gift (like an umbrella or insulated lunch bag). We are now at the point where people thank others for "always being friendly" just to get to the award level. Any ideas on how to keep the process alive without demeaning it?"

I replied, "It sounds like you have a good program in need of tweaking. Remind everyone of the original purpose of the program and put forth criterion or examples of what's appropriate. 'Always being friendly' might be a legitimate behavior worthy of praise if it genuinely helps the other person through his or her day or is tied to customer service. If that's not the case, however, you can simply clarify that the purpose of the program is to recognize exceptional behavior, not day-to-day activities or normal job responsibilities. People will get the message."

Every recognition program needs to be reenergized for one reason or another (sooner, more often than later). Here are some guidelines for revamping your recognition program to make the most of your successes while learning from your mistakes. To see how these guidelines worked for BankBoston's (now BankofAmerica), head to the section "Re-Shining Gold Stars: The Reenergizing Process in Action."

You may also need to revise and expand informal recognition efforts. For example, when I worked with Korry Electronics Company in Seattle, Washington, the company had an excellent, informal, decades-old recognition program that made use of *pogs,* the milk bottle cap-style tokens popular in the 1990s. Employees received pogs as a simple and immediate form of thanks for work well done, and they could redeem the pogs for company merchandise, logoed T-shirts, and similar items. Seemed pleasant enough, yet the program had flaws. While some managers handed out pogs like candy, others hardly dispensed them at all. Reintroducing the program, reminding managers of its purpose and intent, and counseling errant managers helped to breathe many more years of life into what had been a successful program.

Reassessing program effectiveness

If left unchecked, formal recognition will not just lose its luster, but it will often grind to a halt! I was working in a corporation and stopped to read a plaque honoring annual top achievers, only to discover that the last entry was 12 years old!

In this section I outline steps you can follow to reenergize any recognition program.

Step 1: Take stock of what's working

The first step in reenergizing any recognition program is to take stock of what is working well and what needs to be fixed. This process can and should include tapping into the perspectives and opinions of those you are most trying to motivate — and especially those employees who are vocal critics of the existing program. You can get their perspectives through an employee survey, select interviews, or focus groups.

It may seem strange, but I've found that if you can incorporate the feedback of the most vocal recognition program critics, you stand a good chance of converting them to being the revised program's strongest advocates by fixing all the issues they had problems with the original one.

The recognition committee can select a group of volunteers who represent all functions or departments in the organization to target for these surveys, interviews, and focus groups. Start by asking the volunteers questions related to the purpose of the recognition program: Was it achieved? Does it need to be revised? A well-defined program purpose and targeted performance goals should drive every recognition program.

Step 2: Find out what people think about the existing program

Next, collect perceptions of the program from other members of the organization, especially those who are critical of the existing recognition programs. Ask questions such as the following:

- ✔ What do you like about the program? What would you like to change?
- ✔ Do you understand the mechanics of how the program works?
- ✔ Do you think the incentives offered are significant and have value?
- ✔ Have you been a recipient or nominee of the program?

These are the types of questions that can help you obtain a frontline assessment of what you need to change.

Redesigning and implementing program changes

From the data they collect, task-force members should list changes that seem to be the most needed and prioritize those recommendations. In some instances, they may need to expand a program; in other instances, they may need to delete certain awards. In some situations, employee perceptions may be inaccurate, in which case, recognition task force members may need to disperse additional information about the program. Ideally you would strive to keep those aspects of the recognition program that are working well while eliminating those aspects that are not working.

Revamping recognition at the Commonwealth of Virginia

Recognition programs at the Commonwealth of Virginia in Richmond had become stale and ineffective. The HR department spearheaded a recognition program revitalization effort that sought to increase the frequency with which recognition occurred within the agency.

Human resources conducted a preprogram employee survey that indicated most employees felt employee recognition was inadequate. In addition, the HR department found that, because various units throughout the agency administered existing recognition programs, recognition efforts often fell between the cracks.

To correct the situation, the Commonwealth produced a *Recognition Guide* to increase awareness of existing recognition programs, which was distributed along with copies of my *365 Ways to Manage Better* perpetual calendar and *1001 Ways to Reward Employees* (now in a new edition entitled *1501 Ways to Reward Employees*) — to all managers and supervisors. Standing Ovation Recognition pocket cards were also created to remind managers of what to recognize their employees for.

A follow-up employee survey showed a significant increase in the number of employees who responded positively to the item "employees in my work group are recognized" for the work they do. Focus groups within the organization also revealed a significant increase in recognition.

When you know what elements of your program you want to expand, modify, or end, organize the changes on a timeline and assign committee members to handle each change. If the task is especially significant or requires extensive work by itself, you can have a subgroup work on it. This is what they did at Petco when I worked with them. They called each subgroup and the work plans they developed "workstreams," and the process was very effective.

Market your success

After the team has revamped the recognition program, it's time to relaunch it with all the gusto of a celebration. Hold a special launch meeting to feature the revised program. You want to give as much emphasis to the program's renewal as you gave to the initial rollout, ideally having an extra spark for the rerelease. As you present the revised program, share these points:

- Review the successes of the previous program, especially focusing on the results achieved and the levels of participation, if significant.

- Explain the program changes and improvements, emphasizing that these improvements came from employees.

Taking the time to reassess and revamp a recognition program can be a minimal investment of effort that offers great returns. No program or initiative lasts forever, and the sooner you catch a faltering program and make needed changes, the stronger your overall recognition culture becomes. Over time, you can make the overall recognition effort more robust by adding new elements, expanding successful programs, or focusing on increased participation. After all, the best organizations continually look to be better.

Re-Shining Gold Stars: The Reenergizing Process in Action

The project of reenergizing a recognition program does not always go smoothly, but the results can still be spectacular. One such case worth looking at is the Service Star program used at BankBoston. The Service Star program is an informal recognition program wherein any employee can give embroidered gold stars to another individual or team, accompanied by an acknowledgement — written, faxed, or e-mailed — of a deed well done. The nominator selects from three delivery options: The gold star can be sent directly to the person, given to their manager or executive to be presented to the recipient, or presented to the recipient at an upcoming meeting. Furthermore, nominators can even call a hotline number to check on the status of the nomination or to get any questions answered.

When the Service Star program first began, some 30 gold stars were given out daily. By the end of four months, the number had climbed to 200 gold stars a day. Eventually, an individual or team star was being awarded every three minutes! The program, which initially had a turnaround time of three days from nomination to gold-star presentation, now had a turnaround time of 12 hours or less. "All Stars" were selected from all Service Star recipients once a quarter. The organization aimed to select 125 All Stars each quarter.

Like any program, however, even BostonBank's successful Service Star program began to show some age, and the company took steps to find out what could be improved to keep the program alive and well.

As this example from BostonBank shows, taking the time to reassess and revamp a recognition program can be a minimal investment of effort that offers great returns. The sooner you catch a deenergized or faltering program and make needed changes, the stronger your overall recognition culture will become.

Evaluating the program

To evaluate the program after it had run for several years, BankBoston created a "MAD" ("Make A Difference") project team. Half the members were volunteers and half were "targeted members" — cynics, skeptics and nonusers of the existing program. The MAD team's job was to determine whether the program aims were being achieved and whether the program needed to be revised, expanded, or cut back.

The feedback indicated that employees felt that

✔ Too many Service Stars were awarded and as a result the recognition had lost its specialness.

✔ The program was expensive.

✔ The program was not supported by executive management.

This kind of feedback is typical of recognition programs in decline. What's interesting about the perceptions of the surveyed BankBoston employees was that they were at odds with the facts:

✔ Although thousands of Service Stars had been awarded, 90 percent of employees who received Stars reported the recognition was the most meaningful moment of their career.

✔ The Service Star program at BankBoston was not that expensive; it cost only $1.33 to award a Service Star to an employee and, in a recent year, the overall budget decreased by 56 percent through various cost-saving initiatives.

✔ The Service Star program was actively supported by executive management who, in aggregate, had nominated over 340 employees annually for the award and who, on average, spent an hour each week per executive personally delivering Service Stars to employees.

Taking action to save the program

It quickly became obvious that these misperceptions would have to be rectified by communicating the relevant facts throughout the organization. This awareness, along with other data collected from employees — many of them the harshest critics — was very useful in making recommendations for needed improvements to the program. Employee input revealed that the existing Service Star program could be enhanced by

✔ Having greater management involvement

✔ Making recognition more specific

✔ Making changes to recognition events to make them more meaningful and less expensive

More management involvement

To increase management involvement with recognition at BankBoston, a refresher module, entitled "Managing Made Easy," was offered for all managers, and an employee-recognition toolkit was made available to every manager. This toolkit included recognition technique recommendations, recognition program criteria and nomination forms, and recognition tools and reminders such as thank-you cards. Notification packets were distributed to the managers of All Star winners. Included in the packet were congratulations for the manager, as well as directions for the manager to notify All Stars within one to two weeks. Senior managers were also notified of the All Star award winners in their division and encouraged to call each recipient.

More specific recognition

For recognition to be even more meaningful at BankBoston, managers needed additional guidance in effectively recognizing employees, and greater patience needed to be shown for those managers who still didn't implement recognition very well. Nomination forms were modified to provide additional examples of the guidelines that were explained. When nominations seemed questionable, nominators were asked to provide more details as to why the person or achievement was worthy of the award.

More meaningful recognition events

Employees liked that they could invite a guest to recognition events, that executives served as hosts, and that the events were fairly casual. They were less pleased that the events were often boring and awkward, the monetary awards often meager, and recipients' immediate managers had a bad habit of not showing up.

This information inspired many changes: Managers and executives started receiving notification packets about the individuals being honored, quarterly recognition events became semi-annual celebrations, and the organization began leveraging their relationships with other companies to barter for unique and creative recognition celebrations that created extensive interest and buzz. For example, the company was able to arrange player appearances with the New England Patriots and hold celebrations at the Boston Aquarium and the Museum of Fine Arts.

Marketing the program like a product

"We marketed the program like a product — it was not mandated or required of anyone — which forced us to sell the program so people would want to use it," says Kathe Farris, recognition consultant at BankBoston at the time. "Once you met their needs, you never had to sell the program again."

To market the program, BankBoston added new communication and marketing efforts to the program's relaunch, including a nomination challenge (during the first 30 days, anyone who nominated another employee received a surprise gift), which incentivized people to use the program; an overview of the recognition program included in the new employee orientation program; and expanded efforts to ask employees for their opinions on the company's strategies and employee issues.

The company also designated a specialist to clarify any vague written nominations with the nominator so that no program nominations were declined. Additionally, managers received monthly participation reports that identified which employees in the managers' areas were using the recognition program and marketed some aspect of the program, and program champions were paired with program skeptics.

Bringing a Program to a Close

In some cases, when it takes far more effort to revitalize a recognition program than the program is worth, it's probably time to retire it — or at least put it aside until some later date when you can reintroduce it.

It's difficult for any program — no matter how good — to last forever. It's also difficult to meet all motivation needs with a single program. If a recognition program has lost its focus, start over by asking what behavior or performance you are trying to impact and brainstorm other ideas and incentives that would get people excited about achieving the desired results. In this way an effective recognition initiative is vibrant, constantly evolving with the needs of the organization.

How can you tell when a program is a candidate for closure? Sometimes it's painfully obvious that a program's been degraded beyond recovery, which was the case at one company that had a spontaneous recognition program that included the phrase "You're the best!" The program had been successfully used for over a year but then became stale, and its catchphrase became an all-purpose sarcastic joke. If someone had a bad day, a coworker would say, "Remember, Joe, 'You're the best!'"

Here are some general tip-offs that a program's run its course:

- ✓ **You set a time limit for the program at the outset, and you've reached the end of the program's planned duration.** It's better to shut down a successful but declining program a bit earlier than necessary, than it is to allow a marginal or counterproductive program to remain in place long after it should have been retired — especially if you have some new recognition ideas or activities that are likely to be more motivating to employees. And who knows? Maybe it'll be ripe to bring back later!

- ✓ **Staff generally ignores the program, no matter how much you publicize it and encourage its use.** Although you can change the program (refer to the earlier sections), take caution about changing a program too dramatically. If you want to radically change a recognition program, it might be more desirable to end the program and begin a new one.

- ✓ **Employees do not value the rewards you give, no matter what items you use.** Perhaps they weren't involved in the selection of reward items or perhaps the program was underfunded so that nothing that employees received seemed to have much of any value. Whatever the reason, it's probably better to stop the program and perhaps try again at some point in the future.

What if your program design is too ambitious to begin with? When they first realize this, senior management's first inclination may be to downsize the program instead of dismantling it (to save the investment of time and possibly funds they've already put in). This is generally not a good idea, since employees might view such action as a takeaway — the removal of a favorable element or program without replacing it — one of the major demotivators of recognition I discuss in Chapter 5). That's why it's so important to heed the principles of organizational recognition design I share in Chapter 11.

- ✓ **Changing market conditions force you to make major changes in your approach.** Timing is a crucial factor in recognition. Sometimes a program launches successfully when business conditions are favorable but then declines when business conditions worsen. If your program is suffering from poor timing, you might want to consider terminating or discontinuing it until conditions improve. Likewise, if the organization is going through some dramatic changes (layoffs, a merger, extensive new product or services launches), you may want to wait until things settle down and then revitalize a recognition program to align with a new direction or new demands.

It's better to shut down a successful but declining program a bit earlier than necessary than it is to allow a marginal or counterproductive program to remain in place long after it should have been retired. There's nothing wrong with terminating a recognition program when it has run its course, especially if you have some new recognition ideas or activities that are likely to be more motivating to employees. And who knows? Maybe it will be ripe to bring back at a later date!

Chapter 14

Troubleshooting Recognition Problems

. . . .

In This Chapter

▶ Identifying individual, team, and organizational recognition mistakes

▶ Avoiding recognizing the wrong things

▶ Preventing common organizational demotivators

. . . .

Despite the best intentions, recognition can go wrong. And when recognition goes wrong, it can lead to far more problems for an organization than having no recognition program at all. Possible mistakes abound: Managers recognize the wrong people and recognize people for the wrong things; the chosen awards can turn out to be meaningless or even insulting to those who receive them; and recognition tools and programs can be ignored altogether. The result? Decreased morale, lowered performance, and a lousy place to work.

If you're implementing recognition efforts that just don't seem to be working, this is the chapter for you. In the following pages, I review the most common recognition mistakes at the individual, group, and organizational levels, and give you some tips on how to avoid each. Let the troubleshooting begin!

Identifying Individual Recognition Mistakes

In many ways, one-on-one thanks is the most important form of recognition in the day-to-day working lives of employees because individual recognition is very personal and, thus, more meaningful to employees. You can give individual recognition to anyone at any time — you don't need permission, have to submit a nomination to a committee, or get approval from top management. However, sometimes, individual recognition goes astray.

In this section, I outline some of the most common mistakes I see managers make when it comes to recognizing individuals. If your recognition is falling flat, check this list for possible causes.

Missing recognition opportunities

Probably the most common problem with individual recognition is ignoring or just missing opportunities to use it. The reasons include being too busy to acknowledge an employee who does a good job, believing that employees don't need to be recognized, or thinking that giving positive feedback once a year in employees' performance reviews is sufficient. Missed opportunities can especially be a problem for good performers, who managers feel must already know they are good because they've been told so in the past.

Recognition that's not timely

Waiting too long to thank someone is almost as bad as completely missing an opportunity to recognize them altogether. The longer you wait to recognize someone, the smaller the recognition's impact. After a certain point, delayed acknowledgement shows your employees just how out of touch you are with them and their accomplishments. They may even forget what they had done to warrant your appreciation! Saying, "Gary, I really appreciate the way you handled that problem with the client last month" is liable to leave Gary scratching his head and wondering what problem or what client? Conversely, they may remember all to well what they did to deserve recognition but, when you finally get around to delivering a thank you, view your effort as too little, too late.

Being insincere or mechanical

One of the hallmarks of effective recognition is sincerity. If you're not being earnest with your praise, your employees can see right through it, and that's probably why it isn't working. Mechanical and superficial recognition can completely backfire. Recognition you deliver mechanically — you offer thanks without really thinking about it or walk around the office the same time each week to dole out boilerplate thanks — doesn't seem believable. Instead of your efforts feeling genuine to your employees, they leave the impression that you are only going through the motions because it's expected or you have a checklist item you want to mark off. Instead of doing the same stuff all the time, change your recognition activities up — and recognize from the heart!

Publicly recognizing private people

Does your overachieving employee seem to shun your recognition? Although, as a general rule, people value public praise, some people are uncomfortable with public recognition. Forcing public recognition on someone who does not want it is demotivating and can very well have negative ramifications. For example, one gentleman who was going to be given a perfect attendance award at an all-company awards banquet was so nervous about going up on stage — with the possibility of having to speak publicly — that he called in sick on the day of the banquet. Then there's the story of one self-conscious employee-of-the-month recipient who never used his designated parking spot close to the building, so a few of his buddies removed the sign and posted it in front of his car out in the middle of the employee parking lot.

You've probably also heard the rule to "recognize publicly, reprimand privately." For certain, this approach is more effective and respectful. Public reprimands can be very demoralizing — and have the opposite effect of what you intend. The founder of one computer company publicly berated employees who ran behind schedule. The result? Other employees started hiding when they were running behind schedule or having trouble with a project — or they rushed to turn in less-than-perfect work.

Undercutting praise with criticism

If your recognition never seems to be good enough for your employees, maybe it's because they don't feel good enough, either. It's very common for managers to immediately follow the thanks they give with a note of criticism: "You did a great job on that report, Betty, but I noticed quit a few typos in it," for example. Doing so sends a confusing message. Are you pleased? Are you disappointed?

This approach undermines the positive impact of the recognition, and the employee is left thinking about the negative feedback you shared — or what a jerk you are! Save constructive feedback for a future developmental discussion and just focus on what the person did right for now!

Giving recognition that is not rewarding

Many times, well-intended managers defeat their best intentions by doing something that ends up being demotivating — or worse, even insulting — to the recipient. One Canadian woman told me about a new boss who took her to a baseball game as a reward — something she had never been to before. Her initial excitement was soon dashed after she asked a question about the game, and the boss replied, "What, are you stupid?" She spent the rest of the game petrified, staring blindly in cold silence at a game she didn't understand, and she reported it as being "One of the worst experiences of my life."

You can avoid this problem by simply asking the person what he or she would like as recognition, or running your idea by him or her in advance. In the example involving the baseball game, perhaps the employee would have confessed that she had never been to a baseball game before and thus better help set expectations.

Overcompensating

If you're reprimanded for how poorly you treat employees and then, in trying to make it better, you suddenly start thanking all your employees for everything they are doing, you could be overcompensating, which suffers the same fate as insincerity in that it lacks honesty and meaning.

Overcompensating can be made worse when the overcompensating manager then stops all recognition and returns to his or her former mean or indifferent self. This Dr. Jekyll/Mr. Hyde approach to recognition confuses employees. It's better that you start small in identifying a few truly deserving employees, recognizing them for a few things they've done well, and then sustain or build on that practice going forward.

Being manipulative

Some managers use recognition as a way to manipulate employees — for example, saying, "Gary, here are some movie passes for helping out yesterday — can you work late again tonight?" Manipulative managers lose credibility with their employees, who learn to not trust communication at face value and constantly look for the hidden agenda behind the recognition.

 For recognition to work, it needs to be honest and sincere, with no expectation of a favor in return. Consider the employee who received a report back from her manager with glowing comments on it. She was upset when she later learned that her manager had not actually read the report, making his praise meaningless!

Looking at Team Recognition Mistakes

All the individual recognition mistakes can also apply to teams, yet recognizing teams provides some additional challenges as well. What makes team recognition especially difficult (and more prone to misfires) is that determining who on any given team is truly performing and who is slacking off can be difficult. If you give a nonperformer the same reward as a high performer, you risk invalidating the recognition in the eyes of the members of the team. And if you fail to recognize the team stars, you risk alienating them. Read on for some other recognition mistakes that often arise with groups.

Treating everyone the same

Also called "jellybean motivation," this strategy fails to differentiate between the deserving and those merely riding the productive team members' coattails. Guess who best knows who on the team is not performing? The members of the team. By rewarding everyone on a team equally — say with public recognition or a team bonus — when some people clearly did not perform up to the standards of the rest of the group, you risk losing credibility in the eyes of the high performers, precisely those you can least afford to alienate. Worse yet is to give more work to the team member who does good work, while allowing a nonperformer more time because he or she didn't finish an assignment.

If you don't have a close working knowledge about the work the team is doing, you can solicit individual feedback from team members: Query the group about their efforts working together and ask who contributed the most to the team results and who contributed the least. You can then use this information to provide added recognition to those that are most deserving.

Leaving someone deserving out

Say you recognize a team but notice one of the employees seems surly or hurt. What happened? Sometimes when a group is recognized, individuals are left out, either inadvertently or perhaps because group membership has changed. Sometimes, only the manager gets credit for the entire group's work, which can be especially demotivating to the group. It's up to you to ensure that *everyone* who contributes to the success of a team effort is recognized for his or her contributions.

Again, the best way to know who deserves recognition is to be up to date on the group, its efforts, and successes. At the very least, being updated on the group's latest membership helps you avoid praising individuals that may no longer be on the team and missing new members who have been added.

Failing to involve the group in determining recognition and rewards

Too often, groups are not allowed any say in how they'd like to be thanked. As a result, the thanks can miss the mark completely. By involving the team in deciding how to recognize or reward the team's success, the recognition will likely be more motivating and meaningful to the group.

A team leader in a chemical plant wanted to thank her project team for work they had done, so she purchased T-shirts for team members. Their response: "We saved the company all this money, and all we get is this lousy T-shirt?!" The manager, smart enough to use the incident as a learning opportunity, asked the team, "What would have been more motivating?" The manager made amends by doing something else for the team.

Making Mistakes at Organizational Recognition

Because of their scope and complexity, organizational recognition efforts have the greatest likelihood to go awry. Following are common problems that arise in organizational recognition efforts.

Rushing to recognition

Although delaying recognition of individuals can cause problems, too little planning when executing organizational-level recognition is also a no-no. If you hurried to launch your recognition program only to have it fall flat, you shouldn't assume that the lack of success means your idea was a bad one. Perhaps you simply needed more preparation.

Some action-oriented companies tend to take a ready-fire-aim approach to planning, and more than a few of them have rushed to roll out initiatives but neglected one or more important components. The result? The initiative fails. Where a systematic plan is highly desirable for individual and team recognition, it is absolutely essential for organizational recognition. Big ideas sometimes require big planning and careful thought and follow-through.

Many times I've seen the awards offered in recognition or incentive programs create more problems than they solve because of lack of planning and due diligence. Suppose, for example, that you want to reward high achievers with a trip to Mexico. At first, such a trip seems like a great reward for desired performance, but questions quickly arise: Employees may ask "Can I bring my family if I win?", "If my children can't come, can the company pay for someone to watch them while we're gone?", "Will I have to get new clothes, luggage, etc. for the trip?" Suddenly, that nice reward becomes a headache to pull off because adequate planning was not done. In this case, selecting what was thought to be a desirable reward without thinking through the potential consequences, questions, and problems created an expanding challenge for the incentive organizer, and the reward missed the motivational mark.

Assuming that one size fits all

Giving everyone the same reward seems like the ultimate in fairness, right? So why are your employees upset? Well, another basic mistake managers make is to provide — out of a false sense of fairness — the exact same recognition or reward to every employee. Few things are as unfair as the equal treatment of unequals. You need to adjust the recognition you use to the individual preferences of those you are trying to motivate. And as the number of people you want to recognize increases, the possibilities for what you can do also should increase as well.

People (and their accomplishments) vary in many ways, and the best forms of recognition and rewards need to vary as well. What is rewarding to one person could actually be demeaning to another. Ideally you want to customize recognition to the people who will receive it and match the reward to what those recipients most value. Unless it's a form of celebration which would involve others, you need to allow individuals in the group a greater choice. Although it's true at every level of recognition (individual, team, and organizational), the problems of a one-size-fits-all approach become more problematic as the group gets larger — or involves the entire organization. The worst example of this is when a company does something for all employees that it thinks everyone will appreciate (perhaps based on the idea of just a single person or committee), and no one does. This mistake is simple to avoid with a little due diligence and involvement of a greater number of people in deciding and designing the best way to recognize everyone.

Younger employees, for example, often want to be highly engaged and passionate about their work or to have greater social interaction at work. Give them leeway and the chance to pursue their ideas and learn new skills. Challenge them with interesting work or give them full responsibility to take control of a situation. For example, a young man recently told me that he felt most motivated when his company gave him full contact with a key client, trusting that he would do what needed to be done to meet that client's needs. A younger employee might prefer to be given responsibility, and an older employee might prefer to have a choice of assignments. Of course, you can minimize the guesswork simply by asking each employee what most motivates him or her and do those things as he or she performs well.

Losing freshness and relevance

If you've had the same recognition program in place for years (even if it's a good one), but your employees don't seem excited about it anymore, the program might be past its use-by date. You can't expect a recognition program to remain effective forever. I see many formal recognition programs that were once very good but along the way ran out of energy, got boring, or lost the ability to inspire enthusiasm by those who ran them. The longer the program has existed, the greater the chance that it will become stale. This is often the fate of years-of-service awards and employee-of-the-month programs.

One employee told of feeling good about receiving his 10-year pin until a new employee came up to him and said, "How did you ever make it working here 10 years?! I'm ready to quit today!" He found himself having to defend why he had been with the company so long. What had at one time been an honor had morphed into an endurance award. Having lost touch with those it was meant to excite, the recognition program had become a joke in the organization.

At another corporation, employees didn't view years of service as a feat that warranted recognition at all. Because everyone eventually reached that milestone, it didn't seem special. Making it even less noteworthy, the award was delivered very impersonally, and the only feedback managers got about the program was negative (like "You misspelled my name!").

Even the best programs need to be reevaluated and renewed from time to time — usually sooner rather than later. As a general rule, the shelf life of a typical recognition program today is closer to 12 weeks than 12 years, so if you're having problems and haven't reassessed your program in some time, now's the time. Find out what's working and what's not and adjust the program accordingly.

Having priorities that are confusing

It's amazing how many organizations send confusing and conflicting messages in their recognition practices and systems. Without realizing it, mixed messages make it unclear just what achievement warrants recognition, and employees feel confused rather than guided. "Maximize production!" "Quality is job one!" "Give customers your complete attention!" "Reduce customer contact time!" "Increase long-term profits!" "Reduce costs immediately!" "Work faster!" "Work safer!" "Be innovative!" "Don't make mistakes!"

If everything is a priority, nothing is a priority. In these situations, employees sense that management is confused about what it really wants. When performance expectations are unclear, employees waste a tremendous amount of energy trying to figure out what is really expected, and individuals can end up working at cross purposes.

Recognizing subjectively

Sometimes, I look at a client's newsletter and find photos of employees and the company president with an award or plaque. When I ask what the reward is for, more times than not, the client doesn't know. "Why do you suppose these people are in this photo then?" I ask. The telling answer: "Management's favorites."

Too often, managers give recognition based on subjective impressions, which are notoriously inaccurate. Subjective recognition is uneven at best, and wrong and unfair at its worst.

One thing to be aware of is the tendency to recognize employees based on a *halo effect*: Once you perceive certain people to be top performers, you *always* perceive them as top performers who can do no wrong. Conversely, a *horns effect* often exists around employees whom you perceive to be somehow inadequate. When you give (or withhold) recognition due to one of the these effects, recognition becomes more of a demotivating influence than a motivating one.

To avoid these pitfalls, use carefully defined, objective criteria when crafting your recognition. Checklists can be helpful to identify behaviors and results that are worthy of recognition. The tendency of supervisors to give some people more recognition than others can also be counteracted by using a recognition log, which helps keep track of who is receiving recognition and how often. This log is also a valuable feedback device for the supervisor or manager who wants to improve the quality (and quantity) of his or her recognition giving.

Breeding an entitlement culture

You try to give recognition all the time, but someone always finds something to criticize! What gives? A common problem when you do recognition just to be nice is that it becomes expected, leading to a culture of entitlement. For example, if you bring in donuts on one Friday to be nice and the following Friday you bring in donuts again, on the third Friday (and perhaps subsequent Fridays) the donuts will be expected. At one company, employees complained that a recognition dinner was a buffet, while the previous year it had been a sit-down affair. And when the company spent thousands of dollars buying popcorn as a spontaneous thanks to all employees, people complained that the popcorn wasn't that fresh. Employees in this company even complained that the tissue paper in the restrooms wasn't as soft as it used to be!

Recognition should be special, not routine. Too often, recognition becomes a general activity, such as a department or company celebration and not a specific form of thanks. When recognition is routinely expected, it loses its value and its authenticity. Entitlements that everyone receives (such as employee benefits) are fine. Just don't make recognition one of those!

Too much recognition is almost as bad as too little recognition, especially when it is not tied to performance. If you come to recognize everything, it has the same impact as if you recognize nothing. Recognition should be viewed as a valuable organizational resource — and should be used as such. Remember, recognition is a strategic business resource, not simply a form of psychological compensation.

ANECDOTE

The corporate turkey

A defense contractor in Los Angeles had a good year and wanted to thank employees and thus motivate their future performance. Someone in upper management announced, "Let's give everyone turkeys!" which seemed like a nice gesture since it was near the end of the year and the holidays. The turkeys were distributed.

Instead of accolades, management got letters of complaint about the size of the turkeys: "So-and-so got a larger turkey than me." To fix the problem, the following holiday season, the company tried to order 12,000 turkeys, each weighing exactly the same amount. Because that wasn't possible, each turkey was boxed and distributed with a letter from the company's

president stating, "The exact weight of your turkey is not an indication of your level of performance over the past year." Still people complained: Some wanted ham instead of a turkey. Vegetarians wanted fruit baskets.

The program, which had not been effective to begin with, spun so out of control that the company hired someone just to manage all the administration and choices! That person's formal title? Turkey Administrator.

I've heard various versions of this real example from other firms. At one manufacturing plant, the employees even took their frozen turkeys to the boss's house and dumped them on his lawn!

Doing too much or too little

Sometimes recognition is too small or too large. Telling someone in the hall-way that she did a nice job at the completion of a two-year project can be as inappropriate as giving a cruise to the newest employee-of-the-month (a real-life example — and in this instance, the recipient was ultimately fired within the year because he fudged his performance numbers). Recognition accompanied by a large monetary payment can easily be overwhelmed by the reward itself.

Giving too much recognition can make the activity less meaningful. Giving too little recognition undermines the performance you were trying to encourage and the relationship between the provider and the recipient. So how do you determine the right amount of recognition? This is one of the challenges of recognition that makes it a bit of an art, refined by experience over time. By trying to learn what worked or what did not as you use recognition, you can assess whether your recognition was effective or was too little or too much, and then adjust accordingly.

REMEMBER

It is very important to differentiate recognition from rewards. Recognition is positive reinforcement for something well done. A reward is something tangible that often accompanies recognition. Rewards are often used as a proxy for recognition and, too often, rewards are given to employees without sufficient recognition.

Zero-sum recognition

In *zero-sum* games, in order for somebody to win, somebody else must lose. Although zero-sum games might make sense in competitive sports, they don't make sense in the collaborative workplaces of today. There needn't be any losers in a positive work environment. Singling out one outstanding employee at the expense of others is problematic. For example, company contests typically result in one or a few winners and many losers. A top salesperson winning a trip to Hawaii, the number two salesperson getting a bottle of champagne, and the rest of the sales staff (and support staff) getting nothing also focuses on a single winner. Likewise, in employee-of-the-month or employee-of-the-year programs, there is one winner, and everybody else loses.

Competitive recognition can be detrimental to an organization's goals, and it sends the wrong messages about teamwork — that it isn't important. When establishing an organizational recognition program, *every* employee should be able to win. This doesn't mean that rewards shouldn't be earned; they should. But why can't a lot of employees be employees of the month? Isn't that what organizations ought to be striving for? Even better, how about celebrating many employees who have excelled — consider them "employees of the moment"! Avoid having one employee's gain be another employee's loss; instead set objective recognition criteria in which everyone who meets the standard is recognized.

Untimely recognition

Delay is the enemy of recognition. One of the challenges of organizational recognition is how to keep it streamlined and nonbureaucratic so that people can receive timely recognition. If every form of recognition needs management approval, many — if not most — recognition opportunities will be missed. Avoid recognition decisions that have to go through level after level of approvals, and always allow some forms of recognition, such as an on-the-spot award or a traveling trophy, that require no additional levels of approval. Or use a mix of recognition in which some forms are spontaneous while others are more formal and planned.

Recognizing the Wrong Things

At any level of recognition, but especially at the organizational level, it's critical to identify exactly what you're rewarding.

If your organization isn't getting the results it wants or the behaviors needed to achieve them, perhaps you're just confused about what you want. It's amazing how many times organizations do what management expert Steven Kerr calls "the folly of rewarding A while hoping for B." In his classic article of the same name, Kerr gives a wide range of examples of undesired outcomes that are, usually inadvertently, being reinforced. Read on.

Misguided recognition

Here are some examples of my own that you and your organization might be facing:

- **Many organizations want profits but recognize *any* sales revenue.** It's amazing how many salespeople receive recognition — and significant cash rewards — for closing *unprofitable* deals. Recognizing sales revenue, period, can result in a big top line and a small — or nonexistent — bottom line.

- **Many organizations want teamwork but recognize internal competition.** If there isn't enough teamwork in your organization, you probably don't have to look beyond your recognition system. In fact, most performance evaluation systems pit employees and departments against each other in an internal competition for scarce rewards. When he was dismissed as CEO of Digital Equipment Corporation, founder Ken Olsen admitted that his major failing was not getting his engineering managers to team up with product and marketing managers.

- **Many organizations want quality but recognize inspection.** For years, companies tried to improve quality by *inspecting-out* defects. Factories that shipped no defects were recognized, even though they wasted millions of dollars on scrap and rework . . . and quality was never built in. Some software firms even went so far as to give employees cash rewards for finding bugs in their products, creating an incentive for employees to plant these bugs in the first place and then (hopefully) catch and fix them before the products were released to the public.

- **Many organizations want effective training but recognize trainee attitudes or training time.** The desired outcomes of training should be business-critical skills, job knowledge, and improved business results. However, rather than recognizing this, most organizations recognize the *amount* of training that employees receive and the attitudes of trainees toward training events. Both of these factors have very little bearing on whether the skills are valuable, and the extent to which they will be used on the job, much less the impact on organizational effectiveness. I've seen many training courses that receive rave reviews from trainees, but the skills aren't used when the trainees get back on the job. This is often because no one ever recognizes (or reinforces) applying new skills (which requires more effort than using existing skills).

✔ **Many organizations want high performance from employees but recognize seniority.** There's nothing wrong with celebrating service anniversaries, but not at the expense of performance. Some companies not only tolerate mediocre performance; they encourage it by giving mediocre performers the same recognition they give outstanding performers. What kind of message does this send? To get high performance, you must recognize it.

✔ **Many organizations want problem-solving but recognize problem-hiding.** What happens when an employee speaks up about a problem in your organization? In many companies, problem-finders are viewed as troublemakers. No one can solve problems that are being hidden or ignored. Does your organization recognize whistleblowers or punish them? Remember that problems are really opportunities for improvement, and then trumpet those who make efforts to uncover them.

✔ **Many organizations want knowledge-sharing but recognize individual expertise.** You might be surprised by how many organizations are investing heavily in knowledge management but don't have the most critical enabler in place: a recognition system that recognizes knowledge-sharing and not knowledge-hoarding. As long as you recognize individual expertise above corporate expertise, this will continue to be the case. Make sure to reward collective knowledge!

✔ **Many organizations want creativity, but recognize conformity.** No organization can be successful without some degree of conformity. However, no organization can be truly successful without a significant amount of creativity. Creative behavior manifests when employees go beyond the "normal" requirements of the job and take initiative. Unfortunately, in many organizations, creativity is often punished rather than rewarded because it's messier and often causes problems associated with innovation. Many employees try to be creative, only to encounter resistance (not recognition) in the form of phrases like, "It won't work," "We've never done it that way before," and "That's just not feasible." Resistance also comes in the form of bureaucratic and cumbersome suggestion systems that purport to welcome ideas but do the opposite. Ensure your systems are welcoming of and recognize creativity!

✔ **Many organizations want safety but recognize *not* reporting accidents.** Recognizing lack of accidents often encourages employees simply *not to report* accidents or injuries. There are two ways to achieve excellent safety records: (1) maintain a safe workplace and recognize employees who engage in safety behavior or (2) recognize employees for not reporting the accidents that will inevitably happen, especially in an unsafe workplace. Which approach do *you* think is the better one?

✔ **Many organizations want cost containment but recognize bloated budgets.** How many times do you get "rewarded" for being under budget by getting your budgets cut the next year? In fact, that is the most frequent consequence of managerial frugality. Managers learn that the best way to defend against organizational cost cutting is by having a bloated budget!

In addition, across-the-board cost-cutting hurts those who have been running a tight ship much more than those who have bloated budgets and redundant staffs. This kind of cost-cutting actually reinforces budget padding, buffer stocks, and inventory cushions to protect against future shocks.

✔ **Many organizations want excellent customer service but recognize lack of complaints.** Really outstanding hospitality organizations realize that it's virtually impossible to improve customer service *without* customer complaints. In fact, the best customer-service organizations actually solicit complaints! Research has verified that effective recovery from a customer service problem is one of the key drivers of customer delight and building customer loyalty.

Recognizing desired results

Recognition is a wonderful thing, but recognizing the wrong things can actually undermine your organization's competitiveness and threaten its very survival. So, then, what should be done about this problem? In short, you must take an inventory of what is being recognized in your organization and then change it, if necessary, so that the recognition inspires the desired behavior or outcome. That means

✔ If you want profits, recognize profitable sales.

✔ If you want teamwork, recognize collaboration.

✔ If you want quality, recognize process improvement.

✔ If you want effective training, recognize business-critical skills used on the job.

✔ If you want high performance, recognize the results achieved.

✔ If you want problem solving, recognize problems found and solved.

✔ If you want knowledge sharing, recognize organizational expertise.

✔ If you want creativity, recognize creative ideas and solutions.

✔ If you want safety, recognize safe behaviors and conditions.

✔ If you want cost containment, recognize reduced spending.

✔ If you want customer service, recognize customer loyalty — which means that customer complaints are solicited and solved.

Avoiding Common Organizational Demotivators

There's one more thing I want you to consider before leaving this topic: built-in demotivators. Here are some of the most common demotivators that can be inadvertently built into a recognition program:

- **Unclear expectations:** Sometimes, due to poor design, planning, or communication, employees simply don't know what to expect from the recognition program. They don't know what their roles and responsibilities are, or what is supposed to happen during the program. This uncertainty makes them feel anxious and insecure (not the ideal conditions for a program that is supposed to be motivating). The solution, of course, is to make sure that expectations are very clear and unambiguous.

- **Unnecessary rules:** Recognition programs are sometimes so full of rules and guidelines that employees perceive them as being just more bureaucracy. Keep recognition programs simple.

- **Lack of follow-up:** Nothing's more demotivating than expecting a positive outcome and not getting it. Too many recognition programs make promises that cannot be kept, at least not in a timely fashion. Promise only what you can deliver and make sure your initiative delivers on all promises.

- **Constant change:** Change is particularly demotivating when employees perceive that the rules keep changing. When you change recognition programs, make sure that you are making them better (such as adding new recognition opportunities) and not simply changing the rules to the organization's advantage (such as making it more difficult for people to attain existing recognition levels). If you do need to raise the bar to address *recognition inflation* (when more staff keep reaching the goals), for example, consult with employees and explain the necessity of the change.

- **Unfairness:** If employees view recognition in your organization as unfair, your entire recognition program might be in serious jeopardy. Organizational recognition is particularly vulnerable to this concern, since the recognition criteria in one area of the organization could differ from the recognition criteria in another area. Don't think that employees don't compare — they do! The antidote: Keep the perception of fairness in mind while you are designing the program and keep track of any recognition disparities in different areas of the organization.

✔ **Hypocrisy:** Nothing is more demotivating than managers who say one thing and do another. Many recognition initiatives have been sabotaged by inconsistencies between *talk* and *walk*. There is no quick fix for hypocrisy. The countermeasure is to make executives aware of this pitfall and to monitor employee feedback that may indicate whether hypocrisy is still a problem. Then provide feedback to those who may be inadvertently sending the wrong messages.

✔ **Rewarding poor performance:** If employees see that poor performers are being recognized, the program (and whoever put it into place) will lose credibility. Recognition should always be earned. Never recognize those who don't deserve recognition! Here are some tips for ensuring you don't reward poor performance, from the book *Why Employees Don't Do What They Are Supposed to Do and What To Do About It,* by Ferdinand Fournies (McGraw-Hill Education):

- Examine the consequences you deliver when an employee fails to perform or creates problems.

- Don't reward nonperformance with attention, lunch, coffee, or lengthy discussions about personal problems.

- Don't personally correct errors made by nonperformers. Make sure that the employee responsible for the mistake also makes the correction.

- Give your attention to people who do the things the way you want them to be done without creating havoc for you.

- Don't assign someone else to take over work from the nonperformer. Work with him/her until either performance improves or you replace the nonperformer.

- When an employee is difficult to control, apply the necessary controls and negative consequences. If performance improves, provide immediate verbal recognition and praise.

- If an employee repeatedly complains about work assignments that are both fair and unavoidable, ignore it. Respond to the person with verbal rewards only when they correctly perform the job.

✔ **Management invisibility:** Too often, senior managers are visible during the initial launch of the recognition initiative but then disappear! This makes employees believe that the program is not really important to the organization and is, therefore, not deserving of their efforts or attention. Keeping a recognition initiative healthy requires continual management visibility. Senior managers should have specific roles to play in a recognition program (such as in presenting recognition to recipients) so that they will remain a visible part of it.

Part V
Issues and Challenges in Recognizing and Engaging Employees

Five Ways to Retain High-Performing Employees

- ✔ **Conduct *stay interviews*.** Rather than rely on the tradition of conducting exit interviews after employees give their notice and you can't do anything to keep them with the company, implement a practice of stay interviews, wherein you take time with each high-performing employees to find out what they like about their jobs, what they find challenging, and what it would take to have them stay for a long period of time.

- ✔ **Create a development plan for each employee.** Find out what your high-performing employees want out of their professional experience and make a strategy to help them achieve it. Give them experiences to grow, get promoted, and increase their skill-sets in ways that support their vision and goals.

- ✔ **Don't micromanage.** High-performing employees especially value autonomy and authority to do their jobs as they see fit. Give them the leeway to accomplish their tasks in their own ways.

- ✔ **Provide financial and nonfinancial rewards.** As your high-potential employees perform well, reward them well. You can give them financial rewards — like bonuses and raises — as well as nonfinancial rewards: opportunities to get involved in decisions, public recognition, and work that's interesting and challenging.

- ✔ **Grant them flexibility.** If they need a day off to do personal business, give it to them. If they need to work from home a couple of days a week, grant that to them. It's highly likely creative arrangements like this will lead to them performing at higher levels for you.

Find out more about what motivates and how to recognize different generations in the workplace in my online article at www.dummies.com/extras/recognizingandengagingemployees.

In this part . . .

- ✔ Understand how to use the right language, research, and angles when you pitch the idea of adopting recognition to your senior managers

- ✔ Put your business case together successfully to make recognition part of your company

- ✔ Learn about the impact Millennials have on the world of workplace recognition and discover how best to work with them

- ✔ Identify your high-performing employees' special motivation and recognition needs and meet those needs

Chapter 15

Selling Recognition to Senior Management

. . . .

In This Chapter

▶ Talking to executives in their own language

▶ Creating a pilot program to try out recognition

▶ Identifying the differences between senior management and employees that make it a hard sell

▶ Recognizing senior managers for recognizing you

. . . .

Sooner or later, you have to sell senior management on the benefits of recognition. For some, this time comes before they launch a new recognition program; for others, it comes when they need to continue or expand funding. The support and credibility that comes from top management endorsement is essential for a successful recognition initiative. With active support from the top, recognition initiatives take on a new urgency, encouraging employee participation at every organizational level. Without it, recognition programs and activities tend to be considered optional — or fads — and will consequently flounder or fail.

The road to recognition program success almost always passes through the offices of senior management, but as the preferences and priorities of top management vary widely, so, too, do the best approaches for selling them on recognition. Typically, however, no matter who's the boss, you are bound to run into resistance on the topic sooner or later. And when you do, following the strategies I outline in this chapter for influencing senior managers will help your executives recognize the importance of employee recognition and identify the roles they can play in making it happen more successfully in the organization. As Larry Colin, president of Colin Service Systems put it, "We realized that our largest asset was our work force and that our growth would come from asset appreciation."

The CEO/CFO Perspective on Human Resources

Whereas almost every executive claims, "Our people are our greatest asset," the typical CEO/CFO also realizes that people typically represent the greatest costs to the organization as well. Costs are *inputs* and reflect a historical value, or *sunk costs,* in the business. Assets are *outputs* and represent the future value of the organization. Because the CFO sees people as being either revenue generating, revenue maintenance, or overhead, you need to be able to show how any employee in the organization, if positioned well to do so, can more productively help the organization be successful. Then, as recognition drives results that are important to your organization, the return on the investment that was made in recognition will be more significant, and the case for further investment in recognition will be enhanced.

A paycheck is not a thank you, even though many, if not most, executives feel it should be thanks enough for a job well done. Yet the fact is that a paycheck is a contractual obligation for doing a job; recognition, on the other hand, is the appreciation for having the job done *well* — something that is not required as part of any work contract. In some ways, recognition is a more powerful tool for managing because the behavior *is not required*. That is, because recognition is an optional behavior, employees who receive recognition feel that their managers have been sincere in their thanks. As Roseabeth Moss Kanter, professor at Harvard University puts it, "Compensation is a right, recognition is a gift."

Best yet, recognition is free, so from a financial perspective, it has an infinite rate of return. Even an incremental 1 percent of payroll expenditure on recognition and rewards (the average company spends 2 to 3 percent of payroll on incentives) can have a significant impact on shaping employee behavior, whether that behavior relates to achieving the company's strategic objectives, living its core values, embracing cost-saving ideas, or going above and beyond to serve customers or help team members.

When I was in college, I held a part-time job working at a 7-Eleven. It was the late 1970s during an economic recession. I remember the regional manager coming in to talk with all the employees of our store one day, and he specifically went out of his way to say, "It's a tough employment market out there, so each of you should be glad you have a job, and if you aren't, there's the door." I felt insulted that this guy thought the only reason people were working was because they had to and that this was the best job we could get. His words revealed that he believed it didn't matter how management treated us. I quit the next day.

Seven Strategies for Obtaining Executive Buy-In

Many different ways exist to persuade others, but no single magic bullet works for everyone. And because different people are persuaded differently, you need to be able to call on different strategies when it comes time to make your case with upper management. In this section I explain seven strategies that I have seen successfully implemented in organizations to sell the topic of recognition to upper management.

One way to obtain executive buy-in that I like to advocate is to look at how other initiatives — for example, a new investment in a computer system, product, or market service — were sold in your organization. The same steps and justification that were made for that decision will most likely serve as a good template for selling a new or expanded recognition and rewards initiative in your organization.

Talking in terms they understand

To communicate effectively with any other person, you have to speak that person's language. The language of top management reflects their focus and priorities, and it typically includes concern for achieving the organization's strategic objectives, a cost/benefit analysis of potential management actions, and the financial bottom line" — the profit returned to the organization for any financial investment made from the organization's budget. Emphasize the importance of motivated employees for increasing sales revenue, productivity, quality, safety, customer service, or other key performance objectives.

To make a business case for recognition, point to the financial returns or specifically share the bottom-line impact that other companies have realized from recognition programs. Here are some examples:

- One oil refinery saved $18.8 million in two years through the use of various recognition gift programs and contests.

- The Travel Related Services division of American Express attributed a 500 percent increase in net income over 11 years due in part to recognition programs such as the Great Performers poster campaign.

- American Airlines, using a points-for-merchandise recognition program, was able to purchase a new airplane with $50 million in savings derived from employee suggestions.

By pitching recognition as a means of enhancing productivity, performance, and profitability, you can convince upper management that employee recognition is not just a "feel good, nice to do" activity, but a key driver for successfully achieving whatever objectives the organization has targeted.

For example, in many industries, tenure (how long someone stays working for the company) is important. The longer someone stays, the more that employee's knowledge, training, and experience can be leveraged to the benefit of the organization. According to the National Society for Human Resource Management, the costs of replacing a typical professional employee tend to average 1.5 times that person's annual salary. This amount doesn't even take into account the loss of organizational knowledge and training investment that occurs whenever anyone leaves an organization. You can examine your company's turnover statistics and calculate the cost of that turnover. If increasing recognition can lower the number of people that leave the organization by, say 20 percent, you can calculate the financial benefit of implementing more employee recognition. For example, if 100 people leave the organization in a given year and their average salary (with benefits) is $50,000, the cost of replacing those employees would be $75,000 $\times$ 100 = $7,500,000. Reducing that number by 20 percent equals $1.5 million of potential savings that would accrue from having a greater culture of recognition.

Sharing studies and statistics

Most top managers are analytical by nature; therefore, you can influence them by including evidence from research studies and surveys in your proposal. Research and statistics that connect recognition to goals and objectives that are important to the organization give you instant credibility. To obtain the latest recognition research, visit my website (http://www.drbobnelson.com) or go to Recognition Professionals International's website (http://www.recognition.org).

Here are a couple of examples of compelling research findings that may be useful:

- ✔ Robert Half International, the nationwide staffing firm, recently conducted a survey of why people leave their jobs and found the number one reason to be a lack of praise and recognition.
- ✔ According to the People, Pay, and Performance study, conducted by the American Productivity Center in Houston, it generally takes 5 percent to 8 percent of an employee's salary to change behavior if the reward is cash; if the reward is noncash, it takes approximately 4 percent of the employee's salary.

With research in hand, you can make a formal presentation to your manager or the organization's management team about the benefits that would accrue from creating a stronger culture of recognition. You could provide an analysis of the need to make the change, what that change would cost in financial resources or otherwise, benefits that you believe would accrue, and a timeline for proceeding — all supported by independent research (or internal calculations). Many organizations use an external firm or incentive service provider to help them set up, manage, and administer their recognition and rewards program. You can find such a firm through a request for proposal (RFP) that you distribute to various service providers.

Sharing industry best practices

The information you share with upper management should also include industry best practices. If you can show how, by being innovative about how they manage and motivate their employees, other successful companies like yours are producing bottom-line results, even the most hardened top managers are apt to listen more closely.

Aside from the two sources I mention in the preceding section (Robert Half International and American Productivity Center), you can find other best practices, survey, and research findings by doing a bit of searching on the Internet. Check out human resource organizations such as the Society for Human Resource Management (http://www.SHRM.org), the U.S. Department of Labor (www.dol.gov), and the Human Capital Institute (www.hci.org), among others. Be sure to include this information in the presentation you make to management.

Looking at the competition

Sometimes, data that hits closer to home has a greater impact on upper management than do general statistics. Although the glut of authoritative research on the value of motivated employees should be persuasive to any reasonable executive, it's also human nature to feel that, somehow, all those studies about other organizations are unrelated to the specific needs and circumstances of your company or industry. You can help bring a sense of relevance and urgency to the topic by citing your own evidence or what your company's competition is doing on the topic.

Imagine being able to say to key executives, "Yes, I can understand why you don't want to 'coddle' employees, but at the same time, some of the employee recognition practices and programs that our competitors currently use have been quite effective. These efforts are making it easier for them to attract the talent they need to stay competitive, to get a better return on the investment they're making in that talent, and to hold on to that talent longer. Unless we act soon with a more comprehensive plan on this topic, we will likely lose our ability to attract and keep talented employees."

You can often find out what your competitors are doing by looking at their websites and seeing how they're positioning their companies as great places for employees to work.

Surveying your employees

Demonstrating the impact of employee recognition, rewards, and motivation and tying those performance results to specific recognition efforts can be difficult. However, you must be diligent in trying to do so. To help quantify the impact, ask yourself these questions:

- ✔ What are the benefits of having employees who are more motivated?
- ✔ What are the liabilities if employees are not motivated?
- ✔ If the recognition initiative is successful, what will be different and improved, and what impact would that improvement have?

An essential starting point for this analysis is to survey your employees to determine what their current *motivational baseline* is. Many organizations do this through an annual or biannual employee survey that includes specific items about employee motivation, recognition, and/or engagement, such as "I feel valued for the job I do," "My manager appreciates my efforts and tells me so," "I receive the information I need to do a good job at work," "I'm thanked or recognized when I do good work," and so forth. Employees can rank each of these items on a 5-point scale from "least agree" to "most agree."

I recommend creating an index of a core number of questions, such as those listed previously. Doing so will give you a more robust measure than just a single variable. If it is unclear what the survey responses mean, hold one or more focus groups with employees in order to probe the questions more fully and obtain a clearer perspective as to those things that are important (or not) to employees in your organization. Include these survey results in any proposals you give to upper management.

If you're initially unsuccessful in presenting your proposal to create or enhance the organization's recognition and rewards program, gather feedback and learn from the process so that you can strengthen your proposal; then select a future time to again present your proposal to management for consideration.

Creating a pilot program

You can create your own success and build momentum for your recognition efforts by initiating a pilot program in your company and developing your own results. This strategy has the advantage of yielding data that is more relevant to your organization than general industry research would be because the pilot involves your own employees, performance goals, culture, competitive pressures, and managers.

You can influence the success of a pilot program by carefully selecting positive, proactive participants and closely monitoring what is done to ensure things don't get off track. Say, for example, that you have a department or facility that is especially interested in increasing employee recognition. The people in this department would be perfect candidates for a pilot program because they are ready and willing to try something new rather than being forced to participate because their performance or morale is low or their turnover is high.

When you discuss a possible pilot program with the leadership of the group you will be working with, talk about the following:

✔ When the pilot would start, what it would entail, and what objectives you hope to attain.

✔ What the time frame for the pilot will be. You want to allow enough time for changes to be made, but not so much time that the focus of the effort gets lost; a good time frame may be three to six months, for example.

✔ What success looks like. It's important to know in advance what success looks like because it's usually difficult to determine impact after the fact, when the evaluation becomes very fuzzy ("People seemed to like what we did, but it's unclear if there was any lasting impact").

✔ What the motivation baseline is. To find this, survey employees so you have something to use to demonstrate your pilot's results!

Here are some suggestions to give your pilot program the best chance at success:

✔ **Keep the pilot simple.** The fewer moving parts, the better. Otherwise, you are bound to lose sight of what variables impact the results you are able to attain.

✔ **Integrate employees from the selected area to help own and drive the changes you are attempting.** If people feel a sense of ownership, the program is more likely to be successful. Ideally, they would feel the pilot program was an opportunity to try something they were excited about doing.

✔ **Monitor initial efforts to try to get some immediate wins and excitement about the pilot.** Doing so can create momentum and excitement that becomes contagious to others in the group (and subsequently to other groups who can serve as the next areas to rollout the program!)

If, despite your efforts, the pilot is not successful, learn from it so as to be able to do a better pilot on the next attempt.

Making a personal appeal

If the logical approaches fall short of selling top management on the value of recognizing employees, you might try a personal appeal. At some point, most executives must make a leap of faith on this topic, so you need to reassure them that recognition is the right thing to do and that the organization can become known as a workplace where people come first. After all, if people truly are the organization's most important assets — as many company mission statements proclaim — then treating those people right should be a priority, not an afterthought, to the success of the organization.

Whether you can sway someone varies widely based upon many variables: the relationship you have with that person, the person's personality, and his or her hot buttons — the issues that he or she is especially passionate about. Sometimes, however, an effective approach can be as simple as asking the executive you are trying to persuade to trust you that the proposed solution will work; then you need to be committed enough to the strategy so that it does.

If your CEO doesn't believe the value of an incremental investment on behavior, use the example of an airline rewards program. Is your CEO loyal to any particular airline and, if so, do frequent flier points have anything to do with that loyalty? Chances are they do. The favored airline's points program drives the executive's preference to fly one airline over another often for a very nominal incremental financial benefit. This example is the same value that any manager can realize by making an effective use of employee recognition and rewards.

Boomerang Returns 3x Results with *DealerRewards*

Boomerang Tracking/LoJack is the North American leader in recovering stolen vehicles, heavy equipment, marine equipment, and other valuable property, and the company wanted a way to drive sales of the Boomerang/LoJack device and gain a competitive advantage in the auto dealer sales market.

In-depth online surveys revealed 77 percent of dealers believe an incentive attached to aftermarket items would influence their selling approach. Even more compelling, 94 percent of respondents said they were more likely to sell an aftermarket product that offers an incentive. Boomerang/LoJack saw an opportunity to increase its selling potential by implementing an attractive and user-friendly dealer incentive program.

Unfortunately, management in the firm questioned the need for incentives to drive the desired behavior. They weren't sure whether recognition was really what was needed, and they worried that the seemingly frivolous, difficult-to-measure activity might end up leading to a perpetual cost that could never be stopped. Some executives warned that the incentives were going to get out of hand. Overcoming a strong executive bias against the use of incentives, Boomerang launched a recognition initiative that achieved unprecedented results of 3x sales.

Starting with a limited pilot program and working with just a couple of agents in the company's call center, Boomerang took an incremental, grassroots approach to determining how best to roll out the program. Discussions with agents revealed obstacles of their jobs, what "going the extra mile" meant, what incentives would be meaningful to help encourage the desired behavior, and what recognition agents needed or wanted from their peers.

The four-month test with just five agents created an excitement and buzz that made it easier to expand the pilot program, which led to multiple loops of testing, integrating, and soliciting feedback for improvements on the incentive program. Boomerang launched DealerRewards in its largest market, where the program quickly exceeded the expectations and was expanded to several other major markets for the company. The DealerRewards incentive program has helped Boomerang achieve a 97 percent customer retention rate.

An online survey conducted two years into the program revealed how much dealers were engaged in DealerRewards. Here are some highlights of that survey:

- ✔ 30 percent of respondents find DealerRewards more motivating than other programs

- ✔ 60 percent find the program motivating

- ✔ 92 percent are satisfied with claim time, and 54 percent describe it as ""fast/very fast."

Other significant benefits include changes in company's corporate culture, as well as in the dynamics of the organization's teams and how the teams communicate what they are doing and their successes. Employees came to feel that "If you go the extra mile, you'll get more for your effort." Says Marc Roth, Incentives Manager, Boomerang/LoJack, "Pilot programs rule the day! If it's working, it's working; if it's not, keep communicating!"

Recognizing Why Convincing Top Management Isn't Easy

For all the evidence that points to the impact and importance of recognition and rewards on employee motivation and the desired behaviors and outcomes that result from that motivation, you'd think the topic would be easier to sell to top management. So why isn't it? Two reasons come to mind: different values and different senses of time.

Differences in values and time frames between executives and employees make recognition implementation more difficult to attain, yet the benefits of the effort far exceed the challenges of making it part of your workplace culture.

Different values from a different time

In my doctoral research, I found that, of the 140 variables I examined to see which one(s) most differentiated recognition-users from nonusers in the workplace, the demographic variable of *age* had the greatest significance. That is to say, the older someone is, the less likely he or she is to believe recognition is, or should be, important to today's employees. Perhaps this is because they grew up in a different time in which employees perhaps truly did feel lucky just to have a job or to be with a quality employer for the long term.

I know this sounds like a broad, politically incorrect generalization, and of course, exceptions to this research finding abound. I'm often inspired by top executives, regardless of their age, who truly get the importance of treating people right and valuing the contributions they make in frequent, sincere, and personal ways at work. Still, the exception is not the rule. Although we need to simply appreciate the fact that different people see the world differently, we also must persist in making the case for what might work best to inspire exceptional performance from employees.

Different executive and employee time frames

Executives think in terms of the business cycle: quarterly, semiannual, and annual periods of time. Employees, on the other hand, tend to focus more on daily and hourly activities. These different time perspectives influence each person's outlook and priorities at work. While employees look for more of a "here and now" recognition for the value they are adding in their job, an executive may be more comfortable in letting her employees know once a year in their performance reviews that they are doing a good job. Getting these two groups in the same time zone — or at least getting their time frames to overlap — can help to minimize differences in their respective outlooks at work.

Thus, in a fundamental dichotomy found in all organizations, management must constantly show employees how the immediate work they do ties to the long-term success and objectives of the organization, its mission, vision, and values while also appreciating employees for the successes they are having "here and now." They should not put recognition off to some future time, such as the end of the year review, or — worse — fail to acknowledge employees' successes at all.

Getting Top Managers to Model Recognition

Getting top managers to practice recognition sets the tone for all managers and sends the message, "If *I* can make time to do this, no one else in the organization has an excuse not to." For example, the publisher of *The Washington Post* writes hand-written notes to reporters, which tend to become career milestones to the recipients. The CEO of the Phoenix Textile Corporation hosts a monthly breakfast for representatives from each department of the company to acknowledge the representatives' efforts and see how the organization can better meet its employees' needs.

In this section, I cover some effective strategies for getting executives personally involved in using recognition.

Assessing what managers are able to do

You have to determine what top managers are able and willing to do and then help structure a specific plan that keeps them to their commitment.

For example, I worked with an introverted president of a company who confessed that he was terribly uncomfortable with directly praising employees. Telling such a person he must personally praise employees would be counterproductive and likely unsuccessful. So I told him, "You don't have to praise employees, but you do have to do something to recognize them." We brainstormed possibilities, and the executive decided to hold monthly lunches with small groups of employees (one from each department in the company) in which all present shared what they were working on in their jobs that excited them. Over the course of each meal, he got to know his employees better, and his employees, given the chance to ask questions, got to know him better as well. Both the employees and the CEO benefited from the activity.

Steve Wittert, former president of Paragon Steakhouse Restaurant, a restaurant chain based in San Diego, California, told me that he knew appreciating employees was important, but at the same time, he found that he didn't do as much of it as he wanted because he was so busy. One day, he concluded that being busy was simply an excuse, and so he decided that, no matter how busy he was, he could always take a few minutes at the end of each day to reflect on the outstanding performances of his people — those who wowed a customer, helped a coworker, or turned in a cost-saving idea, for example — and to jot a personal thank-you note to each of those individuals. To help keep his commitment to this activity, Wittert bought a stack of thank-you cards and placed them on his desk by his telephone to serve as a daily reminder. Although he didn't write notes every day, he did so on a majority of days, in part because of the grateful response he received from his employees. He found that, although the notes took just a few moments to write, they were often a highlight of the recipients' day or week.

Providing choices

Everyone likes to have alternatives and options. So give those in the top tiers of management a choice for their level of involvement. Outline different roles they might play in the recognition program and get their commitment to one or more of them. For example, Shimadzu Scientific Instruments in Columbia, Maryland, has a simple, but successful way to personally involve top management in its recognition program: Outstanding performers in the organization are "promoted" to special assistant to the president for two weeks! Not only is this a great source of recognition for the employees, who return to their jobs with a new appreciation of senior management challenges, but it also helps the CEO connect with top performers in the company. Communication is improved and misconceptions are minimized.

Here are some other ways you can personally involve top managers with recognition in your organization:

- ✔ Host a recognition kickoff meeting in which your top executive explains the strategy and importance of the topic.
- ✔ Have the CEO or other executives present top individual or group recognition awards.
- ✔ Have your executives discuss recognition with their immediate managers and identify recognition opportunities they can act on with their employees.
- ✔ Include an executive on the recognition committee and have that person introduce the recognition committee members at a company meeting.

Helping them look good

If you want upper management to be personally involved in supporting recognition in your organization initially and on an ongoing basis, you need to find ways that they can look good when they are using or advocating recognition. For example, if you want the CEO to write a letter or e-mail to endorse a new recognition program or an upcoming recognition event, draft the letter for that executive so that the CEO sounds well-educated on the initiative (and you get bonus points for making his life easier!).

If you are having your president present formal awards at a banquet, research some personal stories about each recipient for the president to share at the ceremony, and go over the pronunciation of the names of those being honored prior to the event. Then you might arrange for the senior manager to personally meet with the honorees prior to the awards banquet. If you are trying to get your CEO to be more visible in the office or on the plant floor, escort him or her through those facilities so that you can make introductions (most CEOs don't know the names of employees they may have seen only on select occasions).

Here are some examples of how top managers got personally involved in the topic of recognition:

✔ Scott Mitchell, president of Mackay Envelope in Minneapolis, holds a one-on-one, 20-minute discussion with every employee in the organization every year. During these meetings, the employee is free to discuss ideas, improvements, or whatever is on his or her mind. Mitchell devotes more than 170 hours to this task each year, an investment that he feels is time well spent.

✔ Hal Rosenbluth, CEO of Rosenbluth International, now American Express Travel Services, a chain of travel agencies headquartered in Philadelphia, is accessible to all his employees through an 800-number voice mail box. Employees are encouraged to call in with suggestions, problems, or praise. An average of seven employees do so every day.

✔ Mary Kay Ash, founder of Mary Kay, Inc., made a commitment to meet with every new employee within 30 days of hire. She once even turned down an invitation to the White House because it conflicted with a new employee orientation session she had committed to months before. Mary Kay's philosophy: "Make people who work for you feel important. If you honor and serve them, they'll honor and serve you."

Finding an executive sponsor

How do you find an executive sponsor? Identify senior managers who will be most receptive to recognition programs. Make alliances with key senior managers who you think might be the innovators or early adopters for recognition programs — those who are passionate about the topic or are good at championing new causes. Try to find senior managers who are championing programs or initiatives for which recognition might be a natural complement. For example, the senior vice president of human resources might already be interested in improving employee retention or promoting an employee wellness program. Show him or her how recognition can be an integral component of those programs. In other cases, show the linkages between recognition and other improvements in sales, customer service, quality control, productivity, and so on. If you link recognition to desired performance or initiatives that are near and dear to the hearts and personal agenda of senior leaders, you will improve the leverage of the topic.

✔ Herb Kelleher, CEO and cofounder of Dallas-based Southwest Airlines, demonstrates his personal commitment and willingness to be personally involved by helping flight attendants serve beverages to customers when he flies on his airline.

✔ Andy Grove, former chairman of Intel, would conduct a half-dozen or so open forums every year at difference Intel locations. Whenever Grove was in his cubicle (all employees at Intel work in cubicles), any employee was welcome to drop in and speak with him. "Management is about organized common sense," said Grove, "We communicate and communicate and communicate, at every level, in every form. Anyone can ask anybody any question."

Recognizing Top Management for Recognizing Others

After you get your CEO or upper management to use recognition, make sure you notice and thank them for their efforts. Top managers are no different from other employees in their need to be recognized. If you provide positive consequences for top management's involvement in recognition activities, you'll increase the chances of greater future involvement.

Here are some suggestions:

✔ Allow top managers to announce recognition program successes to the organization when a milestone is achieved.

✔ Thank top managers for their recognition efforts in a letter from the employees and/or the recognition committee.

✔ Create a top manager's recognition award, nominated and voted on by employees.

Successfully designing and implementing a recognition program — and getting the leaders in your company to increase the budget for recognition activities — requires not only conviction and persistence, but also a strategic approach to winning over top management. Don't waste time complaining that your organization doesn't have satisfactory recognition programs or support; instead, propose a recognition program and sell management on why it needs to happen now. Do your homework and show management that the behavior or goals the company wants to achieve can be accomplished as a direct result of employee recognition on the part of the executives and all managers throughout the organization. Obtaining the support of top management is a critical step in the implementation of a successful recognition initiative, especially one that crosses organizational lines and requires financial resources.

Chapter 16

Recognizing and Engaging Millennials

In This Chapter

▶ Discovering the profile of Millennials

▶ Reframing your expectations to manage Millennials

▶ Realizing how Millennials are changing the game

▶ Motivating Millennials

Millennials — born roughly between 1980 and 2000 — are currently the largest generation in the workplace and are expected to make up 75 percent of all workers by 2025. An estimated 44 million are already working, and 46 million more will become a part of the workforce in the years ahead. As 10,000 baby boomers a day retire, Millennials will come to dominate the workforce in both number and attitude, and in the process, reshape the work experience for all employees. As a manager of Millennials, you want to know what's important to this generation and how employers can best tap into the potential of this generation of workers.

Understanding this generation is critical if you want to attract Millennials to work for your organization and keep them there. The average tenure of a Millennial (how long they stay with an employer) is currently just 1.8 years. According to the *Harvard Business Review*, 76 percent of currently employed Millennials say they plan to find a new job as the economy improves. Given that it costs employers on average $15,000 to $25,000 to replace every Millennial who leaves an organization, it's worth taking a closer look at how you can best recognize and engage Millennials in your organization today so that they give you their best efforts and stay with your organization.

Profiling Millennials

Known by a variety of names (Gen Y, the Nintendo Generation, the Microwave Generation, Generation Next, the Net Generation, Generation Why, the Echo Boomers, and the Trophy Generation), Millennials are well-educated, have high aspirations for themselves and their careers, and have a lofty sense that who they are and what they do matters. They love all things high-tech, have and expect instant connections, and are highly optimistic and socially responsible. Millennials bring some tremendous skills and attributes to the workplace, which can at times be offset by perceived negatives of their generation.

Looking at the upsides

Millennials have a lot to offer, and if you can play to their strengths, you and your company will reap enormous benefits. They are techno wizards; they are not only at complete ease with today's technology, but they are also avid users, more so than any generation to come before them. They are quick learners and very resourceful — good at finding answers from whomever and wherever. They are multitaskers, able to quickly change focus from one item to the next and then back again as needed. They are optimistic, hardworking, and high-achieving, systematically setting and then achieving goals in rapid sequence. Although high achievers of any age or in any generation can possess these characteristics, a majority of Millennials has these traits, not just a select few. And better yet, these attributes all happen to be ideal characteristics that almost every employer needs from its employees to be competitive today.

Checking out the downsides

Millennials also tend to have a downside as well. Knowing the challenges that Millennials can present in the workplace enables you to better work through those challenges. For starters, Millennials expect to have meaning and purpose in their jobs from the very first day of work. They look to be challenged — some might say entertained — constantly. They tend to have an inflated opinion of themselves and are overconfident, especially given their limited work experience. They want to earn more sooner and to have both job status and respect, regardless whether either has been earned. They are impatient and not interested in "paying their dues" to earn such respect. Notably, they need and demand instant feedback and praise on an ongoing, daily basis.

Other generations tend to react negatively to these attributes, feeling that Millennials are a generation of spoiled, entitled youth that need to wake up to the realities of work in which everything does not revolve around them. They need to "pay their dues" and earn the respect of their colleagues and management before they are trusted with greater responsibility. However, if managers can look past or work through Millennials' perceived shortcomings, they will have an easier time tapping into the vast potential this generation has to offer.

Reframing Expectations

To work successfully with the Millennial generation, you should do your best to check and possibly shift your expectations. What was once expected treatment of a new employee is no longer the norm. This generation feels entitled and expects more from its employers. Millennials have been raised to believe they are special; they are from a generation that has been told they can achieve anything. They have big dreams and plans, which they are in a hurry to achieve.

These are positive attributes, but they need to be channeled — and that's the job of their managers (like it or not). I'm not talking about abdicating your role as a manager or about letting them do whatever they want. I'm talking about painting a bigger picture of the organization's mission and vision and showing them how they fit in that picture, connecting their values and skill-sets to the work that you need them to do. I'm talking about channeling their energies in ways that will be productive for them, their managers, and the organization.

Yes, work can seem easier when everyone is the same, when we all value the same things, act the same way, and conform to the same norms, but for Millennials, it's just as easy to accept the notion that people can be who they are — different from one another — and still stay clearly focused on what is needed to get the work done.

If you give your Millennial employees a reason to get excited, they can and will show an extraordinary work ethic and passion to get the work done and to have fun in the process. Keep the focus on the work and not on things that may not matter anyway to the quality of work (for example, dress, informality, nontraditional working hours, communication preferences, and so on). Consider the lesson to be learned from social networking giant Facebook, based in Palo Alto, California. Facebook is known for its open culture and lack of enclosed workspaces, walls, or cubicles. Neither the COO nor the CEO has an office, and at the Microsoft office in Portland, Oregon, employees can even work in their pajamas.

Work's most motivating aspects to employees in general are things that don't tend to cost much, if any, money. This is especially true of for Millennials; in fact, 88 percent of Millennials don't feel money is their main motivator, and 78 percent say they will work for less if challenged. Taking time to get to know them, asking for their opinions and ideas (and encouraging and supporting them in pursuing those ideas), involving them in decisions (especially those that affect them and their work), creating opportunities to connect with others at work or otherwise, focusing on learning and development opportunities — these are the motivational opportunities that any manager can deploy that this generation of workers most values.

How Millennials Are Changing the Way People Work

The influx of the Millennials into the workforce is changing many traditional rules that earlier generations of workers have grown accustomed to. This generation of workers has entered the workforce with different attitudes, expectations, and ambitions than those held by their predecessors. They are considered the best-educated generation ever and the first truly globalized generation of workers. They expect positive work culture, work-life balance, meaningful work, and social responsibility. Perhaps most significantly, they expect to use technology and social media as a matter of course in any job.

Relying on technology more than ever before

Millennials have grown up with technologies that have shrunk the workplace, expanded their horizons, and made them feel comfortable operating in a borderless world. Having grown up with technology, they expect it to be an ever-available tool for all they do and especially when it involves their work. They bring their integral knowledge and access of technology to their jobs and, along with it, increased efficiency in problem-solving, creativity, and innovation. They are quick to apply technology tools and apps to get routine work assignments done in efficient, new ways that their managers may have little or no knowledge about.

For them, the digital workplace also means dealing with colleagues from different cultures in different time zones in a virtual world. There is a universality to the Internet in which everyone has equal access. Thus, they more easily assimilate perspectives from different cultures and backgrounds and are perhaps better able to evaluate contributions based on the merits of the idea as opposed to the background of the person suggesting the idea. The benefits of diversity in the workplace are well-documented, and the Millennials bring a rich opportunity to challenge established notions, refresh practices, and tap into new thinking, technologies, and attitudes.

Expecting a positive work culture

Eight-eight percent of Millennials consider a positive work culture to be essential. For this generation, the workplace is not solely about work; it is a place for social interaction, shared learning, and meaning and purpose in their lives. Workplace culture, relationship-building, and ongoing learning are thus critical to these individuals.

Consider these examples:

- ✔ According to Jeff Ellman, Homescout Realty cofounder and managing broker, the Chicago-based agency was built around Millennials. "I care more about culture than anything," says Ellman. "We won't hire someone if they don't fit. We have a culture-based interview based on the five Fs: Fit, Family, Fun, Fortune, and Freedom. If you don't fit in our culture, this won't be the right fit for you."

- ✔ Google, based in Mountain View, California, has a policy that requires each new office to have a tenured "Googler" as one of its first ten employees. The Googler's role is to ensure that the culture is passed along from veterans to rookies. The company has also developed "Culture Clubs," made up of volunteers who help maintain the culture.

Expecting increased work-life balance

For Millennials, the lines between their work and personal lives are blurred. They are the first generation to have been raised in a 24/7 environment, where people are connected to both their work and social lives at all hours, year-round. The social media revolution has made that possible, and the Millennials for the most part love it.

Issues involving work-life balance are important to Millennials because the boundaries between the two are ill-defined. For Millennials, there needs to be some level of compromise.

The workplace itself is evolving to meet some of these requirements:

- ✔ SAS, the world's largest privately held software business, based in Raleigh, North Carolina, gives employees flexibility in their work schedule to help promote work-life balance. SAS allows employees to work a schedule that is best for the employee as long as they get their work done. "We focus on results and not the micromanagement our employees' time. We trust our employees and treat them with respect. Many company policies and practices are in place assuming the worst in their people; we assume good and deal with those who prove us wrong as we need to," says Jenn Mann, vice president of human resources.

- ✔ Chicago-based Total Attorneys, a process-improvement firm that helps small law offices and solo practitioners streamline their practices, does its best to give Millennial employees a sense of ownership and belonging, while providing opportunities for their personal lives to blend into their work lives. CEO Edmund Scanlan has lunch with all new employees, where he tells them they have freedom to do what they want — for example, decorating their offices in unique ways or checking their Facebook pages. Employees enjoy an on-site gym, a TV room, and beer-and-wine Fridays. They can also attend corporate events that the company hosts.

> ✔ Euro RSCG, the Chicago-based marketing and advertising agency, offers greater integration of work with other pursuits, including outreach and community programs, extensive training, lunch-and-learn sessions, art-making events, and a Ping-Pong table to its workforce. Millennial employees have access to senior employees, and the CEO regularly sends e-mails and letters to keep them abreast of the agency's operations.

As a manager of Millennials, devise creative ways to work with the blurred boundaries between work and personal life rather than get put off by them. If you can show your Millennial employees that your organization offers flexibility and fluidity in the work done, they will be more likely to want to put in the time necessary to do the best job possible for you!

Expecting more from their careers

The issues of career paths, responsibility, and promotion frequently arise in regard to Millennials. Some people say this population of workers is overly ambitious, even impatient. What's apparent is the significant focus Millennials have on making the most of opportunities and advancing their careers. This tendency can affect decisions concerning job stability and tenure. Members of this generation need to be constantly engaged and excited about what they are doing, and they have a low tolerance for waiting for their next job opportunity to become available (especially if that next job is their manager's!)

The Millennial definition of a career path differs from the traditional job ladder that older employees are familiar with. With a job ladder, an employee might expect a promotion every five years or so to a higher paying, higher status position within the firm. Millennials, on the other hand, tend to view a career path as a "job lattice" in which they are given a series of varying job opportunities, not necessarily of higher position status or pay, but each one being a learning opportunity that is exciting to them. As it turns out, such a varied career progression suits many in this generation just fine and allows them to develop a portfolio of constantly exciting opportunities to engage and hold their interest and passion.

The task of recruiting and managing Millennials can seem bewildering, especially for managers whose approaches are based on old notions of command and control. Understanding the varying needs of the different generations — everything from communication style to management techniques to organizational structures — becomes important if you want to meet all your employees' needs. When generational differences are better understood, you stand a better chance of creating a high-performing workplace in which everyone works better together to achieve common objectives.

Employers worldwide are adapting to these behaviors and striving to get the best out of the diversity that characterizes the Millennial generation. Critical to recruiting and motivating this generation is an understanding of their social and cultural drivers, allowing them to be who they are at work.

Valuing ethics and social responsibility

The Millennials bring new approaches to the issue of ethics, the environment, and social responsibility in the workplace. They are more likely than previous generations to want to work for firms that have a good reputation for ethical and environmental responsibility, and they are ready to tell others when their employer is doing well or doing poorly. They are acutely sensitive to the changing fortunes of brands and the way in which social, ethical, and cultural influences can enhance or destroy corporate reputation. Note that

- ✔ 61 percent are actively worried about the world.
- ✔ 72 percent want to make a direct social impact.
- ✔ 60 percent value a sense of purpose in an employer.
- ✔ 81 percent donate to one or more charities.

These stats mean that many Millennials are very attuned to what the company they work for does, and if it doesn't align with their own personal values, they are less likely to stay. They want to do good work for others.

If your company's mission isn't directly tied into that effort, you can ask your Millennial workers if they would be interested in forming a specific committee just to tackle these concerns. Many companies involve the younger generation with much success when addressing issues of corporate and social responsibility. Not only is it a perfect outlet for the Millennials' values, but it usually impacts companies in a very positive way, both inside the organization and in the public's eye.

Millennials' Five Key Job Expectations

All the attributes just discussed influence Millennial job expectations. According to Pew research, half of Millennials would rather have no job than a job they don't like. So what makes for a job they do like? In a survey of 150,000 recent graduating students from 1,000 universities, research firm Experience, Inc., found that these are the attributes Millennials most wanted in a job:

- ✔ Career advancement opportunities (55%)
- ✔ Salary (52%)
- ✔ Interesting and challenging work (42%)

  ✔ Benefits (30%)

  ✔ Training/mentorship (27%)

By simply being aware of these five preferences, you can make a concerted effort to include them in your ongoing management of your Millennial employees. When you bring on new Millennial employees, make sure to sit down with them and discuss these attributes. Also talk about how your Millennial employees sees these attributes playing into their career planning. Make a plan to include these aspects in the employee's work accordingly; then actively and regularly follow up on it.

Several companies employ innovative strategies to engage new hires even before they join the organization include. Consider these examples:

  ✔ Software company Intuit, in Mountain View, California, has developed a Rotational Development Program for new hires to switch between finance, marketing, and product development every 6 to 12 months (see the nearby sidebar for more on how Intuit taps and fosters its younger employees).

  ✔ Defense contractor Lockheed Martin in Fort Worth, Texas, reaches thousands of students and potential new hires during National Engineers Week in February through various hands-on projects and presentations that show how engineering impacts everyday life.

  ✔ FactSet, a software company based in Connecticut, sends new hires who are college seniors a gift basket and a good-luck note before they take their final exams.

  ✔ L'Oreal USA created the L'Oreal Brandstorm Competition for college students to play the role of a L'Oreal brand manager and help develop marketing and advertising campaigns. Winners receive a trip to Paris to interact with top L'Oreal managers.

Intuit: Igniting creativity in younger employees

Scott Cook, founder of Intuit, believes that the newest and youngest employees are often the most valuable when it comes time to make changes and inject fresh ideas. He makes an effort to spend time with them and believes that he can learn from them. He's found that this approach ignites the creative process and makes employees feel more valued.

The practice at Intuit has been so successful because Cook doesn't just solicit ideas from younger employees; he lets the younger employees stay truly involved in the projects they dream up. For example, rather than take accepted proposals and assign them to more senior managers, Cook lets the employees who introduced the concept take the project and run with it. Not only does this put less visible employees at the head of very visible projects, but it also encourages innovative thinking and shows that the company truly values input from all employees, no matter their rank.

Motivating the Millennials

The key to motivating the Millennial generation is harnessing these aspects of the work relationship: managerial time, work direction, personal development, social interaction, feedback, praise and meaningful rewards. As a manager of Millennials, you should understand the complexities of each of these areas and strive to put into action various practices that meet your Millennial employees' needs.

Managerial time

In studies of this younger generation, one motivator that consistently ranked highest was time with one's manager. According to Pew research, Millennials are five times more likely to quit if they have poor relationships with their managers. Managers need to make special efforts both to be available and to actually connect with younger employees on a more frequent basis at work.

To meet this need, managers in some organizations have one-on-one discussions with employees who report directly to them at least once every two weeks. During these meetings, employees set the agenda, which typically includes questions they need answered, items they want to discuss, or advice they need from their managers.

Here are some other examples of companies that make time with a manager a priority:

- Larry Meadows, a manager at Chick-fil-A in Asheville, North Carolina, makes a special point to call individuals into his office on a regular basis to discuss how things are going and to hear their concerns.

- New hires at ViaSat, the satellite communications company based in Carlsbad, California, are free to approach upper management with questions or to contribute new ideas. The door to executive leaders is always open.

- The law firm of Kelly Kronenburg, P.A. in Fort Lauderdale, Florida, values collaboration and promotes an open-door policy for younger associates to chat with more seasoned attorneys.

Work direction

Millennials want and expect to be constantly excited about how they are spending their time at work, and they want to do so on their terms. Sixty-nine percent want more freedom at work, 89 percent want to choose where and when they work; and three out of five expect to be able to work remotely.

They are consummate multitaskers, able to do a variety of tasks in fast succession, often utilizing the power of technology. Easily bored, they want and need to be challenged, which can be a blessing for managers who want to take advantage of their energy, skills, and resourcefulness, or a curse for managers who feel they don't have the time or energy to constantly assess whether these workers are excited about the work they are doing.

According to the Gallup Organization, only 28 percent of Millennials are currently "engaged"' in the workforce — the lowest employee engagement of any generation at work. If their current job does not excite them, they are quick to look for another job opportunity: 47 percent of Millennials report they plan to look for another job with a different organization.

Provide clear work expectations but allow Millennials to bring their own imprint to their jobs. Show them the big picture — how their jobs relate to the mission, strategic objectives, and core values of the organization. Ask for and use their ideas as much as possible or encourage them to pursue their own ideas when those have merit. This generation is very socially conscious, so clearly and directly linking the work they do to your organization's mission and its clientele has a strong impact. Likewise, supporting their efforts at volunteering is recommended because 72 percent of Millennials want to make a direct social impact on the world.

Consider these examples:

- ✔ At Zubi Advertising Services, Inc., headquartered in Coral Gables, Florida, manager Michelle Zubizarretta gives younger staffers a seat at the table. She asks them how they would talk to young consumers for a business pitch. Another initiative is the creation of innovation groups, setting up teams to develop ad-related iPhone apps and other original ideas.

- ✔ Marketing software company HubSpot in Cambridge, Massachusetts, believes in transparency and revealing everything to its employees — from cash burn rates to comments on the company's Wiki page. CEO Brian Halligan says that this transparency is just one aspect of HubSpot's push toward a corporate culture of teamwork and collaboration. Halligan believes that the Millennial generation has radically changed the way HubSpots' employees work and live and that companies need to change the way they manage. HubSpot works to create an extremely flat and transparent organization to meet the expectations of its employees. Halligan himself doesn't have an office, and his salary is not that different from other employees. HubSpot has its own Wiki, and people have no problem calling out Halligan in the Wiki. Halligan believes that employees today, who have grown up with social media, expect transparency and authenticity from their leaders.

Keys to the kingdom

Carmen Villarma, President of the Management Group, a property management firm based in Vancouver, Washington, and Portland, Oregon, says she had a new 416-unit apartment complex that she needed to rent out in a hurry. She went to a group of Millennials that worked for the company and said, "Here are the keys to the office. You can work whenever you want; you can do whatever you need to get this apartment complex rented!" The young team of workers rose to the occasion, starting a Twitter campaign, making a bunch of YouTube videos, hosting parties for open houses, and so on. They succeeded in getting all units in the complex rented in record time. They then decided to celebrate their success (they already received greater compensation for their work), and they went to Las Vegas as a group. Although one of the team members didn't make her goal on the project, the others wanted her to go to Las Vegas with them because she had been a supportive team member and helped the others along the way. When the group returned from the trip, they asked Carmen, "Do you have any other apartment complexes you need rented out?"

Personal development

Millennials expect constant learning and personal development and growth, and they expect their managers to serve as coaches and mentors (75 percent of Millennials want mentors). Therefore, Millennials' managers need to take the time to help coach their Millennial employees and, in the process, show them how they can make a positive, meaningful impact at work.

Redefine the time frame for this generation's focus and show them how the things they are doing now can lead to things they want to do in the future. Talk with them about their interests and the ways they can apply their skills; talk about career paths and needs of the organization; and discuss strategies for learning and opportunities that they can pursue to help them prepare to meet future opportunities.

Following are examples of training or mentoring opportunities that appeal to Millennials:

- Junior employees at Hitachi in Portland, Oregon, get an average of 300 hours of training a year.
- Chicago-based investment firm Morningstar sends its entry-level employees through a two-year rotational process called the Morningstar Development Program. The new employees learn the business and where they fit into it. They stay in one role for one year and can then move to different roles to learn skills in other areas. The firm also gives its Millennial employees relatively high levels of responsibility.

✔ Chicago-based insurance company Assurance has many initiatives to motivate millennial employees. Because many of these employees have no insurance background, 75 percent participate in continuing education. Employees get $100 when they pass a class. Fun programs include the Assurance Casino (employees get a chip when they meet goals, increasing their chances for winning cash prizes), an Employee Appreciation Day, and an Assurance 5K run. Instead of using a suggestion box, the agency created Ivan Idea, a mascot shaped like a light bulb, to collect ideas from employees. Employees get $5 for every business improvement idea they submit. The best idea wins a $250 gift card.

✔ Accounting firm Deloitte & Touche, headquartered in New York, makes new recruits immediately eligible for its Future Leaders Apprentice Program, a development program that helps them grow professionally and learn applicable job skills.

Talk to Millennials in terms of development opportunities and the long term, referencing time frames that exceed the given task or assignment. If you shape the context for your relationship with Millennials as extending years into the future and focus on how you will help them grow and gain experience, they will be more likely to remain with your company rather than look to change jobs at the first sign of frustration or disappointment.

Job-shadowing: Bringing hands-on training to light

Job-shadowing (having one person follow another around in his or her job) offers employees experiential, hands-on learning opportunities, and Millennials have a special affinity for it. Shadowing affords a current or prospective employee the chance to be immersed in the actual job environment, making it possible to see an experienced worker apply the skills and traits needed to accomplish the work. An insightful observer can glean information about the personal characteristics that contribute to success in the position.

Some employers prefer to orient new employees before involving them in job-shadowing to build on the new employee's existing knowledge of the company. Post-orientation job-shadowing can reinforce loyalty, strengthen the orientation (or "onboarding") process by which Millennials integrate into the company and their jobs, and shorten the time it takes a new hire to get up to speed.

Pamela Genske, human resources director for Blue Cross & Blue Shield of Rhode Island, says her firm's employees learn about shadowing opportunities in orientation and can ask for a shadowing assignment any time after joining the company. "People remember what happens in situations they've been placed in much more effectively than they recall a theory they've been taught in a classroom," says Genske. The Indiana Department of Corrections and the YMCA are other organizations that offer job-shadowing.

Social interaction

Millennials are very social and perhaps more peer-group-oriented than previous generations. Most of their upbringing and educational and social experiences has revolved around groups, be it playing interactive video games, participating in group sports, or connecting on Facebook with their friends.

Use these generational preferences to your advantage by allowing Millennials to work together on projects and assignments, hosting team-building activities and celebrations — even organizing nonwork social situations such as outings, team sports, or charity events. If they tend to work best with others and if they get into a project by talking it through with coworkers, let them do that. Make clear what you need the end result to be, but let them bring the imprint of who they are to the task so they can be excited about the work and even have fun getting it done (you may not need your job to be fun to get it done, but don't fault them if that's their preference!).

Some real-life applications of this concept include the following:

- Umpqua Bank in Oregon has outfitted its branches with cafes and couches and often provides recreational activities in the office for its employees.

- Oregon Cascade Plumbing and Heating, based in Salem, Oregon, regularly hosts contests and awards a Kermit the Frog Statue to whoever has the best decorated office or the ugliest shirt.

- Kimley-Horn and Associates, an engineering firm in North Carolina, holds regular lunchtime forums for employees to network, share advice, and plan social get-togethers.

- Marriott Hotels offer a Teamwork-Innovations program for employees to improve efficiency by working together and scheduling their own hours.

Feedback and praise

One of the most defining characteristics of the Millennial generation is its significant need for constant feedback and praise at work. This need can be frustrating for other generations to understand, as in, "I just told you last week that you were doing a good job. Do I really have to tell you again?" It's easy to dismiss this need as being a symptom of a generation spoiled by parents who showered them with constant praise and protected them from the harsher realities of life, or to believe that Millennials have frail egos and constantly need to be puffed up.

Evolution Fridays

Huan Ho, cofounder of Rallyteam, an engagement and social media platform that allows employees to connect and collaborate with a suite of social productivity tools in a single, unified platform, uses what it calls Evolution Fridays to evolve and constantly improve. Every second Friday, employees meet as a team to discuss what they can do to improve their company; they then break out into small groups to work on those items. The purpose of these sessions is to break out of the mold, think outside the box, and work on initiatives that will evolve the company's systems, processes, and/or team. The only rule: It cannot be operational work, and you must have fun doing it!

For the team meeting, each person takes the lead on facilitating one of the following sessions:

✔ **Round Table:** 15 minutes to discuss evolution projects and goals, to hold each other accountable, and to share ideas and provide feedback.

✔ **Lessons Learned:** 15 minutes to share any lessons learned over the past two weeks. Sometimes this session takes longer if a team member wants to do a more formal training session. Guest speakers have also been brought in from other teams as well.

✔ **Leaders Journey:** 15 minutes to discuss how they can become better leaders. This often entails discussing examples of good leadership and reading and discussing articles on leadership.

✔ **Challenge/Debate:** 15 minutes to complete a team challenge or debate (When I visited, I had a box of mind benders to help facilitate this.) The challenges and debates were often unrelated to work, but it helped participants develop their team communication and collaboration skills.

After the sessions, participants have the rest of the afternoon off to work on the evolution projects. These projects can be anything from developing new forecasting models to organizing the next volunteer event. Huan Ho has implemented Evolution Fridays with his team for over two years, and they love it! Apart from building a stronger team, they've improved their systems and processes, which had a direct impact on the company's bottom line.

But instead, consider this perspective: The Millennials are smart enough to realize that in fast-moving, constantly changing times, people need constant feedback to be on the mark and to adjust their performance accordingly. Think about the level of video game feedback, something that's second nature to this generation. Reportedly, someone playing a video game gets feedback over 50 times per minute. Because job requirements and expectations are constantly in flux, yesterday's feedback may no longer be relevant today. Constant feedback, thus, is necessary, not as a way to pump up a frail ego but as a practical way to show employees when they are on track so that they can continue to do good work day after day for their managers and employers. Feedback and praise serve as an emotional reinforcement as well as a practical mechanism for communication for this generation — they love it.

By "constant feedback," I don't mean *micromanaging,* a negative term that is almost always associated with an ongoing stream of negative feedback on even the smallest of items and corrections that a manager makes to control an employee's performance. No one feels micromanaged when the boss tells them in specific detail what he or she most liked about a great job the employee did.

Make it a high priority to provide greater and more frequent praise and recognition in a greater variety of forms. Equally important, but far less often (perhaps quarterly), would be having *developmental discussions,* in which you can focus on ways the employee can improve. When you build on a strong foundation of ongoing positive feedback, employees are more likely to trust that you are on their side and thus be more willing to accept constructive criticism from you when it is offered.

As you offer praise and feedback, keep these suggestions in mind:

- ✔ **Base your (frequent) feedback employees' performance.** But be aware that this may be a new perspective for many of them, if they grew up getting trophies even when their team lost or got all As a result of rampant grade inflation in schools.

- ✔ **Provide a context for how Millennials' contributions relate to team and organizational goals, to the organization's customers, and even to society.** This systematic framing of feedback and praise elevates it from unearned hype to practical information that can help shape desired behaviors and results you need from them.

- ✔ **Be authentic.** Provide direct and honest feedback and evaluations that can best help Millennials excel and help them build trust in you, their manager, all the more in the process.

Meaningful rewards

When they have done good work or an outstanding job, Millennials want rewards that are meaningful and exciting to them. Obviously, these rewards include financial incentives, although 88 percent of Millennials don't feel money is their main motivator, and 78 percent will work for less if they feel challenged.

Millennials who do express a desire to be paid more, however, may have less-than-realistic expectations as to what accomplishments are needed to earn more money, and that's where you can help them out. Show them the skills they need to learn and the contribution they need to make to earn more money. Also show them the path that will get them where they want to go, both in their life and in your organization and help them see that you will help them succeed to the best of your ability.

This translates into discussions in which you as a manager need to state things like, "I can't just pay you more because you want to make more. I can pay you more when you have increased your level of contribution to the organization to a level that warrants earning more. Let's talk specifically about what that would look like and come up with a plan for how you can get there." Then you can channel the person's energy into things he or she can directly impact, such as taking on greater responsibility, doing exceptional work, implementing a cost-savings idea, delighting an important customer, helping to streamline a process, bringing in a new account, and so on. Of course, limits do exist regarding what any employee is paid by your organization; in that case, you can focus on skills you are helping your employees develop that they can use throughout their careers and in future jobs.

Millennials expect that their reward experience be fun and exciting — not the same old boring thing the company has done for years. They increasingly expect rewards that are creative, varied, and personalized:

- ✔ **Creative** in that the rewards are fun and unique. Millennials don't want the same certificate, plaque, or trophy that has been passed out to employees for years. Scottrade, a firm based in St. Louis, Missouri, has implemented a peer recognition program, Above and Beyond, that allows employees to earn rewards such as iPods.

- ✔ **Varied** in that not everyone gets the same reward. It's not very motivating for Millennials to receive the same reward as everyone else. Take time to offer different items and experiences that match not only the achievement itself, but the individual employee. A gift card for coffee or a "thank you" might be a great option for a smaller achievement, but a more significant achievement deserves a more significant reward.

- ✔ **Personalized** in that the reward needs to be tailored to the employee's unique interests, which can be a hobby, travel, or a life experience. Give employees a choice and a say in what reward they receive for doing a good job. The days of one size fitting all are long gone when it comes to employee motivation. What thrills and delights one employee may be boring and insulting to another. Avoid this problem by allowing employees to choose what best motivates them — be it the latest electronic merchandise, an experience, or a charity donation.

Chapter 17

Engaging and Retaining High-Potential Employees

In This Chapter

▶ Identifying the three key attributes of high-potential employees (HIPOs)

▶ Discovering six strategies for better engagement of high-potential employees

▶ Realizing the importance of mentoring to high-potential employees

*O*rganizations invest millions of dollars to identify and develop high-potential employees (also known as "high potentials," or "HIPOs") within their workforce. Executives and managers often peg this cream-of-the-crop top talent for leadership roles early on in their careers. HIPOs are also usually the first to participate in innovative leadership development programs. Despite the considerable amount of time and effort companies put into guiding them, however, studies show that many High Potentials remain unengaged in their work and continue to actively pursue other opportunities.

In recent years, as many as 30 percent of HIPOs have left their organizations, a number that is expected to increase as the economy further improves. Over 50 percent of executives feel their organizations are ineffective at managing and keeping top talent, and 90 percent of CEOs rank a retention plan for the organization's high-potential employees as a top priority for their organization. As Jim Wall, national director of human resources at Deloitte & Touche, says, "Our only competitive advantage is having talented people. We need to keep them."

Identifying High-Potential Employees

High-potential employees, those individuals who are thought to have the ability and capacity to be future leaders in an organization, are critical to the viability of any organization. The first step in better managing these employees is identifying exactly who they are.

Some companies have a formal process for identifying this group of future leaders that includes systematically pinpointing such individuals, discussing their potential among senior staff members, and closely monitoring their progress over time. Some firms even categorize these potential leaders as "promotables" (those ready to be promoted when an opportunity arises) and "high potentials" (those that with the potential of being promoted to a higher level with the right development).

Some organizations launch a program for high potential employees without ever clearly defining who those employees are. How does your organization identify high potential employees? Find out. And if there isn't a way, make one! One thing is certain: If you wait until a crisis to find these people — such as an unexpected departure of a key leader in your organization who you now need to replace — it will often be too late to engage in a thoughtful, rational selection process, even if you wanted to. And in the case of a serious illness or death of a key leader, the topic of succession may become completely taboo. Why? Because the discussion at that time often seems disrespectful to the ailing senior leader or to the memory of a recently deceased leader. It's best to discuss and implement a way to identify and develop your HIPOs now, before you need them!

Often, people confuse high-potential employees with top performers, but they aren't necessarily the same. People can perform their current jobs excellently but still not be viable candidates for promotion to top management. According to the Corporate Leadership Council, 70 percent of top performers lack critical attributes essential for success in future roles.

To decide who best falls into the high potential category, the Council recommends that you evaluate and systematically rank HIPOs according to established criteria. This process involves first interviewing the candidates and then validating your findings through interviews with managers who have worked with the candidates.

In these interviews, you should evaluate employees on the attributes of ability, engagement, and aspiration:

- ✔ **Ability:** This is the most obvious attribute. To be successful in progressively more important roles, employees must have intellectual, technical, and emotional skills (innate and learned) to handle increasingly complex challenges. Candidates with exceptional ability are typically well-known by their managers and peers.

- ✔ **Engagement:** Engagement refers to the level of personal connection and commitment the employee feels toward the firm and its mission. You shouldn't just assume or take for granted this attribute; you may need to do some work to really assess this. For example, just asking employees whether they are satisfied with their jobs isn't enough. Instead, you need to probe deeper, perhaps by asking a question such as, "What would cause you to take a job with another company tomorrow?" Questions like this prompt employees to share their underlying criteria for job satisfaction and perhaps to identify what's currently missing from their jobs.

✔ **Aspiration:** Aspiration can be more difficult to measure than the other two attributes. It refers to the desire for recognition, advancement, and future rewards, and the degree to which the employee's desires align with the company intentions for him or her. Because knowing what people are thinking is difficult, evaluating a person's level of aspiration really requires a discussion with that person. Be direct and ask pointed questions about what the employee aspires to and at what price: "How far do you hope to rise in the company?" "How quickly?" "How much recognition would be optimal?" "How much money?" And so on. To get the full picture, weigh these responses against individuals' "softer" objectives involving work-life balance, job stress, and geographic mobility.

The two-step evaluation process of interviews (interviewing the employee and then validating your discoveries by interviewing managers who have worked with the employee) is important because shortcomings in even one of these three attributes can dramatically reduce a candidate's chances for ultimate success as a future leader in your organization, and the cost of misidentifying talent can be high. You may, for instance, invest tens of thousands of dollars and time in a star employee who jumps ship just as you are looking for him or her to take the lead on a significant project for the firm.

AMN Healthcare is a good example of how an organization considers all three attributes. The company built its annual talent-assessment processes around measures for ability, engagement, and aspiration. As part of its annual succession-planning process, AMN typically conducts interviews with more than 200 rising leaders, specifically to get a read on their engagement and aspiration levels. This information, combined with managers' assessments of ability, gives AMN a clear picture of its bench strength for talent.

Current Challenges with HIPOs

There are three primary challenges with high-potential employees in any organization today: high turnover, low engagement, and "troubling" performance.

✔ **High turnover:** In a study by the Corporate Executive Board, the turnover rate of high-potential employees (the rate at which HIPOs are leaving their current jobs) is 30 percent. And a survey of 174 North American organizations by OI Partners corroborated this finding by identifying that HIPOs are the organizational level with the highest turnover, followed by frontline employees (27 percent), middle managers (26 percent), and senior executives (20 percent).

Currently, 14 percent to 33 percent of HIPOs are actively job hunting, according to a study published in the *Harvard Business Review*, and the executive staffing firm Challenger, Gray, and Christmas reports that 42 percent of employers are worried other companies will steal their top talent. As you can see in Table 17-1, these statistics are of great concern to CEOs, 90 percent of whom report they are most concerned about losing their high-potential employees. According to the Corporate Executive Board, over 50 percent say their organizations are ineffective at managing and keeping top talent.

Table 17-1	Employee Turnover and CEO Concern	
Employee Type	*Turnover Rate (%)*	*% of CEOs Concerned about Retention of Employees*
High potentials	30%	90%
Frontline employees	27%	72%
Middle managers	26%	60%
Senior executives	20%	45%

✔ **Low engagement:** According to research by the Corporate Executive Board, 33 percent of emerging stars report feeling disengaged from their companies, 20 percent believe their personal aspirations are substantially different from (as opposed to being aligned with) their organization's mission and vision, and 40 percent report having little confidence in their coworkers and even less so in senior management of their organization. The *Harvard Business Journal* amplified these findings when it reported that the discretionary effort on the part of disengaged workers can be 50 percent less than other employees.

✔ **Troubling performance:** Worse yet, for a group that you would expect to naturally have the highest level of performance in the organization, research suggests that is anything but the case. The Corporate Leadership Council reports that 40 percent of HIPOs have "troubling performance," 40 percent of internal job moves by HIPOs end in failure, and less than 15 percent of direct reports are ready for immediate transition to subsequent roles.

Why do high-potential employees fail? It's not that they lack ability. Most fail because they are not engaged and because their assignments don't inspire or interest them. Based on this research, focusing more on engaging HIPOs could have a significant impact on their current level of performance, their level of engagement, and their subsequent level of retention with the organization.

Following are six strategies that can help you better engage your organization's high-potential employees.

Get to know them and their aspirations

The first strategy is to get to know your high-potential employees personally and discover their aspirations for the future. There's a big difference between what employers think motivates HIPOs and what actually does. HIPOs tend to value chances to directly influence and direct their own careers, challenging assignments (or even the choice of assignments), and real risks (and rewards!) for the work they do. Spend time with each of your high-potential employees to discuss these things and explore their preferences for future work assignments and career paths.

One activity that can help candidates explore their inner values and aspirations is to have them mentally construct an "Ideal Day" ten years into the future, divided into 15-minute segments. Where did they wake up? What time was it? Who were they with? If they went to work, where did they work? What was their job? What were they working on? And so on. This activity can help establish the direction high-potential employees want their careers and lives to take. I've seen this exercise inspire many people to make major changes to put their lives on the path they most want to go.

Align their aspirations with the organization's mission and strategy

When you know what makes your HIPOs tick, try to align their goals with those of the organization and its vision, mission, and strategies. Have HIPOs spend time with the firm's executives so they can learn and better understand these organizational objectives. Also, align the opportunities your HIPOs value with these organizational elements.

Johnson & Johnson managers select individuals they believe could run a business (or run a bigger business) in the next three years to participate in a nine-month program the company calls LeAD. During these nine months, participants receive advice and regular assessments from a series of coaches brought in from outside the company. They also must develop a growth project — a new product, service, or business model — intended to create value for their individual units. Each candidate's progress is evaluated during a leadership session that is held in an emerging market such as China, India, or Brazil (which increases participants' global knowledge). Graduates leave the program with a multiyear individual development plan and are periodically reviewed by a group of senior human resources heads for further development and reassignment across the corporation. Johnson & Johnson managers believe that the LeAD process has accelerated individual development of the company's high-potential employees. More than half of the LeAD participants moved on to bigger positions in the company during the first three years of the program.

Focus on real and important work

When your organization's vision, mission, and strategy are clear and you've discussed the different opportunities HIPOs have in your organization, it's time to assign them work that matters, that contributes to the organization's success and well-being. To truly engage high-potential employees, give them assignments that have significant impact on the organization and truly challenge them.

Procter & Gamble managers in the company's flagship Family Care division identified a set of complex, high-impact positions that offered particularly quick development and learning — for instance, brand manager for a leading product, for example, or director of marketing for a new segment or region. Division managers dubbed these "crucible roles" and began a concerted effort to fill 90 percent of them with high-potential employees. Candidates had to pass through three screens to be eligible: They had to have 1) adequate qualifications to perform well in the particular crucible role, 2) stellar leadership skills, and 3) a clear developmental gap the crucible role could help fill. Through this program, Procter & Gamble has measurably increased the percentage of employees qualified for promotion: More than 80 percent of P&G's high-potential employees are ready to take on critical leadership roles each year — putting the company at a tremendous talent advantage when the going gets tough.

Connect them with mentors committed to their development

Once you've assigned high-potential employees real, meaningful work, the next strategy is to find them a mentor — a senior executive in the organization who can advise, coach, and counsel the HIPO. Typically, a mentor is in a different chain of command so that the relationship can have some objectivity as well as give the participants the ability to candidly discuss challenges in the HIPO's reporting relationships.

Finding the right mentor can be tricky. The personalities should fit, and each party must have adequate time and motivation to make the relationship work. Some companies use informal mixers to provide opportunity for mentors and mentees to find each other.

Here are examples of companies and industries that have successful mentorship programs:

✔ SC Johnson has developed a Mentoring Steering Committee responsible for pairing mentors and mentees according to similarities in work experience, interest, and skills. Over a period of 18 months, pairs contribute a total of 45 hours to the commitment. All participants in the program, mentors and mentees alike, have reported a positive experience that left them with a sense of personal and professional growth.

✔ Rockwell Collins matches mentors and high performers using a web-based program.

✔ IBM has three distinct mentoring programs: expert mentoring, career mentoring and, for new hires, socialization mentoring.

✔ Phillips Electronics EVP and co-COO Gerard Kleisterlee has three priorities when he travels: meet local management, meet a key customer — and lunch with a HIPO manager.

✔ The learning and development team at Banner Health works alongside the executive office to develop mentorship programs for leaders. The result has been two effective programs that have produced hundreds of leaders:

- *New Leader Experience seminar:* Every month, this three-day seminar is held at the company's headquarters and introduces new managers to the company's overall goals. In addition, the managers are presented with resources on how to guide employees effectively.

- *Leadership symposiums:* These weeklong development programs give leaders the chance to renew their skills and interact with other leaders in the organization.

Head to the nearby sidebar "Just what the doctor ordered" for mentoring ideas used in the health care industry.

Does mentoring work? A five-year study of 1,000 Sun Microsystems employees found that 25 percent of mentored employees enjoyed salary grade changes, compared to only 5 percent of the control group. Those who were mentored were also promoted 6 times more often than others. Providing mentorship programs — or simply encouraging employees to assume a mentorship role — allows employees who have grown within the company or who have significant career experience to pass on what they have learned to other employees. Many times, individuals in entry-level or mid-level roles are promising or aspiring leaders but lack the guidance and direction to achieve their goals. Employees with a desire to further develop their skills and career path are eager to learn and welcome new opportunities, something that serves any company well, especially in a downturn.

Just what the doctor ordered

Another great illustration of mentorship at work comes from the healthcare industry. Newly graduated nurses often face culture shock when moving into a full-time role in a hospital environment. To ease this transition and ensure the success of newly hired nurses, some hospitals have made adjustments to their entry programs, many of which you can modify to fit nearly any industry or company. Here are some of their ideas:

✔ Provide online evaluation systems to track progress.

✔ Establish regular meetings with a mentor to discuss the evaluation.

✔ Develop an easily accessible curriculum program.

✔ Select individuals from various departments to conduct training so that newly hired employees establish relationships beyond the people with whom they work directly.

✔ Recruit volunteers, especially previous or retired employees, to serve as mentors if existing employees cannot afford to take the time.

Hospitals that adopted all or some of these strategies have reported positive results, including a drastic reduction in new-hire turnover, a reported increase in on-the-job confidence among new nurses, and an ability to attract qualified applicants from the outside because of their employer's growing reputation in the industry.

Invest in a variety of ongoing learning and development activities

Another strategy is to invest in a variety of ongoing learning and development activities for your HIPOs. The best organizations realize that providing employees with opportunities to learn pays dividends for both the firm and the employees. The firm gains workers who are better skilled, more versatile in their work assignments, and motivated because they are challenged and encouraged to grow. Employees get the opportunity to learn new skills, gain new ways of viewing things, and network with coworkers. When employees get the chance to learn and better themselves within the organization, they can sense the firm's commitment to them; enhanced trust and loyalty follow suit.

All development is self-development, 90 percent of which occurs on the job. Therefore, explore with your HIPOs the challenging assignments within their current jobs as well as supplemental learning and development activities outside of their jobs. In its Mini Retention Survey, the Society for Human Resource Management (SHRM) found that employees are most hungry for tools, information, and knowledge they can take as their own. "Many companies are hesitant about providing such development programs for fear that those employees will up and leave with their newfound skills and credentials," says SHRM spokesperson Barry Lawrence. "The irony is that the more tools you offer, the more likely employees will stick around."

Advocate-mentor: A different kind of mentoring

A riff on the traditional mentor is the *advocate-mentor*. This mentor does the usual mentoring things but is also an advocate for the high-potential employee. This advocate, a confidante, keeps the HIPO current on what's happening in the company, provides counsel, identifies internal resources, and helps clear obstacles that impede performance. The advocate-mentor also helps to resolve conflicts that can easily develop when, for example, a newly rotated HIPO is assigned a critical role and the operating unit head would prefer a more experienced person in the job. The advocate also keeps senior management up to date on the HIPO's performance.

Following are some real-life examples of employee development:

✓ At pharmaceutical giant Eli Lilly and Company, learning for new MBA grads is structured so that HIPOs receive 20 percent of their learning from coaching, 70 percent from their work, and 10 percent from formal education.

✓ At Epson Computers (now Epson), high-potential employees rotate through executive internships that allow them to actively participate in meetings and decisions at the executive level prior to returning to their job.

Says Robert Lukefahr, one of the founders of Third Millennium, "Training is one of the best motivators. The opportunity for high potentials to increase their portfolio of skills through training, either formal or informal, ranks high on their list." As several staff accountants at Price Waterhouse point out, learning is a significant piece of the new contract that will bind people to their firm. "I'm here because I keep learning," says one 30-year old. "Whenever I get a little bored, a new project comes along with opportunities for learning. For me, stagnation would lead to restlessness."

Additional development ideas for high-potential employees include

✓ Leading or being a part of supplier and process improvement teams

✓ Engaging in formal executive education programs through a leading college or university

✓ Shadowing (following a key leader around in their job)

✓ Attending closed-door strategic briefings

✓ Swapping job with colleagues in other functions

✓ Performing stretch assignments and problem solving

✔ Participating in specialized skills training like project management, Six Sigma, or data analytics

✔ Developing and presenting proposals to senior leaders

✔ Representing the company at industry meetings

Reward and recognize high performance

After you have an overall learning and development plan in place, the next strategy is to reward and recognize high performance as it occurs. To start, let your high-potential employees know they are special by telling them your plans for them! Sixty percent of employers don't do this, and their HIPOs have no idea there is a larger plan for their development and future with the organization — a real shame because research indicates 33 percent of HIPOs who are *not* told of their status and the company's plans their futures will seek jobs at other firms. If they are told, however, the percentage that seeks outside opportunities drops to just 14 percent. Research by Maritz Motivation produces a similar conclusion: Recognized employees are seven times more likely to want to stay with their organization than those who aren't recognized.

I was speaking about high-potential employees at a recent Talent Management conference and a fellow attendee shared that a company she didn't work for informed her that she was on that company's high-potential employees list. She was flattered, of course, and then she realized that her current firm had no such plan for her. Who do you think she's working for now?

Consider hosting a recognition event for your top performers. These can be national or regional. The event gives management and executive leadership direct interaction with their high performing partners, which can be motivating to both the employee and the manager. These face-to-face opportunities give partners a clear understanding of the organization's brand message and goals for the company.

Retaining High Potentials

Doing a better job of engaging high-potential employees, using the strategies I outline earlier in this chapter, goes a long way toward keeping them in your organization, but you may need to go further if your HIPOs start (or are already) leaving, especially if they are in hot professions that currently have an explosive demand for workers — software development, finance, or nursing, for example. Read on for some additional strategies you can deploy on a proactive basis or as the need arises to hold on to your top talent.

My wife managed a dozen software engineers for a high-tech start-up. One day, to her surprise, one of her direct reports told her he was leaving his job and the organization. When she sat down with him to find out why, she learned that months prior, when the head of the division was giving a staff update on the state of the organization, that executive made a passing remark about one project being behind. Her employee was one of a number of employees who worked on that project and he took that one remark, spun it around in his head many times over the following weeks, and concluded he was at risk of being laid off from his position. Nothing could have been further from the truth, but the concern was very real to this technical worker who geared up a job search and accepted a new position with another firm. At that point, the die was cast for this employee, so she couldn't keep him with the company, but it got my spouse thinking about her other team members, and she resolved to check in with each of them with a one-to-one meeting. To her surprise, she found several employees with similar concerns; fortunately, she was able to reassure them and keep them committed to their jobs and the department.

Conducting stay interviews

The previous tool of choice was an exit interview, conducted as employees left an organization, but these interviews occur when it's too late to do anything that would lead the employee to stay. To influence employee attrition and reduce employee turnover, managers must measure employee job satisfaction and engagement on an ongoing basis. Enter the *stay interview* — a new strategy that companies are turning to in force. These interviews give employers a chance to have conversations with high-potential employees about what they like and don't like about their current jobs and what would keep them in those jobs longer.

Robert Half International found the number one reason employees leave organizations is because they aren't given recognition for the work they do. Not asking how they are doing in their job and what could make things better may be number two.

Asking the right questions

Beverly Kaye and Sharon Jordan-Evans, authors of a book about stay interviews entitled *Hello Stay Interviews, Goodbye Talent Loss: A Manager's Playbook* (Berrett-Koehler Publishers) recommend that managers conduct stay interviews early and often, especially with their best employees, those they most want to keep. The act of taking time to focus on the employee demonstrates the value you see in that person, and asking open-ended questions allows you to better learn about that person.

For example, the question, "What about your job makes you jump out of bed in the morning?" immediately conjures an image of excitement and gets the employee thinking about why he or she is excited about going to work. It's an unexpected question about job satisfaction, and it can elicit some fascinating responses: "The project I'm working on" or "I love my colleagues (or customers)!" A manager stands to learn more about their employees just by asking this probing question.

"What makes you hit the snooze button?" is the flip side of the initial question. It's a safe way to ask employees what they do not like as much about their jobs. Employees can answer this question in many ways: "I'm just not an early morning person," might be one way. In this case, perhaps the manager could provide a little flexibility regarding that person's start time. Another talented employee said he dreaded Monday morning staff meetings and therefore delayed his trek to work for as long as possible. Could that staff meeting be shorter or made to be more fun? I'm sure it could.

Here are some other sample questions Bev and Sharon recommend asking:

- ✔ What are you passionate about?
- ✔ What's your dream job?
- ✔ If you changed your role completely, what would you miss the most?
- ✔ If you won the lottery and didn't have to work, what would you miss?
- ✔ What did you love in your last position that you're not doing now?
- ✔ What makes for a great day at work?
- ✔ If you had a magic wand, what would be the one thing you would change about your work, your role and your responsibilities?
- ✔ What do you think about on your way to work?
- ✔ What's bothering you most about your job?

Probing for understanding

Just asking the open-ended questions is only part of the process. Managers need to truly listen to the answers and encourage employees — verbally and nonverbally— to share more. As you probe for additional information, you're trying to answer questions such as, "Does he want a chance to learn something new?" "Does she want visibility with the senior team?" "Is he ready to manage his own project?" and so forth.

Be careful not to react negatively to what you hear; otherwise, you can shut the person down. This is a time of exploration, and the mood needs to be one of openness, trust, and sharing.

According to Bev and Sharon, the top "stay factors" are work that is exciting, challenging, or meaningful; recognition, respect, and being valued; supportive management/a good boss; the potential for career growth, learning, and development; job location; job security and stability; fair pay and good benefits; flexible work environment; pride in the organization and its mission or product; a fun, enjoyable work environment; working with great coworkers or clients; feeling loyalty and commitment to coworkers or boss.

Addressing stay interview challenges

The most common fear managers express about stay interviews is that employees will ask for a promotion or a raise that isn't in the budget. That's an unfounded fear. "We've had very few stay interviews come in with pay being the thing that makes them stay or want to leave," says Webroot human resources director Melanie Williams. "There were not any requests that we haven't been able to fulfill."

If an employee does bring up pay or a promotion or something else that's out of the scope of a manager's control, the manager should answer truthfully. If you have a budget constraint, say so. If the person is asking for a job they don't have the skills to do, talk about what training opportunities are available to that person. Bev Kaye suggests, "You can say, 'Salaries are frozen, or that job isn't open, but what I really want to do is find things under my control so I can make sure you're getting what you want and what you need. So what else matters to you?' You'll get seven to ten things that are in your control."

Stay interviews create other challenges as well for managers and HR professionals. Sometimes questions uncover unpleasant truths, such as bad feelings toward executive management or employees that don't know about career paths because they've never logged into the HR portal. Accountability for responding to these issues can also pose a challenge, particularly for organizations where employees and managers are already stretched for time and feel overcommitted.

Do stay interviews really work?

Stay interviews can be effective for reducing turnover of key employees. Webroot Software, a Broomfield, Colorado, internet security product development company, implemented stay interviews at a time when the 400-employee company was particularly vulnerable to employee attrition — the period immediately following a recent reduction in force. "We've done other RIFs, and employee turnover has always spiked," says Williams. "Since our RIF in August, we've seen our turnover tick down by a steady 1/10th of a percent each month."

One reason is that the information collected by stay interviews is more actionable than secondary source information, like engagement surveys, because it's specific and forward-facing. Williams says, "You're not filtering through a survey trying to guess what did they mean by that comment or how did they interpret that question?" She adds, "We've gotten feedback from every individual in the organization. We had a 64 percent response to our engagement survey."

"Stay interviews encourage managers to sit down and have a structured talk with their teams about what works and what doesn't work for them," explains Susan Seip, a human resources manager for Geocent, a Metairie, Louisiana, technology company with 230 employees scattered throughout the Southern U.S. It can be a vital part of an overall engagement strategy. "It's a relationship review. What's your relationship to the company, the project team, and your manager, and what is within our purview to do to make those better?"

Stay interviews can also provide valuable data to supplement employee engagement surveys and exit interview metrics to improve engagement in the organization. As such, they can be essential part of your recruitment and staffing strategy that focuses on employee retention. Adding stay interviews to your recruitment strategies can help your organization retain critical employees. "It's the single best tool you can give managers," says Dick Finnegan, CEO of C-Suite Analytics, an employee engagement company.

If exit interviews and engagement surveys aren't moving the needle on your organization's employee attrition numbers (or even if they are), you may want to add stay interviews to your list of engagement strategies.

Creating a development plan and career path

Simply implementing and conducting stay interviews isn't enough. It's what you do with the information you gathered during the interviews that sends the message that you're committed to your top employees and their continued success in your organization. If there are obstacles, be forthright about them, but help your high-potential employees create plans that enable them to move toward their goals; include what you personally will do to help them.

You can use the stay interview as a springboard to shift the discussion to a potential job change or career progression with targeted questions. For example, you can ask employees what top two priorities they are focusing on at this point in their careers. Chance are they're hoping for the following:

- Greater responsibilities and growth
- Lateral exposure to specific areas in their fields
- A better work-life balance
- Compensation and benefits

All of these areas are important, but which one or two are more critical for your key employees at this point in their careers — and what can you do to help them achieve those priorities in their current position?

Most employee development occurs on the job, as employees take on new challenges and assignments related to their current jobs and, in the process, learn new skills. Support your employees in learning new skills and allow them to participate in special assignments, problem-oriented initiatives, and various other learning activities. Also develop learning goals with each of your employees — make them yearly goals or even goals for specific projects — and discuss what was learned at the conclusion of the project or agreed upon time frame.

Periodically, you should also hold career development discussions with your employees — especially with top employees — at least twice a year: as part of their annual performance review and again as a discussion separate from the formal evaluation. Better yet, visiting the topic several times a year and tweaking the plan can help provide momentum and keep the discussion fresh. The latter tactic is especially beneficial when career options and opportunities are constantly surfacing as circumstances change.

If you paint a picture in the future that high-potential employees can aspire to now, you stand the best chance of keeping them in the organization, willing to wait for the opportunities for which you've helped them develop skills.

Jerk alert: Avoid being "micromanager"

"If you ride a horse, sit close and tight. If you ride a man, sit easy and light."

This sage advice from *Poor Richard's Almanac* is relevant today, whether you are a manager trying to get the most from your employees or an employee trying to survive an overbearing manager.

Want to drive high-potential employees crazy? Micromanage them. Micromanagement is a severe management style that undermines employee initiative, crushing the spirit of employees wanting to do a good job. If you constantly find yourself in situations where you are giving your employees details on how to do obvious tasks and then checking on them constantly to see whether the tasks are done properly, you might be a micromanager.

Fortunately, whether you are an employee or a manager, you can learn new approaches and skills for being more effective in your working relationship. For the employee, this means finding ways to assure your manager he can count on you to do what he asked you to do and following through with those strategies. For the manager, it means being clear about communicating your expectations and then giving employees a chance to live up to those expectations. The patience you show can serve you both in the relationship.

Ranked as one of the top motivators for employees in their jobs today is autonomy and authority, that is, having a say in how they do their work and the ability, power, and support to do what is necessary to get the job done. In my research, employees ranked the following items as very or extremely important: being allowed to decide how best to do one's work (89 percent), being given increased job autonomy (87 percent), and being given increased authority in the job (85 percent).

Autonomy and authority create the foundation of trust and respect that today's HIPOs so highly value. It provides them a sense of independence and a *freedom* to bring their own imprint to their work. This freedom is important for fostering employee creativity, resourcefulness, and best efforts, which in turn leads to higher performance and increased employee satisfaction and fulfillment. With autonomy and authority, employees feel more confident in taking initiative with their work and more competent that the initiative they take will pay off, leading to better results and an enhanced ability to take on greater assignments and responsibilities.

If you're an employee of a micromanager

No one likes to work for a micromanager, although it's reported that four out of five workers say they have done just that — and one out of three workers has even changed jobs because of it. To tap into the wellspring of potential every employee has to offer, you need to give them more room and encourage them to take responsibility — and recognize them when they do.

If you currently work for a micromanager, take a look at why this might be happening. Realize that if you are having a problem with your manager, it's inevitable that your manager is having a problem with you. People tend to be quick to blame others for their problems and discount the fact that others are often responding to them and their behavior, often in very logical ways. Here are some ways you can set yourself up to win when working for a micromanager:

✔ **Take responsibility for your relationship with your manager.** Make the first move and be willing to go 90 percent of the way to meet your manager in the middle. After all, you have more to lose from a poor relationship with your manager than he or she does. Take a step back and look at your situation from your manager's perspective. Chances are that your manager micromanages you because he doesn't trust you based on past experiences working with you. Perhaps you have entirely different values of professionalism, for example, so your acceptable standards for work, timing, and thoroughness are not the same. In this case, it's up to you to bring your standards up to his or her level.

✔ **Look for common ground and overlap.** Even if you and your manager are opposites, there should be an area where you can find common agreement. Start by asking some questions: "What would give you the sense that I'm dedicated to doing this task right?" "What time frame would you like this completed?" "Do you want a progress report or just the final completed task?" "You've told me how you'd handle this assignment, but if I can get the same or better results doing it a different way, would that be okay?" Use the answers to these questions to set up some rules for working together. You might find, for example, that your frequent typos make your manager feel you don't proofread your work, and her real concern is getting a chance to review correspondence before you send it out. In this instance, showing your manager you can eliminate typos in your correspondence would help build trust between the two of you. By taking your manager's concerns seriously and acting upon those concerns, you are showing you value and respect your manager and your relationship with him or her.

✔ **Find a new way of working together.** Come up with some new rules for working together without your manager feeling undue risk. Be creative in finding methods in getting your manager to see things differently. For example, some of the administrative support people who have been the best in working for me over the years were the ones that had the clearest idea of what their job was and were not afraid to stand up for their work or themselves in the process.

If you're a micromanager

If you are the micromanager, realize that, by constantly trying to prove that you're the smartest one in the room, you will systematically shut down those who work for you and subsequently drive them away. You have to give your people a chance to find their own ways for getting things done — to allow them the ability to build and learn from their own experiences. Discuss and brainstorm strategies and support them in the execution of their plans, but don't take over their work or assignments. When you do, you demean them and yourself in the process.

I remember charging into the office one day with some silly thing I just had to have done *right away*. The assistant I had at the time said, "Bob, I'd be delighted to do that for you right now, but let me tell you what I'm currently working on so you can decide which is more important." I bit my tongue and had to agree that what she was currently doing *was* much more important than what I was in a dander about. It was perfectly fine for my urgent request to be done perhaps a day or two later.

Offering financial and nonfinancial rewards

Financial rewards matter to high-potential employees. When the financial climate permits, top performers who achieve results expect and should get bigger raises than those who don't. How much more? According to WorldatWork, 50 percent to 100 percent more, although differential rates have averaged just 40 percent to 47 percent in recent years.

Nonfinancial recognition is also important to this group. Although higher salaries offered by other firms are a threat to your employee retention efforts, research shows that traditional pay programs are ineffective for motivating high-performing, committed employees. Compensation has become a right — an expected reward for simply coming to work; however, firms will lose their most valued employees if they fail to offer them the intangible, intrinsic rewards that money cannot buy. Results of a recent survey by the Council of Communication Management confirm this assertion. The study found that recognition for a job well done is the top motivator of individual performance for high-potential employees. In fact, study after study has shown that what tends to stimulate and encourage top performance, growth, and loyalty is praise and recognition. Employees want to

- Feel they are making a contribution
- Have a manager who tells them when they do a good job
- Have the respect of peers and colleagues
- Be involved and informed about what's going on in the firm
- Have interesting, challenging work

"The most important factor is individual recognition — more important than salaries or bonuses," says Paul M. Cook, founder and former CEO of Raychem Corporation. "Most people want to be creative. They want to identify with the success of their professional and their organization. They want to contribute. And their greatest reward is receiving acknowledgment that they did contribute to making something meaningful happen."

Consider using these tactics to recognize your high-potential employees:

- Personal praise, such as a phone call from the CEO congratulating the employee on a success or achievement
- Public praise, such as banner ads celebrating high-potential employees' successes on the company intranet or perhaps naming company initiatives after them
- Autonomy, such as a choice of working assignments
- Authority, such as access to special resources or the ability to spend budget
- Flexibility, such as telecommuting or flexible working hours
- Visibility, such as access to the CEO or top management

Granting high potentials greater flexibility

A key part of any retention strategy — especially for high-potential employees — should include adopting flexible work arrangements. Progressive companies are realizing that restructuring full-time work to include alternative work options, such as flextime, a compressed work week, and telecommuting, can be beneficial to both the employee and the employer. In fact, today roughly 42 percent of employers do offer some form of flexible scheduling, and the result is an increase in profits as well as employee satisfaction. According to the American Management Association, "Allowing flexibility improves work quality: companies with flexible scheduling options report absenteeism is cut by as much as 50 percent."

As an integral part of its ardent effort to retain HIPOs, Ernst & Young developed Lotus Notes, a unique database that encourages employees to test alternative work styles. The purpose of the database is to share information throughout the firm about existing flexible arrangements. "With 27,000 employees across the United States, there were bound to be a lot of terrific success stories around flexibility that weren't known beyond their local areas," says Deborah K. Holmes, then national director of EY's office for retention and the creator of the database. "What's groundbreaking about this database it that we've gone beyond policy and truly focused on practice. We wanted to make sure that places in our firm where flexibility had been thriving could become role models for other places in the firm, and that's what happened."

At Price Waterhouse (now PricewaterhouseCoopers), more than 600 people, including three partners, used some form of flexible work arrangement. The company also introduced a firmwide telecommuting pilot to assess the viability of working from home full-time as another flexible work option. In addition, the firm conducted an in-depth workplace flexibility study to learn more about how, where, and when their employees work — looking at what works and what does not.

In recognition of the importance of personal time for employee well-being, the corporate law firm of Morrison & Foerster expects its lawyers to bill 1,800 hour per year, or roughly 36 hours per week. This compares to an average of about 2,400 a year, or more than 46 hours per week, at most major law firms. This allows the firm's lawyers to create a better balance between work and personal lives — and boosts employee morale and loyalty.

ANECDOTE

Integrating work/life issues: Childcare

Understanding that work/life issues extend beyond flexible work schedules is important for retention efforts of overachieving HIPOs, and a key area that organizations need to focus on is childcare. Finding suitable care is only the first step for working parents. What happens when a child gets sick — or when a childcare provider is ill or school holidays don't coincide with work schedules? Missing a day or two of work can be a cause of panic for most working parents.

Catalyst reported that females make up 46 percent of the working population, and that 40 percent of all women in the labor force have children under 18. One of the fastest growing segments of the workforce is women who have young children. The other fast-growing segment: single, custodial fathers, according to the Fatherhood Project. The childcare issue becomes even more evident when looking at the rise of dual-income families. According to the U.S. Department of Labor, 48 percent of all workers come from dual earner homes that represent over half of all families — up 40 percent over the last two decades.

I was recently presenting in Albuquerque when I heard the story of a company whose new CEO had a bit of an old-school attitude. He demanded that all employees be in their desks by 8:30 a.m. When one woman objected, saying, "I can't do that," the CEO demanded to know why. "I'm a single mother and have to drop my kid off to school and pick them up in the afternoon. I also have an ailing parent who I frequently need to take to doctor's appointments, sometimes with little notice." The CEO was incredulous, responding, "If you're serious about this job, you'll be in your desk by 8:30 am." Not feeling she had any alternative, the employee quit a couple of days later. As it turns out, she was the firm's top salesperson and had been highly motivated because of the flexibility and support the company had previously provided that enabled her to meet the demands of her personal circumstances.

Coopers & Lybrand (now PricewaterhouseCoopers) made great strides in both understanding its employees' childcare needs and in creating programs to help. At first, the firm explored the effectiveness of providing weekend childcare to assist at busy times such as tax season, but this solution didn't work, despite a lot of interest, because, according to then-national director of HR Bob McDowell, people were too scattered geographically, often working at client offices, which made setting child care up at a central location unrealistic. In light of this, the firm opted to provide all employees with a resource and referral program to provide them with child care information as they needed it. The program proved to be very successful. For example, just as one senior consultant was closing a half-million dollar job, her nanny quit. The consultant was faced with the prospect of staying home for a few days to find suitable care — and jeopardizing the deal. Instead, she was able to call the firm's family resource service, interview four candidates that night, and did not miss a day of work. The entire setup cost the company less than $150.

Exploring the childcare needs of your employees will help you determine what types of assistance would be most meaningful and widely used. Sit down and talk with your employees. Ask questions and listen. You might be surprised how much useful information you will uncover.

A Case Study in Developing High Potentials

I had a chance to work with a high-potential employee initiative at Turner Research, a department of Time Warner/CNN, which had 12,000 employees. The company had a program it had started the previous year with good results, and it wanted to expand upon that initial success. The stated purpose of the program was to ensure that a pipeline of internal and external candidates with permanent capability and knowledge was always available to immediately fill key positions as necessary. Their top management did a two-to-three month talent review of staff on an annual basis (although some other divisions did this quarterly). In that process, they identified and updated the list of critical roles in the organization and the employees they considered HIPOs. They also discussed and identified any development needed to make those high-potential employees ready to take larger jobs in these time frames: now, in 3 months, in 6 months, and (the longest time frame) in 12 months.

The talent review was based on leaders' evaluation of high performance of individual staff members, which they observed either while directly managing those individuals or in their experiences working with these staff members on various projects, teams, and initiatives. The leaders didn't conduct interviews of the candidates, nor did they tell the candidates that they had been identified as high-potential employees (they didn't want them to get an inflated ego or see the designation as a guarantee of future positions), although they felt individuals could typically guess their status.

The first wave of the company's high potential development initiative was simply to enroll the individuals in an external executive development program at a local university. In the second year, the company expanded the development opportunities to include internal activities, discussions, and networking opportunities. In the third year, they structured the development even further by taking a high-priority organization initiative, dividing that into a variety of projects, and having each project team led by a high-potential employee. This work was in addition to the job the high-potential employees were being paid to do.

Although the demands of those projects (including the time commitment) were significant, participants reported that the learning and development was extensive, and all were glad to have been a leading part in the corporate initiative. When I asked them what advice they had for other companies that wanted to improve or expand their focus on developing high-potential employees, they replied, "Determine what defines progress on developing high potentials in advance."

Retaining employees today is harder than ever. High-potential employees are — and will continue to be — the most important asset of any organization. Firms must realize this and create a culture that fosters a sense of trust, loyalty, and commitment on the part of their top talent. Employees must know that if they work hard and are loyal they will be appreciated and valued. It's on this belief that successful firms have been founded, and it is on this belief that they will survive. As Carl Camden, CEO of Kelly Services recently told me, "The war for talent is over: Talent won."

Part VI
The Part of Tens

the part of tens

In this part . . .

✔ Get to know the ironies of employee motivation so you don't fall victim to those challenges

✔ Uncover the latest trends in employee recognition so you can keep your program current and fresh

✔ Identify low and no-cost recognition options to stay within your budget and keep your boss happy

Chapter 18

Top Ten Ironies of Motivation

In This Chapter

▶ Ensuring you base recognition on what matters to your employees (not you!)

▶ Preventing formal awards from falling short

▶ Avoiding empty praise

*O*ne of the definitions of *motivation* is "why we do what we do." There are numerous ironies about motivation that make the topic difficult to understand. By examining these ironies, you can better understand the topic of motivation. Following, then, are what I consider the top ten ironies of motivation, in order of importance and prevalence.

Most Managers Think Money Is the Top Motivator

The first irony is all about money (or not). It's very easy to assume money is the only (or biggest) element that motivates employee, but don't fall into that trap! Study after study shows that praise and recognition are the greatest motivators for employees. People want to feel they are making a contribution at work; for most individuals, this is a function of having the respect of peers and colleagues, having managers who tell them when they do a good job, and being involved and informed about what's going on in their departments or organizations.

Catherine Meek, president of Meek Associates, a compensation consulting firm, points out that the number one report they hear from employees is, "We don't care about the money. We just wish my boss would say thank you — just acknowledge that we exist. The only time we hear anything is when we screw up. We never hear when we do a good job."

When you want to motivate your employees, you may be tempted to offer raises or bonuses. That impulse is nice, but those actions alone don't genuinely motivate. According to Frances Hesselbein, president of the Leader-to-Leader Foundation, "People want to feel what they do makes a difference." Money alone does not do this; personal recognition is also needed (see Chapter 5 for more on this). What employees really want is to be valued for a job well done by those they hold in high esteem. As Mary Kay Ash, founder of Mary Kay Cosmetics says, "Imagine that every person is wearing a sign around their neck that says 'make me feel important.'"

What Motivates Others Is Often Different from What Motivates You

Not everyone wants what you want! Managers often identify good wages, job security, and promotion or growth opportunities as the primary reasons their employees work. Why? Because these are often things that motivate them, and they believe their employees are motivated by the same things. Employees, however, report intangibles, such as appreciation for work done, feeling "in" on things, and having empathetic managers as the things they most want from their jobs. To learn more about this disparity, turn to Chapter 6.

To avoid falling victim to this all-to-common assumption, consciously work to reward behaviors with the types of recognition that are valued by and meaningful to your employees, not yourself! Start with the motivational needs of your employees and use their preferences to acknowledge them when they've done good work.

Ask employees what they want, either by engaging in one-on-one discussions or by using other techniques, such as giving employees index cards on which they can list the items they find motivating. You can also conduct a survey with your work group or in a staff meeting to discuss the kinds of recognition your employees find meaningful. By involving those you are trying to motivate, not only are you likely to be more on the mark, but others will also be more likely to take ownership of the recognition program or activities. Involvement equals commitment. The best management is the kind you do *with* your employees, not *to* them.

Things That Most Motivate Employees Are Easy and Inexpensive

One of the saddest ironies is that managers and executives often fail to provide recognition because they think it's costly and time-consuming. In one study of potential workplace motivators (more on that study in Chapter 4), three of the top five incentives ranked by employees had no cost: a personal thank you from one's manager for a job well done; a written thank you from one's manager for a job well done; and public praise. When you implement these simple (and free) forms of recognition in a timely, sincere, and specific manner, employees feel valued and appreciated.

Aside from recognition, there are other ways to motivate your employees that don't cost money or time:

- ✔ **Provide interesting and important work:** All employees should have at least part of their jobs be of interest to them. Find out what tasks your employees most enjoy and use that information in future work assignments. Although OurTown Television Productions of Saratoga Springs, New York, wasn't able to offer its employees the same high salaries as its competition, it did offer its employees jobs custom-tailored to the individual tastes of each worker.

- ✔ **Communicate well:** Information is power, and your employees want to be empowered with the information they need to know to do their jobs better and more effectively. And, more than ever, employees want to know how they are doing in their jobs and how the company is doing in its business. Open the channels of communication in your organization to allow employees to be informed, ask questions, and share information. The Michigan Retailers' Association hosts staff breakfasts to share information and update staff on major policy actions and organizational developments.

- ✔ **Involve employees in decisions:** Involving employees, especially in decisions that affect them, is both respectful and practical. People that are the closest to the problem or customer typically have the best insight as to how to improve a situation. As you involve others, you increase their commitment and buy-in for new ideas or change. Owner Katherine Barchetti assigns each of the salespeople at her self-named clothing stores in Pittsburgh, Pennsylvania, the responsibility for particular items of merchandise — a particular brand and style of belt, for example. Salespeople are granted authority to fully manage the product line assigned to them, including buying, maintaining inventory, marketing, and selling it.

- ✔ **Give them independence, autonomy, and flexibility:** Giving people latitude increases the chance that they will perform as you desire — and bring additional initiative, ideas, and energy to their jobs. All employees at Meredith Publishing in Des Moines, Iowa, must work core hours — between 10:00 a.m. and 3:00 p.m. However, they are allowed to set their own starting and ending schedules as long as they adhere to the core hour requirement. This flexibility allows workers to arrive as early as 6:00 a.m. or as late as 10:00 a.m., and to leave as early as 3:00 p.m. or as late as 6:00 p.m. You might be surprised by how effective flexible hours can be!

✔ **Increase their opportunities for learning, growth, and responsibility:** Giving your employees new opportunities to perform, learn, and grow is a form of recognition and thanks that most people find highly motivating. Management at American Honda Motor Co., Inc., located in Marysville, Ohio, creates energizing opportunities for its employees by assigning them high-risk, high-reward projects. New model development includes trips to Japan, new technology, short timelines, and lots of visibility. Says John Ball, manager of service training, "So when you pull off a successful new model segment, you're a hero!"

Formal Awards Are Only as Good as What They Symbolize

Although a shiny, fancy plaque might *look* good, it doesn't always *feel* good; it all comes down to the meaning. The *recognition value* (the intangible, symbolic, and emotional value) of any award is by far the most motivating aspect for employees. Formal awards are useful for acknowledging significant accomplishments, especially as they span a long period. They can also lend credibility to more spontaneous, informal rewards used regularly by management.

Still, using money, merchandise, or plaques to motivate employees can fall short if the gestures don't have the proper framework. To get the most out of formal awards and to make sure that the focus of the award remains on the performance and achievement — not the award itself — managers must be skilled in the way they present such awards:

✔ **Present in a public forum.** Don't give awards in the privacy of an employee's office; make a big deal of them! Tag onto or schedule a special meeting for the occasion so that you can place the employee in the limelight.

Besides honoring the individual who performed well, recognition is also a message to other employees about the type of performance that gets noticed in an organization. According to management consultant Rosabeth Moss Kanter, "To the rest of the organization, recognition creates role models — heroes — and communicates the standards: These are the kinds of things that constitute great performance around here."

✔ **Provide a context for the recognition.** Managers must provide a context for the achievement and explain how it ties to the larger objectives of the organization. Does this achievement translate into a new product line, more appreciative clients, ongoing cost savings, or other significant goals? How will it potentially impact the overall success of the organization and each person in it? Providing a broader context adds significance to the achievement and to the person being honored.

✔ **Share your feelings.** When presenting an award, emphasize your personal feelings about the achievement or the individual who has achieved. Comments such as, "I was excited by your success," or "I'm proud that you are part of my team" gives energy to the presentation. If your positive feelings are honest and sincere, it adds power to the moment that everyone present can feel.

Fun, Simple, and Creative Rewards Work Best

Despite how well they work, I find more times than not that businesses don't use fun and simple ideas because they think they somehow undermine the seriousness or credibility of the business. Not only is this terribly ironic; it's also a big mistake.

At Walt Disney World in Orlando, Florida, one of Disney's 180 recognition programs is called the Spirit of Fred Award, termed for an employee named Fred. When Fred first went from an hourly to a salaried employee, five people taught him the values necessary for success at Disney. He helped to inspire the award, in which the name "Fred" became an acronym for Friendly, Resourceful, Enthusiastic, and Dependable. First given as a lark, the award has come to be highly coveted in the organization. As this example illustrates, meaningful recognition can truly be created out of thin air!

Recognizing Performance Means the Most to Employees

People don't want something for nothing; they want something for something — recognition for a job well done. Having someone you hold in high esteem at work notice that you performed well and then do something to acknowledge your efforts is the most meaningful kind of recognition. In addition, employees are highly motivated by activities that directly affect the company's bottom line. As Robert Hauptfuhrer, chairman and CEO of Oryx Energy, points out, "Give people a chance not just to do a job but to have some impact, and they'll really respond, get on their rollerskates, and race around to make sure it happens."

Other examples abound:

- ✔ The president of the Pizza Hut fast-food chain asked employees how to eliminate needless paperwork and tasks and improve their working conditions. The result was a company with fewer layers of management, less corporate paperwork, and a 40 percent growth in sales.

- ✔ Goodyear Tire & Rubber, headquartered in Akron, Ohio, believes that providing employees with good company information is motivating. At Goodyear, all workers can access computer files providing information about themselves, their departments, and their plants. Each shift tracks its own productivity. The results are posted on marker boards displayed on the shop floor and updated frequently.

- ✔ Enterprise Rent-A-Car, headquartered in St. Louis, posts the financial results of every branch office and region in plain view of all employees. A friendly rivalry between branch offices ensues, which translates into motivated employees who want to perform at their best at all times. New Jersey manager Woody Erhardt holds his fingers an inch apart and says, "We're this close to beating out Middlesex." He continues, "If they lose, they have to throw a party for us, and we get to decide what they wear."

It Takes Less Effort to Sustain Desired Behavior Than to Initially Create It

The irony behind failing to recognize positive behavior is that you're passing up an easy opportunity. Consider that you don't have to teach your employee the behavior they demonstrated; you just have to notice it when it occurs! Reinforcement theory tells us that after an employee establishes a new behavior, the manager can best perpetuate that behavior through intermittent reinforcement. In other words, don't neglect to recognize the behavior you want just because a program to promote it has ended. Selective ongoing emphasis on the behavior can perpetuate results at a fraction of the original time and effort.

Keep communicating information about performance and achievement. Publish articles about continued results and examples of successes in your organization's newsletter or call them out publicly in meetings. For example, employee suggestions can continue to be highlighted by noting company savings from each suggestion or by interviewing top contributors to encourage role modeling. Have management individually thank employees who have continued to perform as desired. Whether you do it in the hallway, via voicemail, or on a sticky note, keep saying "Thanks!" and "Good job!" to perpetuate ongoing results.

When you provide a vehicle for employees to use to thank one another, you'll discover that praising happens much more often. Tektronix, Inc., a manufacturer of electronic instruments located in Beaverton, Oregon, instituted a simple way for mangers and employees alike to focus on recognizing others for doing something right. They got simple memo pads with a cartoon and the heading "You Done Good Award" that anybody could give to anybody else in the company. On the memo pad, the person giving the award states what was done, who did it, and when, and then gives the memo to the recipient. The idea has caught on and is now part of life at Tektronix. Says Joe Floren, former communications manager for Tektronix, "Even though people say nice things to you, it means something more when people take the time to write their name on a piece of paper and say it. Employees usually post them next to their desks."

AT&T Universal Card Services in Jacksonville, Florida, uses the World of Thanks award as one of more than 40 recognition and rewards programs in the organization. It's a pad of colored paper shaped like a globe with "Thank You" written all over it in different languages. Anyone in the company can write a message of thanks to anyone else and send it to that person. The program is extremely popular — in four years AT&T has used over 130,000 such notes.

Managers Don't Focus on Employee Motivation until It's Lost

So often, managers are too busy focusing on what's urgent, such as dealing with daily crises in their jobs, and forget about regularly motivating and recognizing employees until that motivation is lost. Morale sinks, employees quit, and *then* management scrambles to figure out ways to energize and motivate employees. As you can probably guess, reenergizing employees who have poor morale is much more difficult than doing little things along the way to keep them engaged.

The same type of scenario often plays out as smaller companies grow. Smaller businesses have a lot of inherent motivators — variety of jobs, more direct contact with top management, more room for advancement, and the like. But, as a company grows, these types of motivators disappear and management often fails to supplement what is lost with other forms of recognition. The situation is often made worse by the increase of demotivators that come from having more bureaucracy, policy manuals, approval processes, and the like as the organization grows.

In these situations, an ounce of prevention is worth a pound of cure. Strive to consistently keep motivation and energy high. Ideas like the following help maintain a high level of employee motivation:

✔ To keep up morale, Barr-Nunn Transportation of Granger, Iowa, provides its driver with two monthly publications — a newsletter and a four-hour cassette tape loaded with industry and company news, country music, information on company benefits, and personalized messages such as birthday announcements. Since creating these, the company has experienced a 35 percent reduction in its turnover rate.

✔ To keep employee morale and energy at high levels during particularly busy times of the year, executives at the Cigna Group, an insurance company headquartered in Hartford, Connecticut, personally push coffee carts around the office, serving drinks and refreshments to their front-line partners. Not only do employees appreciate this gesture by management, but they have the opportunity to bring up and resolve customer issues at the same time.

✔ Vice presidents at Nobel/Sysco, a food distribution company in Denver, Colorado, conduct regular employee appreciation lunches where they cook and serve the food. As employees pass through the serving line, the vice presidents tell them how much they are appreciated.

✔ During stressful times at Maritz Performance Improvement Co., in St. Louis, Missouri, the company uses a Thanks a Bunch award. Someone brings in a bunch of flowers to give a hardworking employee who keeps one flower and card and passes on the bunch to another performer who, in turn, repeats the process. At the end of the day, all the cards are collected and a drawing for prizes is hosted.

Helping Employees Develop Marketable Skills Makes them More Likely to Stay

The very definition of marketable skills implies that those who have them can be paid more in the market. Yet, I'm convinced that as you make it a priority to help employees learn and grow, your employees will be more likely to want to stay because they'll know that they're in a very special place. If you don't show an interest in employees — what skills they want to learn, where they want to be in five years, how they are growing in their jobs — you won't be able to persuade them to stay if they get a job offer elsewhere. By clearly showing that you have the individual employee's best interests at heart through your behaviors, you reap the benefits tenfold.

According to Adelle DiGiorgio, corporate employee relations director at Apple Computer, "The message we give employees is that they're responsible for their career development, but we'll help them figure out which paths are the best for them to take." Employers like Apple Computer and others who support their employees' attempts to better themselves (even if it means that they lose good workers) energize their workforce by demonstrating that the company's first concern is the overall welfare of the employees.

Management at Novartis based in Basel, Switzerland, lets its employees know that it does not consider them disloyal for considering career paths that lead outside the company. Novartis believes that offering employees ways to enhance their future employability alleviates the anxiety connected with losing a job and demonstrates that the company truly cares about them.

Skill development is especially motivational for today's younger workforce. These employees constantly want to learn new skills, both to keep their jobs exciting and challenging, and to increase their marketability. In the words of Liesel Walsh, a consultant with Big Picture Marketing in Charleston, Massachusetts, "Young workers today see themselves as marketable commodities, as an item for sale. So if management can help them to see how an assignment we give them today makes them more marketable, how it builds their resumé — that really motivates them."

You Get What You Reward Is Common Sense but Rarely Practiced

Everyone likes to be appreciated. Results of a survey by the Council of Communication Management confirm what almost every employee already knows: that recognition for a job well done is the top motivator of employee performance. Yet how many managers consider appreciating others to be a major function of their job today? Not many. Most managers fail to use the potential power of recognition and rewards. This is true even though 33 percent of managers themselves report that they would rather work in an organization where they could receive better recognition.

At a time when employees are being asked to do more than ever before — to make suggestions for continuous improvement, to handle complex problems quickly, and to act independently in the best interests of the organization — the resources and support for helping them is at an all-time low. What used to be common courtesies have been overcome by speed and technology in today's businesses. Managers tend to be too busy and too removed from their employees to notice when they have done good work, let alone to thank them for it. Technology has replaced personal interaction with one's manager with constant interfacing on a computer display.

John Naisbitt predicted this challenge over three decades ago in his book *Megatrends*. He said the more our work environments become highly technical, the greater the employee need would become to be more personal and human. He called the phenomenon "high-tech/high-touch." And this shift has occurred at a time in which employees are looking to have greater meaning in their lives and in their jobs. So whatever your situation, start today to build on the good work your employees are doing to make them feel valued for the work they do.

Chapter 19

Top Ten Trends in Employee Recognition

Here's a quick history of the incentive industry in just a single story: I had a great employee named Nick who told me that, when his grandfather retired after working for 40 years, his company threw him a retirement party and presented him with a plaque for his years of service. He was so moved, he cried. Nick's father worked his entire career for a defense contractor, and on his 35th anniversary with the firm, he found a coffee mug plopped on his desk, with no one around at the time and no context for the achievement presented. He went into a serious funk for a number of days, pondering, "Is this what my life has amounted to?" Nick graduated from college while he was working for me, and as his graduation date drew near, he called me and said, "Bob, I decided that you should give me a trip to Italy as a graduation gift." Because he was my best employee ever, my reply was simply, "Done." Nick used my frequent flier miles and booked the trip he had earned. He had a great time, and I felt great being able to reward him in a way he valued!

It's clear that recognition has undergone significant changes in just a few generations. By far the most significant current trend in employee recognition is the impact technology is making on the topic, which I discuss in depth in Chapter 12. Following are ten other major ways recognition has evolved in today's work environments.

It's Decentralized and Informal

In the past, corporate headquarters or the human resources department was responsible for designing and implementing incentive programs. Typically, they'd oversee a few formal programs that provided infrequent recognition (often just at year-end). Today, the task of motivating employees falls to each manager in his or her sphere of influence, and recognition has become much more informal.

Informal, spontaneous recognition — specifically tied to what matters most on a day-to-day basis — is even more important today due largely to the increased speed and constant change that occurs in business. Managers need to be more "in the moment" in managing their employees. In addition, employees these days expect more frequent recognition. Managers can't rely solely on formal programs run by HR to motivate their employees; instead, they must take a more hands-on ownership of that task and the connections they build with each of their employees.

 Informal recognition tends to be more personal and fun and thus creates and sustains energy among employees. Some companies are even focusing on fun as a way to enhance employee morale in challenging, often stressful times. Dimension Data Canada, Inc., the network-related technology company, appointed a Chief Fun Officer (CFO) in its Toronto office. This title is given to an employee who's willing to create fun. CFOs get a budget to organize monthly activities, such as paintball or bowling. Cargill, the largest privately held company in America, created a Recognition Committee for each of the company's more than 400 plants across North America to ensure that recognition happens at each local facility.

 Formal recognition touches considerably fewer employees than informal recognition. When you limit your recognition programs to just those very rigid (typically timeline-based) awards, you're missing a lot of opportunities. When I helped to evaluate an electronics firm's formal recognition programs, we discovered that only about 4 percent of the organization's employees were eligible for any of the company's seven established recognition programs. The company realized it needed to increase the frequency of recognition to get everyone in the organization more motivated! We added new tools and programs, and recognition became more prevalent throughout the organization.

It Includes More Reward Options

In the past, rewards tended to be formal merchandise that executives used in formal recognition programs like employee-of-the-month or retirement celebrations. Now options for employee recognition are much greater, and more times than not, managers give employees a choice. Greater choice equals enhanced motivation, because what's motivating to one employee may have no meaning to another. Consider these examples:

✔ **Lifestyle rewards:** Logoed jewelry and crystal have given way to more practical everyday lifestyle merchandise that employees can use themselves (such as a gym bag or first aid kit) or share with their families (like retail gift cards or grills).

✔ **Time off:** Time is an excellent form of recognition for today's time-pressed workers. Boston-based Greenough Communications offers "Winter Fridays," wherein each week, high-performing employees get to leave work early at 3:00 p.m. on Friday. Los Angeles-based company JS2 Communications, Inc., gave each high-performing employee two free "I Don't Want to Get Out of Bed" days to acknowledge the increased demands the company had been placing on all. To encourage a more balanced work life, high performing employees at Eddie Bauer, the clothing store chain based in Bellevue, Washington, are allowed to "call in well" and take time off.

✔ **Experiential rewards:** Increasingly, allowing employees the chance to have a special experience is a very motivating form of thanks. Restaurant Equipment World of Orlando, Florida, treats employees to adventures outside of the office to avoid workday interruptions and give them a greater opportunity to bond. Trips include group cooking lessons, pottery classes, bowling, laser tag, zip-lining, and visits to a factory to make chocolate. Circles, a Boston marketing company, gave CFO Hugh Merryweather a choice of an experience as part of his anniversary reward with the company. He opted for a Red Sox baseball game with special perks and took his young son with him.

✔ **Training and development:** Allowing high-performing employees to attend special training or giving them a choice of projects to work on can be an excellent form of recognition. I feel the future of recognition will include a lot more "opportunity" rewards where, for example, employees can redeem points they've earned in the company's recognition program to attend a conference of their choice or to be on a special task force for the company.

As companies ask employees what they value and then provide those things as they perform, the potential list of recognition possibilities will continue to expand.

It's More Frequent and Comes from More Sources

The days of expecting annual awards or great performance reviews to motivate an employee for the next twelve months of their work are over; you must recognize deserving employees on an ongoing basis. This means that organizations need to have an expanded variety of recognition tools, and managers need to be creative, flexible, and frequent with their recognition. Fortunately, because recognition can come from any direction, the burden on the manager of having to provide 100 percent of the recognition for his or her employees has declined. Others within (and even outside) organizations are expanding the number of recognition opportunities that can occur. Recognition can come from peers and from customers, as well.

✔ **Peers:** Peer-to-peer recognition, as I discuss in Chapter 10, has become prevalent over the last decade, and it will continue to increase. Some examples include the following:

• Employees at SC Johnson, the global manufacturer of household cleaning supplies based in Racine, Wisconsin, nominate and give standing ovations to their peers for remarkable performance.

• Employees at La Posada at Park Centre, a retirement community in Green Valley, Arizona, give each other "You're a Star" cards, which can be redeemed for cash or days off.

• Some agencies of Qsource, a Memphis-based nonprofit health-care management company, erect an "Angels Among Us" table in the office. When someone nominates a peer for doing something exceptional, colleagues decorate the table as a tribute and include a copy of the nomination, an explanation of why the person is being honored, photos of the nominee, and flowers.

• At Montana's Cookhouse, a large restaurant chain based in Mississauga, Ontario, employees praise their peers' work in external and internal customer service, health, and safety. Feedback is entered on the company's intranet and sent to the person's manager, who reads the note to staff; the notes are then posted on the company's website. About 1,500 comments were filed in the first nine months of the program.

✔ **Customers:** You can also enable customers to recognize your employees. One way to do so is to make recognition forms available to customers, such as they do with the Most Valuable Player program at Busch Stadium. Ten randomly selected fans are given two small MVP cards, which they can bestow on any two employees who show them some courtesy. Employees then turn the cards over to supervisors; if the group of workers collects at least 15 of the 20 cards during the game, a drawing is held, and the winner gets a $100 bill. All employees who receive cards from fans are mentioned in a monthly flyer sent out to employees.

You can also recognize your customers and vendors as a strategy for improving relationships, encouraging business, and promoting quality. Four Seasons Flower Shop in Poway, California, for example, recognizes customers by hosting a "Good Neighbor Day" during which the store distributes a dozen free roses to anyone who comes into the store on the condition that the person keep one of the roses and pass the rest of the bunch on to someone else, instructing the next person to do the same. Barbara Bertran, the store's owner, obtained the support of several other local businesses to sponsor this event, in which they distribute some 10,000 medium-stemmed roses. Many auto companies, such as Ford, recognize their vendors for becoming certified in ISO 9000 quality process training, which in turn, increases the quality and consistency of parts and products the vendor supplies.

It's More Customized and Personal

Today, especially with the advent of software that can track employee preferences, you can customize and personalize rewards to fit the needs and preferences of each employee. Employees' award selections get customized based on their past point redemption or order history. You can also track how popular different reward items are by tapping into the comment and rating systems to see what items were "liked" by your employees. At the simplest level, you can use this feature to give your employees a greater range of choice in their reward options or to personalize a gift or achievement certificate you select for them yourself.

In addition, website and system design improvements are enabling a higher degree of individual program personalization as well. For example, you can enable individual employees to customize their home page on the company's recognition software platform in many companies today.

As technology provides increasingly more options for employee recognition, you must remain vigilant that the personal touch still exists. You still need to add your own personal thanks to employees who have had significant achievements; don't rely solely on technology to provide all the recognition.

All Deserving Employees Are Recognized

Executives used to reserve major incentives such as travel for the organization's top sales employees (for example, giving the top sales person a trip to Hawaii as part of the President's Club). Now, managers recognize employees at all levels and in all functions for meeting or exceeding their objectives. I have long advocated that companies allocate some of the recognition budget they traditionally spend on top performers to celebrate the entire team that supported those top performers. You can give top performers recognition tools and resources so that they can thank the employees who supported them; for example, you can give sales reps gift cards to use to thank individuals who helped them close sales. Alternatively, you can host a team or company party to celebrate a new client account or achievement of the quarter's financial goals.

Here are some additional real-life examples:

- Mary Jo Scarpelli, former sales director for Coronet/MTI Film & Video in Deerfield, Illinois, delighted in bringing the entire sales and support team bagels and cream cheese on the last Friday of each month.

- Amtech, a Dallas-based maker of vehicle ID tags, throws a Victory Party for sales support staff and customer-service reps after they land a new account or meet a big deadline. Chairman Michael Corboy says, "Recognition is more important than real dollars, if you pay your people well." In five years, the company has experienced growth of 8,900 percent.

- Alan Ashton, former president of WordPerfect Corporation, told the company that if they doubled its sales in the upcoming year, he would take all 600 employee and their spouses to Hawaii for a week, all expenses paid. The employees achieved this goal, and Ashton sent them all, ten at a time, on their vacations over an eight-month period.

It Recognizes Nonwork Behaviors and Achievements

Increasingly, managers are using incentives to acknowledge achievements other than work tasks. People tend to repeat behavior for which they get recognized, so if employers are interested in saving on their escalating health-care costs, for example, they can recognize healthy habits (exercising, eating healthy, and not smoking, for example) and preventive healthcare (such as getting physicals and vaccinations) and for personal achievements in learning and development:

- **Recognition for health and wellness:** Market trends show wellness initiatives are becoming very popular in the recognition industry and the continual push to make health-oriented technology accessible anytime, anywhere on user's mobile devices creates new recognition opportunities your company can take advantage of. With the use of wearable device — such as Fitbits and smart watches — corporate wellness administrators and company leaders can use mobile apps to track the overall well-being of their employee population, as well as individual employees, and then recognize achievers.

Incentives around health and wellness help company budgets because healthier employees mean lower healthcare costs for the organization. Consider these examples:

- FTEN, the New York City–based financial technology firm, offers its employees a holistic approach to wellness, including nutrition, exercise, and stress-reduction workshops. Workers also receive a healthy daily breakfast free of charge and bimonthly in-house massages. New hires work at ergonomically designed computer desks. With more employees adhering to a diet and exercise regimen, FTEN anticipates that its medical costs will drop.

- Protective Life, a financial services and insurance company based in Birmingham, Alabama, uses the Virgin HealthMiles incentive platform to help employees become healthier. The company also offers an onsite health clinic, massage services, a nutritionist, and health education programs. Just over 60 percent of Protective's employees are enrolled in the Virgin HealthMiles program. Desktop kiosks are available for employees to take biometric readings of their blood pressure, weight, and body fat measurements. Employees get credit for using the kiosks each month and can accrue additional points for walking, running, or doing aerobics, and they are rewarded with gift cards and cash. In a 12-month period, employees can earn up to $400 in cash or choices of gift cards, which are also available via the Virgin HealthMiles platform.

- At its headquarters in Sugar Land, Texas, all employees of Heavy Construction Systems Specialists (HCSS), a Houston-area software developer, are eligible to receive $100 annually for each good result from an annual health screening. The company-paid annual health-insurance premiums fell to $2,318 per employee from $2,950 four years earlier. The company credits this success to its wellness program and to changes it made in its company-offered health plan.

- Chicago-based Radio Flyer, Inc., a toy products company, has a wellness committee that oversees initiatives to encourage healthy behaviors among employees. It devised a benefit in which employees are reimbursed up to $300 annually for activities such as running marathons or taking weight-loss counseling. The workplace efforts extend to Radio Flyer's office in China.

There's a fine line between encouraging and recognizing employees for being healthy and violating employee privacy concerns. Some organizations are starting to charge employees more for their healthcare insurance if they are at greater health risk due to being overweight or having high-blood pressure, for example. And a company my wife worked for actually set an employment policy that they would not hire smokers. Both examples are treading on thin ice.

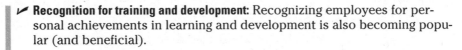

Companies are becoming more health conscious

As employees have become more health conscious, companies are following suit. For example, Dow Chemical, based in Midland, Michigan, has a goal of reducing health risks to its employee population by 10 percent and provides healthy foods in cafeterias and vending machines. Food choices include fresh fruit, yogurt, baked chips, peanuts, and granola bars in vending areas. And the SAS Institute in Cary, NC, a provider of business intelligence and software, has an onsite healthcare center that offers full-time nutritionists who create personalized eating plans for employees. "It's a growing initiative," says Julie Steward, SAS food-service manager. "We got more comments on the healthy food initiative than we've gotten on any other initiative we've done."

✔ **Recognition for training and development:** Recognizing employees for personal achievements in learning and development is also becoming popular (and beneficial).

- Doug Garwood, former director of customer service and product management for Collins & Aikman Carpet in Dalton, Georgia, reports that after 80 employees passed their GEDs (high school equivalency exams), the company hosted a graduation lunch and awarded them class rings.

- Since Western Virginia Water Authority started offering financial planning seminars (as well as a wellness program), the utility reports that its voluntary turnover rate has dropped from 8.93 to 2.28 percent in a two-year period.

- Bruce Power, based in Tiverton, Ontario, offers incentives for employees to reach personal growth goals and behaviors, including use of the firm's extensive wellness program.

- Johnsonville Foods in Sheboygan, Wisconsin, has a personal development team to help individual employees plan career goals and strategies for achieving those goals. Each person has an education allowance to be used however he or she sees fit, and as new skills are learned (budgeting, for example) employees earn an increase to their base income. Today over 65 percent of all employees are involved in some type of formal education.

It Recognizes New Types of Workers

Traditional (regular, full-time) employees have become a minority in the workforce today. In a recent year, 65 percent of all employees were independent contractors, working on either a part-time or project basis, paid by the hour, and typically without benefits, vacation time, or sick leave. The number of virtual workers, those who work offsite, often online, has increased over 300 percent in just the last decade. As contract employees become the norm in the workforce (estimated to increase to over 50 percent of all workers by 2020), managers need to become more aware and skilled in how to motivate workers they may never personally meet face to face. Here are some strategies companies are using today to tap into this expanding workforce.

✔ **Contractors:** Just because some employees are hired to work on temporary projects doesn't mean that they don't need to be recognized when they do a good job. Thank them when they're ahead of schedule or achieve a milestone! Give them a chance to meet others on your staff and be sure you have a good plan for handling questions or problems that arise.

Karla Herzog, president of Total Personnel Service in San Diego, California, knew it was important to stay in touch with the employees she hired and placed with clients, but since she hardly ever saw them after they were hired, the task was daunting. So Karla made it a priority to communicate on an ongoing basis with her workers and was thus able to minimize the gap that might otherwise have existed. She even recognized Star Employees — and personally delivered trophies to them where they were working at the client sites.

✔ **Part-time employees:** Part-time employees can still be long-term employees, so take a long-term view of your relationship you have with them. Disney interviews seasonal hires at the end of each summer to see what went well and what could have gone better from the employee's perspective. They then use all that feedback to make improvements in the next season's part-time hiring process. As a result, a significant percentage of their seasonal hires return each year to work for them.

✔ **Virtual workers:** Virtual and remote workers are another expanding category of worker today whom managers need to have the skills to motivate. Fortunately, with the advent of online recognition services, recognizing such employees is relatively easy. Virtual gift cards, for example, can be sent to employees as a simple form of thanks, wherever they may be physically located.

It Emphasizes a Performance-Based Culture

Organizations — especially larger and older organizations — are moving away from a mindset of "taking care of people" to one of "helping employees help themselves." In other words, companies provide opportunities for employees to learn, grow, perform, and produce in ways that benefit both the organization and the employees themselves. This change is a function of both business demands (companies increasingly can no longer afford to pay employees' long-term retirement pensions, for example) and changing employee expectations. Instead of working for just a paycheck, employees want and expect more thanks, appreciation, meaning, and value in the work they do on a daily basis. Therefore, effective recognition is increasingly being based on performance rather than on just showing up for work.

So that the overall organization can reach its goals, individual employees are being recognized for their contributions toward the organization's objectives. Consider these examples:

- ✔ Newsletter publisher Boardroom, Inc. in Stamford, Connecticut, gives all employees that participate in its suggestion program each quarter a share of the savings accrued. Their program, called I-Power, helped the firm increase its profits five-fold over a three-year period.

- ✔ Plant workers as well as salespeople are eligible for a bonus based on profitability, quality, and continuous improvement at Grand Rapids, Michigan's SSS Spring & Wire.

As a manager, you need to constantly check your attitude to make sure you aren't managing employees from outdated assumptions such as recognizing just for showing up, and recognition not being based on actual achievements. Old school assumptions about human behavior can indicate a manager is out of touch and ineffective in today's organizations.

Socially Responsible Rewards Are Valued

Companies and employees are becoming more socially responsible and environmentally aware in their incentives. As social causes are increasingly important to employees, they are becoming a more significant part of recognition programs everywhere. Managers need to be sensitive and supportive of causes and values that are important to their employees.

Consider the examples set by these companies:

- ✔ PepsiCo encourages associates to get outside by providing lush outdoor grounds, perfect for head-clearing walks, and by offering employees plots of land on which they can start organic gardens.

- ✔ Cox Enterprises in Atlanta, Georgia, has gone green: Its food-service packaging is produced using sustainable, renewable sources like sugar cane and corn — both degrade within 60 days.

✔ San Diego State University uses only trans-fat-free oil for cooking, which it recycles to produce biofuel for campus vehicles. The university also has a food-composting program, and leftover biodegradable food scraps are used for campus landscaping. In one year alone, the university converted 50 tons of waste to compost.

✔ Radio Flyer, Inc., has an employee-run environmental-issues committee that launched a campaign to get employees to reduce their carbon footprints at home and work. The company also introduced a new benefit that pays employees 55 cents a mile to ride bikes to work. These workplace efforts extend to Radio Flyer's office in China as well.

✔ Employees of Pfizer, the pharmaceutical giant based in New York, convinced company leadership to make Pfizer medications free to all former U.S. employees who had been laid off. The program, MAINTAIN, had a big morale-boosting effect within the organization. Employees donated their own money to the program, with the Pfizer Foundation matching all employee donations.

It Has Shifted from Getting to Giving

Charity incentives and employees' desire to contribute money or time for community service are at an all-time high. Many employees donate the financial value of rewards they receive to make a difference in the world. You can incorporate this desire for giving into your recognition efforts as well.

✔ **Cash donations:** One of the easiest ways for employees to support a cause they believe in is by donating money. Companies are finding more ways every day to make it easier to partner with their employees in this effort:

- For $5, employees of participating divisions of Lee Jeans apparel makers headquartered in Merriam, Kansas, can "buy" the right to wear jeans to work; all proceeds go to the Komen Foundation.

- Intuit, a Mountain View, California, tax and financial software provider, lets employees use their recognition awards to make charitable donations to organizations such as the International Red Cross.

- Ford Motor Company encourages employees to participate in various local activities during Breast Cancer Awareness month and Race for the Cure run/walks. Employees sign up their own sponsors, who write checks directly to the charities involved.

A great way for a company to demonstrate its values is by supporting employee charities through matching gift programs. Typically run by the HR department, matching gift programs allow employees who donate to an organization to apply for a matching donation from the company to their charity!

✔ **Volunteer time:** Sometimes, companies and employees go beyond cash donations and give of their time. It's a great way to promote goodwill among employees and a company's image. Here are some examples:

- Robert W. Baird & Co., a financial services company, allows associates to take one paid day per year to perform volunteer service. In addition, many of its departments organize food drives and holiday gift-giving events and support fund-raising walks for local charitable organizations.

- McCormick & Company, a food manufacturer in Baltimore, Maryland, encourages employees to work on one "Charity Day" Saturday every year. Employees donate their pay for the day at time and a half to a charity. More than 90 percent of employees participate.

- The Graham Company, an insurance broker in Philadelphia, allows employees to take time off to volunteer. Bellevue, Washington, accounting firm Clark Nuber, an award-winning CPA and consulting firm, launched Caring, Serving and Giving, a program that lets employees apply for grants of up to $500 to fund community service projects.

- At Atlantic Richfield Company, annual community service awards are given to employees who have made outstanding contributions in the community. The company also matches on a two-for-one basis any employee or retiree donation to a social service organization or college.

Chapter 20

Ten No-Cost Strategies for Recognizing and Engaging Employees

In This Chapter

▶ Involving employees in decisions

▶ Supporting employees' professional development

▶ Sharing praise publicly

The great thing about employee recognition and engagement is that it doesn't have to cost you anything. I conducted a national survey of thousands of employees to find out what motivates them at no cost to their employers. Here are the motivators employees said were most important to them, in order of popularity. Also included are some thoughts and examples of how you might better provide each of these items to your own employees.

#1: Provide Employees Information They Need

The top priority for 95 percent of the employees surveyed is having adequate communication and being informed, and they see it as their manager's job to keep them updated. Employees need information to do their job well, but they also want to know about other things: what's going on in other areas of the organization, what the company's marketing strategies are, what new products and services are in the works, and such. There are many ways to make employees feel informed and included:

- ✔ **Provide the latest information about the employee's job, department, and so on.** Routinely take time to share decisions made by management with your staff and answer any questions they might have. This information is an important part of making it possible for your employees do the best job possible.

- ✔ **Show the big picture.** When you share the organization's purpose and mission, you increase the likelihood that employees will identify with your goals. Explain the strategic objectives for the year and help employees set goals that relate to those objectives in their own jobs. As Frances Hesselbein, CEO of the Leader to Leader Institute says, "No matter what business you are in, everybody needs to know why." Knowing and feeling a part of the company's purpose makes it easier for employees to act in the best interests of the organization.

- ✔ **Share management decisions in a timely manner.** As you share important information, employees will feel more like peers and colleagues than subordinates. Make it a priority to share with your staff within 24 hours what was discussed in management meetings you've attended. Take questions from your employees and find out answers if you don't already have them.

- ✔ **Explain pending changes and how these changes will affect your employees and the organization as a whole.** People should especially hear about difficult changes from management, not from their local newspaper or the rumor mill. Explain how the change will impact the organization, employees, and their jobs. When you provide this information, employees will be more accepting of, and possibly become advocates for, the changes, helping to alleviate fears and concerns.

- ✔ **Give other information they desire.** Ask employees what additional information they'd like to have. The answer may surprise you. At FedEx in Memphis, the most popular column in the company newsletter is about the company's competition. At Subaru's Illinois plant, employees requested information about new car models the company was planning to market, which helped them serve as ambassadors for those products.

#2: Support Employees When They Make Mistakes

Nobody plans to make a mistake, but when mistakes happen, how you handle those mistakes as a manager is important. You can criticize, find fault, and place blame, embarrassing employees in front of their peers and proving that you're the smartest one in the room, *or* you can take a deep breath and say something like, "That's not the way I would have handled the situation, but what did you learn from your mistake?" Employees already know when they've made a mistake; your publicly amplifying that truth isn't going to fix the error and will only leave them focusing on what a jerk you are. Although they probably won't make that same mistake again, if you are overly critical, you risk undermining your employees' self-esteem and permanently losing their willingness to take calculated risks when they face the next problem situation or customer. As William McKnight, former CEO of 3M, once put it, "The mistakes people make are much less important than the mistakes management makes when it tells them exactly what to do."

A better tactic when your employees make mistakes is to roll up your sleeves and pitch in to help fix the problem. Management is about developing long-term relationships with your employees, so every challenge and interaction offers a chance to engage with them and create a stronger bond. In fact, Google attributes much of its incredible success to failure. Founders Eric Schmidt, Larry Page, and Sergey Brin have explicitly stated the importance of "failing forward."

Consider these examples:

- Hershey Foods chairman and CEO Richard Zimmerman wanted to encourage employees to exercise initiative in their jobs and to take risks without fear of retribution should they fail or make a mistake. To encourage such risks, he created the Exalted Order of the Extended Neck. Says Zimmerman, "I wanted to reward people who were willing to buck the system, practice a little entrepreneurship, who were willing to stand the heat for an idea they really believe in." The award has been given out on numerous occasions to celebrate overcoming the odds, including to a maintenance worker who devised a way to perform midweek cleaning on a piece of machinery without losing running time.

- Steve Ettridge, president of Randstad Professionals US, a temporary-employment service based in Wakefield, Massachusetts, had a problem with young workers who would not admit having done something wrong. "Most of the mistakes could have been fixed or minimized, but I never found out about them until they blew up," Ettridge says. "One day I pulled out five hundred dollars in cash, and I told them about a mistake I'd made that week. I said that whoever could top it would get the money. Of course, they were afraid it was a trick." One employee finally admitted to a data-entry error that had caused a $2 million paycheck to be printed and almost mailed out. He got the $500. Since then the company gives out quarterly $100 awards to employees who admit mistakes they have made on the job. Ettridge says the award is designed to allow people to be human and to encourage risk-taking.

#3: Solicit Opinions and Ideas, and Involve Employees in Decisions

Simply asking your employees for their opinions shows trust and respect, and goes a long way in keeping them engaged and motivated. Employees appreciate being asked for their opinions, even if you aren't always able to use the information they provide. Take this tip one step further and involve your employees in the decisions being made, especially those that affect them and their work.

To make sure your employees know that you sincerely want to involve and engage them, you must consistently solicit feedback from your employees. You might ultimately be responsible for the decision, but getting your employees' input helps make your decision a better one. This basic courtesy goes a long way in helping employees feel a part of things — and it's a slap in the face when it does not occur.

If your employees have an idea for how things could be improved, how costs could be cut, or how processes could be streamlined, thank them for that idea and perhaps allow them to pursue it. Who has more excitement for an idea than the person who came up with it? American Strap in Diamond City, Arkansas, found that employees became more and more creative after the company launched its suggestion system. Just finding that their suggestions were being taken seriously changed the workers' attitudes, and they became even more willing to find ways to help the company improve.

#4: Be Available and Get to Know Your Employees

In today's fast-paced world in which everyone is expected to do more work faster, personal time with one's manager is in itself a form of recognition. Busy managers who make time for their employees and answer their questions make employees feel like a high priority, which is quite motivating. The action says, "Of all the things I have to do right now, one of the most important is to take time to be with you." Especially for younger employees, spending time with their managers is a valued form of validation and inspiration, and it serves the practical purpose of facilitating good communication. As Roy Moody, president of Roy Moody Associates puts it, "The greatest motivational act one person can do for another is to listen."

Here are a few ideas and examples of how you can make yourself available:

- ✔ **Just check in:** Randy Niendorff of Lucent Technologies/Audya Communications in Denver, Colorado, stops by employees' desks to "just to see how things are going today." He reports that it's a pleasant surprise for employees to see him and that they appreciate his accessibility.

- ✔ **Listen and learn:** Sue Copening learned an important lesson about listening the hard way several years ago when she was promoted to store manager for a retail chain. Stressed out from the additional responsibilities, she was not taking time to really pay attention to her staff. When two employees quit within a few weeks, one had the courage to tell her that she was creating an unfriendly work environment. Sue realized that, compared to the stress and time involved in hiring and training new employees, spending time to listen to employee concerns and helping them cope on the job was a bargain. She now reports, "A manager's job is 95 percent being sensitive to employees and keeping them happy. It's easier to change your own behavior than to expect other people to adjust to you."

- ✔ **Put people on your to-do list:** A task-oriented top manager at US West Communications (now CenturyLink) in Denver, Colorado, reported that he reminded himself to recognize others by listing his employees' names on his weekly to-do list. Then, one-by-one, he crossed each person off the list after acknowledging that person for something. This was his way to "turn the people aspect of my job into manageable tasks I can focus on each week."

- ✔ **Perform simple, everyday acts of courtesy:** When the Marriott Marquis in Times Square asked 400 housekeepers how management could better recognize them for the great job they do, their overwhelming response was, "Have managers use our names." When employees of AAA of Southern California were asked the same question, they responded, "Have managers get out of their offices more often." These examples illustrate how simple recognition can be, and how even the simplest forms make a difference in people's jobs.

- ✔ **Grant access to management:** You may have a formal open-door policy, in which you encourage employees to approach their managers as needed, but managers also must be truly receptive when employees approach them. At ViaSat, in Carlsbad, California, even the newest hires are free to approach upper management with questions or to contribute new ideas. The door to executive level personnel is truly open.

#5: Support Employees Learning New Skills and Discuss Their Career Options

Today's employees most value learning opportunities from which they can gain skills that enhance their worth and marketability in their current jobs, as well as in future positions. Find out what your employees want to learn and how they want to grow and develop, and then give them opportunities as they arise.

Showing you care about where an employee's career is headed shows a long-term respect for the individual. Managing Personal Growth, an employee development program, outlines a great method that can help managers empower their employees to take responsibility for their own job satisfaction, job performance, and career development. Each employee and his or her manager first separately defines the employee's job responsibilities and the skills required; then the two meet to share their perceptions. From that information, the employee and manager chart a development plan and agree on job priorities. During the following year, employees and their managers meet two to three times to discuss progress and make plans for continued development. The program has been highly successful for better motivating employees (versus more traditional performance evaluations) because employees have a stake in the results.

Another way to help your employees build skills is to delegate. Most managers never stop to consider that what and how they delegate can be a form of recognition. In fact, if properly used, delegation can be one of the strongest forms of recognition — an affirmation of the employee and his or her talents. Here are some tips for getting the most out of the next assignment you delegate:

- **Know your employee's interests.** Effective delegation starts with knowing your employees — their capabilities, interests, and aspirations. Find out what skills they are interested in learning, the types of work assignments they like best, and where they'd like to go in their careers.

- **Match assignments to employee interests.** As work needs arise, consider who would be excited about the assignment, not just who has done the task before or happens to be available. The person who views the assignment as an opportunity is likely to be most motivated to do the best job possible.

- **Provide a context when delegating.** Tell the person why you selected him or her for the assignment, what skills or attributes made you think of that person for the task, and what you think can be learned from the assignment. Provide encouragement and say you have confidence in the person's ability to do the assignment.

✔ **Be available to assist.** Delegation is not abdication. When you have given an assignment to someone else, be available to discuss progress or answer questions. Set a time for the person to check back with you. Much learning can occur when you discuss approaches and strategies for completing an assignment — and debrief the assignment afterwards!

#6: Allow Autonomy, Increase Authority, and Give Assignment Choices

The ultimate form of recognition for many employees is to be given increased autonomy and authority to get their jobs done, whether they need to spend or allocate resources, make decisions, or manage others. Giving greater autonomy and authority says, "I trust you to act in the best interests of the company and to do so independently and without approval of myself or others." For example, to demonstrate trust in their employees, when managers leave a Midwestern printing plant for their annual offsite meeting, employees run the show. Managers are not allowed to set foot inside the plant or call in unless an employee asks for assistance. So far, no manager has ever been called.

Award increased autonomy and authority to employees as a form of recognition. Autonomy and authority are privileges, not rights, and should be granted to those who have most earned them, based on past performance, not simply based on tenure or seniority. You can also reward top performers by assigning them to exciting new projects (or by letting them choose their own assignments). If that's not possible, give the top performers more variety or responsibility in their existing jobs. More responsibility tells employees you trust them and respect them and want them to grow on the job.

Taking on a special project or managing a task force can give an employee valuable experience. Here are some examples of these concepts in action:

✔ At Xerox, one customer service center turned decisions about work schedules over to the employees. With employee work teams in charge of scheduling, the company reported higher morale, better customer service, and a 30 percent reduction in absenteeism.

✔ Reference International Software in San Francisco, California, allows one day a week for customer service reps to work on any project they choose. Some results have included better systems and new, salable products in addition to greatly enhanced employee morale.

✔ AT&T has a program called Resource Link that lets employees from diverse backgrounds and with varied management, technical, or professional skills "sell" their abilities to different departments for short-term assignments. It has greatly increased retention and employee satisfaction.

✔ Employees at AT&T Universal Card Services can use their own judgment about whether to waive late fees or raise credit limits when talking to customers on the phone. This has not only made customers happier, but also improved efficiency and given employees a greater sense of autonomy and control over their jobs. Employees at the Container Store are likewise given autonomy to make decisions involving customers. If a customer notices an item is scratched, for example, the employee can decide to offer a discount for the item.

✔ George MacLeod, a restaurant owner in Bucksport, Maine, allows his employees to run the restaurant by themselves one Sunday every month, and then splits the profits among them to help pay for their health insurance. Participating employees have made enough money to cover the entire cost of their insurance premiums.

#7: Thank Employees for Doing Good Work and Praise Them in Front of Others

Although you can thank someone in 10 to 15 seconds, most employees report that they are never thanked for the job they do — and especially not by their managers. Systematically thank your employees when they do good work, whether it's one-on-one in person, in the hallway, in a group meeting, on voicemail, in a written thank-you note, or via e-mail. Better yet, go out of your way to act on and amplify good news — even if it means interrupting employees to thank them for the great job they have done. By taking the time to say you noticed and appreciate their efforts, those efforts — and results — are likely to continue.

One excellent — and very inexpensive — way to recognize employees or peers is simply to give verbal feedback when you notice something you like: "Chris, you did a great job handling that angry customer," for example, or "Robin, the shelves you stocked are really looking good." If your feedback is immediate and sincere, the other person will feel gratified that you've noticed and strive to do the same thing again.

Verbal praise from one's manager is a top motivator for employees today and consistently ranks high in surveys of workplace motivators. Here are three possible ways to give verbal praise. Try each of them and see what works best for you!

- **Directly, face-to-face.** Telling someone directly that he or she did a great job is an effective way to make the person feel valued for the work done; it is also a demonstration of what you would like more of from the employee. Praising that is immediate, sincere, and specific has the most impact. Tie the person's achievement to a larger context, for example, the department's goals, the company's values, and so on, and — for maximum impact — add a personal touch. For example, "Gary, I really appreciate the way you pitched in to help others today; that's exactly the type of teamwork we've been striving for."

- **In front of someone else.** Praising in front of someone else lets the recipient know what he or she did well and also communicates to others that you value the employee. For example, "John, I know you're in the middle of a meeting, but the second quarter numbers just came in and I had to come over to tell you that you blew past your goals. Congratulations! We'll talk more about this later. I just had to come by to tell you how proud I am of you and your group."

- **To others when the recipient is not around.** It's funny how praise about someone often gets back to the person mentioned ("Sally, your boss was really singing your praises to upper management in yesterday's executive meeting!"). In fact, some employees consider this the most powerful form of praise, because the manager explicitly has nothing to gain; that is, the manager isn't asking for a favor after having given a praising.

Other ideas include the following:

- Nikki Burns, Miami Valley Hospital, in Dayton, Ohio, says she tries to say "Thank you" to every employee as he or she leaves for the day. She has received feedback from employees regarding how much that means to them.

- Hugh Fleming of the Spotsylvania Mall restaurant in Fredericksburg, Virginia, makes a point of catching people doing something right every day and praising them on the spot.

- At Domino's Pizza (now Domino's) headquarters in Ann Arbor, Michigan, Eric Schmaltz tries to acknowledge at least five people every day, whether they are employees or customers. He found that the behavior closely correlates to effectiveness in sales.

#8: Grant Flexible Working Hours and Time Off

Today's employees value their time — and their time off. Especially as work-life boundaries get more blurry every day, giving time off can be extremely powerful: It refreshes employees and shows that you respect them as people, and not just as workers. Having flexible working hours is increasingly important to employees. In a recent survey by Robert Half International, 66 percent of workers said they would take a cut in pay in exchange for more flexibility. Granting flex time or time off is a way of showing that you area aware of all the times they work from home or put in extra hours. It's your chance to pay them back.

This can be as simple as allowing employees to leave work early for doctor appointments and school programs, or letting them have an ongoing flexible work schedule. You can reward employees with an extra hour for lunch or an extra day or half day off around the weekend. Some employers even allow employees to negotiate work hours with coworkers so that if something comes up and they need to attend to personal business, they can swap work hours or arrange for someone to cover their duties.

Here are some other ideas:

- **Take the day off:** Jeff White, a Chick-fil-A manager, rewards individual team members with a paid day off based on excellent performance.

- **Call in well:** As a result of its commitment to a more balanced work life, employees at clothing outfitter Eddie Bauer can "call in well." The company's Redmond, Washington, store has even created a Balance Day, an additional day off for all employees.

- **Ferris Bueller's day off:** Integrated Genetics, a biotechnology company located in Westborough, Massachusetts, surprised all employees with a movie and refreshments and asked that they each take a paid day off in the next year to do something fun. Los Angeles-based JS2 Communications offered a similar benefit when it gave each employee two free "I Don't Want to Get Out of Bed" days to use at their discretion over the following year.

- **Let the best decide:** A McDonald's franchise in St. Louis gives first choice of work schedules to those employees who have the best attendance records. This practice promoted better attendance and — because many employees are students — gave them the chance to better coordinate their work and class schedules.

✔ **Three-day weekends:** Employees at TRW and other defense contractors in San Diego work nine hours each workday and have every other Friday off. Surveys of employees report that this "9/80" work schedule ranked highest in importance to employees — even above their health-care benefits!

✔ **Summer hours:** Karen Cora, then-executive vice president at Deland, Gibson Insurance Associates, Inc., in Wellesley Hills, Massachusetts, reported that the company rewards employees with summer hours from Memorial Day to Labor Day. Everyone takes 15 fewer minutes at lunch four days a week and leaves an hour early on Fridays. It's a big hit and employees love it. Workman Publishing in New York City offers May Days, in which all employees can leave work Friday afternoons throughout the summer.

#9: Provide Written and Electronic Praise

A simple note can go a long way in making someone feel valued. It only takes you a moment to write but is often a highlight to the recipient — and sometimes it's even a milestone in that person's job or career. You can take this recognition up a notch by having a letter of praise placed in the employee's personnel file. Likewise, a simple e-mail of thanks and praise serves the same purpose. Employees also report valuing positive e-mail messages that are forwarded to them. For employees, this simple action represents a validation of the job they're doing and the appreciation you have for their efforts. I know employees that collect such good news and place it into a "Victory File" to take out and read through when they're having a tough day.

Following are some creative ways businesses have found to give written praise:

✔ **The Gold Star Award:** Markeeta Graban, associate director of the Department of Psychiatry at the University of Michigan Health System reports, "It's really true that anything can be a significant form of recognition. Over three years ago, I drew a star on a piece of scrap paper, colored it, and gave it to someone for helping me out that day. They in turn gave it to someone who gave it to someone else. It took on special significance with each use. Now we have it on a magnetic backing and people pass it on to recognize those who have helped or those who are having a rough day. People love it!" At La Posada at Park Centre in Green Valley, AZ, employees give each other You're a Star cards, which can be redeemed for money or days off.

- **The Praising Board:** "I post notes from other departments that have had something positive to say about any of us," explains Connie Maxwell of West Des Moines Community Schools. "This way, people who work with me are more inclined to write one to someone else, so there's a mutual sharing of thanks. It's become a point of pride to have a note that one wrote posted." I've also seen some companies do this with an erasable white board that anyone can add a comment or note of praise to.

- **The Thank You cod:** The New England Aquarium allows employees to recognize coworkers with a Thank You Cod (a card shaped like a cod fish) — a play on New England accents. Half of the card goes to the employee and the other half into a quarterly lottery for gift certificates for paid time off, items at the company store, and local restaurants.

- **Secret Agent Dad:** "An engineer on my staff spent an extended amount of time on the road doing environmental evaluations of companies," reported Michael L. Horvath when he was director of environmental projects for FirstEnergy Corporation. "I sent a letter to his three school-age children explaining why their dad was gone so much lately and that he was doing special 'secret agent' work that was very important for our company. His wife called the next day to say how excited their kids were that dad was a 'secret agent!'"

- **Say it electronically:** Katherine A. Kawamoto, then-director of Americas Sales Contracts in Irmo, South Carolina, shared the following tip: "Everyone knows about electronic greeting cards. There are many services. They all have a great selection and are really a pick-me-up for our employees when they are having a bad day or are far away on business. People may not realize, however, that you can plan to send anniversary and/or birthday cards up to a year in advance. It just takes filling out a form electronically, and the services send reminders out via email when the date approaches."

- **E-mails sent automatically:** At aircraft manufacture Boeing, based in Chicago, employees complete an online form and the program automatically sends e-mails to the giver's and the recipient's managers. The company publicizes the program by sending fliers to employees' homes and through monthly e-mail reminders. Employees receive electronic cards or points that can be redeemed for merchandise.

- **Pass the praise around:** ComDoc in Uniontown, Ohio, encourages employees, who refer to themselves as partners, to recognize each other as "Passionate Partners." "One partner sends an e-mail or letter recognizing a Passionate Partner to me," says Judi Adam, Manager of Corporate Administration, "and I, in turn, send out a Passionate Partner e-mail to all ComDoc partners recognizing that person for their accomplishments, good deeds, acts of kindness, or whatever it is for which they are being recognized." Often this prompts other partners to send appreciative e-mails to the Passionate Partner. It further reminds everyone to think about others who need recognition.

#10: Publicly Share Customer Letters and Recognize Employees in Meetings

In general, most employees value public acknowledgment, so look for opportunities to sing their praises in department or company meetings. When your employees receive a positive letter from a customer or client, encourage them to share that letter with your group. Have them read it out loud at your next staff meeting to remind everyone what you are trying to achieve together. Post it on your department bulletin board. Add a note to the letter and forward it to your manager for his or her information.

Here are some other real-life customer recognition examples:

✔ Edward Nickel, then-regional training and development manager for Nordstrom, Inc., in Oak Brook, Illinois, reports that some Nordstrom stores recognize employees before the stores open by sharing over the store intercom great letters received from customers about employees' exemplary service. Letters are then posted on an employee bulletin board for all to read. Each store manager has his or her own routine, but there is never a dearth of material to read, and hearing the examples motivates other employees to do similar things.

✔ Kym Illman, managing director of Messages on Hold in Perth, Australia, shares, "Our client contact is over the phone, so we need our people to wow those clients to overcome the distance factor (Perth being the most remote city on the globe). I read the compliments I receive in a team meeting and ask the person to pick from a deck of playing cards. For cards 2 through 9, they receive the dollar value. For a 10 or picture card, they receive $10, and $20 for an ace. It's fun and helps to spur all the reps to wow the clients."

✔ In keeping with the theme of appreciating great performances, employees are applauded for doing a great job at the Kansas City Symphony, according to Barbara Tate, then HR director and current director of business operations. As an example, she was applauded when she presented a new benefits plan at a company meeting. Employees at SC Johnson, the global manufacturer of household cleaning supplies based in Racine, Wisconsin, nominate and give standing ovations to their peers for remarkable performance.

✔ Rather than wait for a weekly or monthly report, store managers at the St. Ann branch of Famous-Barr department stores, based in St. Louis, Missouri, go to each employee at the end of the day to see what went well for that employee that day. Those positive items are worked into the next morning's store rally. "It's been a very effective way to reinforce good news on a timely basis and charge employees up to do their best every single day," said Dan Eppler, then-merchandise sales manager for the company.

Index

• F •

• G •

Math & Science

Algebra I For Dummies,
2nd Edition
978-0-470-55964-2

Anatomy and Physiology
For Dummies, 2nd Edition
978-0-470-92326-9

Astronomy For Dummies,
3rd Edition
978-1-118-37697-3

Biology For Dummies,
2nd Edition
978-0-470-59875-7

Chemistry For Dummies,
2nd Edition
978-1-118-00730-3

1001 Algebra II Practice
Problems For Dummies
978-1-118-44662-1

Microsoft Office

Excel 2013 For Dummies
978-1-118-51012-4

Office 2013 All-in-One
For Dummies
978-1-118-51636-2

PowerPoint 2013
For Dummies
978-1-118-50253-2

Word 2013 For Dummies
978-1-118-49123-2

Music

Blues Harmonica
For Dummies
978-1-118-25269-7

Guitar For Dummies,
3rd Edition
978-1-118-11554-1

iPod & iTunes
For Dummies, 10th Edition
978-1-118-50864-0

Programming

Beginning Programming
with C For Dummies
978-1-118-73763-7

Excel VBA Programming
For Dummies, 3rd Edition
978-1-118-49037-2

Java For Dummies,
6th Edition
978-1-118-40780-6

Religion & Inspiration

The Bible For Dummies
978-0-7645-5296-0

Buddhism For Dummies,
2nd Edition
978-1-118-02379-2

Catholicism For Dummies,
2nd Edition
978-1-118-07778-8

Self-Help & Relationships

Beating Sugar Addiction
For Dummies
978-1-118-54645-1

Meditation For Dummies,
3rd Edition
978-1-118-29144-3

Seniors

Laptops For Seniors
For Dummies, 3rd Edition
978-1-118-71105-7

Computers For Seniors
For Dummies, 3rd Edition
978-1-118-11553-4

iPad For Seniors
For Dummies, 6th Edition
978-1-118-72826-0

Social Security
For Dummies
978-1-118-20573-0

Smartphones & Tablets

Android Phones
For Dummies, 2nd Edition
978-1-118-72030-1

Nexus Tablets
For Dummies
978-1-118-77243-0

Samsung Galaxy S 4
For Dummies
978-1-118-64222-1

Samsung Galaxy Tabs
For Dummies
978-1-118-77294-2

Test Prep

ACT For Dummies,
5th Edition
978-1-118-01259-8

ASVAB For Dummies,
3rd Edition
978-0-470-63760-9

GRE For Dummies,
7th Edition
978-0-470-88921-3

Officer Candidate Tests
For Dummies
978-0-470-59876-4

Physician's Assistant Exam
For Dummies
978-1-118-11556-5

Series 7 Exam For Dummie
978-0-470-09932-2

Windows 8

Windows 8.1 All-in-One
For Dummies
978-1-118-82087-2

Windows 8.1 For Dummie
978-1-118-82121-3

Windows 8.1 For Dummies
Book + DVD Bundle
978-1-118-82107-7

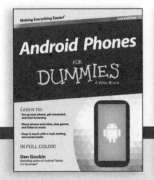 **Available in print and e-book formats.**

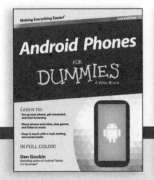   

Available wherever books are sold. **For more information or to order direct visit www.dummies.com**

Apple & Mac

iPad For Dummies,
5th Edition
978-1-118-72306-7

iPhone For Dummies,
7th Edition
978-1-118-69083-3

Macs All-in-One
For Dummies, 4th Edition
978-1-118-82210-4

OS X Mavericks
For Dummies
978-1-118-69188-5

Blogging & Social Media

Facebook For Dummies,
5th Edition
978-1-118-63312-0

Social Media Engagement
For Dummies
978-1-118-53019-1

WordPress For Dummies,
6th Edition
978-1-118-79161-5

Business

Stock Investing
For Dummies, 4th Edition
978-1-118-37678-2

Investing For Dummies,
6th Edition
978-0-470-90545-6

Personal Finance
For Dummies, 7th Edition
978-1-118-11785-9

QuickBooks 2014
For Dummies
978-1-118-72005-9

Small Business Marketing
Kit For Dummies,
3rd Edition
978-1-118-31183-7

Careers

Job Interviews
For Dummies, 4th Edition
978-1-118-11290-8

Job Searching with Social
Media For Dummies,
2nd Edition
978-1-118-67856-5

Personal Branding
For Dummies
978-1-118-11792-7

Resumes For Dummies,
6th Edition
978-0-470-87361-8

Starting an Etsy Business
For Dummies, 2nd Edition
978-1-118-59024-9

Diet & Nutrition

Belly Fat Diet For Dummies
978-1-118-34585-6

Mediterranean Diet
For Dummies
978-1-118-71525-3

Nutrition For Dummies,
5th Edition
978-0-470-93231-5

Digital Photography

Digital SLR Photography
All-in-One For Dummies,
2nd Edition
978-1-118-59082-9

Digital SLR Video &
Filmmaking For Dummies
978-1-118-36598-4

Photoshop Elements 12
For Dummies
978-1-118-72714-0

Gardening

Herb Gardening
For Dummies, 2nd Edition
978-0-470-61778-6

Gardening with Free-Range
Chickens For Dummies
978-1-118-54754-0

Health

Boosting Your Immunity
For Dummies
978-1-118-40200-9

Diabetes For Dummies,
4th Edition
978-1-118-29447-5

Living Paleo For Dummies
978-1-118-29405-5

Big Data

Big Data For Dummies
978-1-118-50422-2

Data Visualization
For Dummies
978-1-118-50289-1

Hadoop For Dummies
978-1-118-60755-8

Language &
Foreign Language

500 Spanish Verbs
For Dummies
978-1-118-02382-2

English Grammar
For Dummies, 2nd Edition
978-0-470-54664-2

French All-in-One
For Dummies
978-1-118-22815-9

German Essentials
For Dummies
978-1-118-18422-6

Italian For Dummies,
2nd Edition
978-1-118-00465-4

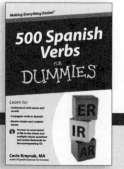 **Available in print and e-book formats.**

 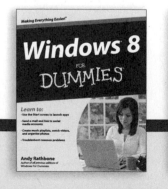 

Available wherever books are sold. **For more information or to order direct visit www.dummies.com**

About the Author

Bob Nelson, PhD (San Diego, California) is a leading authority on employee recognition, engagement, and retention, and president of Nelson Motivation, Inc. (www.drbobnelson.com), a management training and consulting company. He serves as an Executive Strategist for HR Issues and has worked with 80 percent of Fortune 500 companies. He has sold over 4 million books on management and motivation, including *1501 Ways to Reward Employees* (Workman), *The 1001 Rewards & Recognition Fieldbook: The Complete Guide* (Workman), *1001 Ways to Energize Employees* (Workman), *Motivating Today's Employees* (Successories), *The Management Bible* (Wiley), *Managing For Dummies,* 3rd Edition (Wiley), and *Ubuntu!: An Inspiring Story About an African Tradition of Teamwork and Collaboration* (Crown Business), among others. He has frequently appeared in the national media, including the *New York Times*, the *Wall Street Journal*, CNN, CNBC, CBS's *60 Minutes,* and National Public Radio. Dr. Bob holds a BA in communication from Macalester College, an MBA in organizational behavior from UC Berkeley, and a PhD in management education from the Peter F. Drucker Graduate School of Management at Claremont Graduate University in Los Angeles, California. You can reach Dr. Bob directly at bob@drbobnelson.com or by phone at 1-858-673-0690.

Author's Acknowledgments

Dr. Bob would like to thank his coauthors Dr. Dean Spitzer (*The 1001 Rewards & Recognition Fieldbook: The Complete Guide*); his long-time friend, Peter Economy (*The Management Bible*; *Managing For Dummies,* 3rd Edition; and *Consulting For Dummies,* 2nd Edition), and Dr. Stephen Lundin (*Ubuntu! An Inspiring Story About an African Tradition of Teamwork and Collaboration*). He would also like to thank former professor, the late Dr. Peter F. Drucker; his former mentor and co-author, Dr. Ken Blanchard (*Exploring the World of Business*); his colleague and coach, Dr. Marshall Goldsmith; and his colleagues James Key Lim and Dr. Rick Garlick. Plus, the great folks at John Wiley & Sons, including Executive Publisher Matt Holt; Acquisitions Editor Stacy Kennedy; Project Manager Michelle Hacker; Development Editor Tracy Barr; and Editor Sarah Sypniewski— great job, all! Finally, he would like to thank his family: his loving spouse of 31 years, Jennifer; his son, Daniel; his daughter, Michelle; his sister, Alice; and his brother, Douglas for all their ongoing love and support.

Special thanks to Aberdeen Group for the use of their proprietary research in Chapters 1 and 3. Aberdeen Group is the leader in integrated data science and content marketing. They provide solutions that deliver precise targeting and predictive analytics combined with compelling content and demand generation programs. Their customers achieve superior returns on their marketing and sales investments by having the right conversation with the right targets at every stage of the buying journey. They work with companies of all sizes and industry segments: from aggressive startups to established industry leaders. Sales and marketing professionals turn to them to help uncover their best opportunities and deliver targeted content that results in increased conversion rates and accelerated sales wins. For more information about Aberdeen's research and services, please visit www.aberdeen.com or call 1-800-577-7891.

Publisher's Acknowledgments

Acquisitions Editor: Stacy Kennedy

Contributing Writer: Sarah Sypniewski

Project Manager: Michelle Hacker

Development and Copy Editor: Tracy Barr

Production Editor: Suresh Srinivasan

Cover Image: © Ken Colby